LAOS

T0291249

TAX GUIDE

VOLUME 1
STRATEGIC INFORMATION AND REGULATIONS

International Business Publications, USA
Washington DC, USA - Laos

LAOS
TAX GUIDE
VOLUME 1 STRATEGIC INFORMATION AND REGULATIONS

UPDATED ANNUALLY

We express our sincere appreciation to all government agencies and international organizations which provided information and other materials for this handbook

Cover Design: International Business Publications, USA

2017 Edition Updated Reprint International Business Publications, USA
ISBN 978-1-5145-2437-4

For additional analytical, business and investment opportunities information,
please contact Global Investment & Business Center, USA
at (703) 370-8082. Fax: (703) 370-8083. E-mail: ibpusa3@gmail.com
Global Business and Investment Info Databank - www.ibpus.com

Printed in the USA

For additional analytical, business and investment opportunities information,
please contact Global Investment & Business Center, USA
at (703) 370-8082. Fax: (703) 370-8083. E-mail: ibpusa3@gmail.com
Global Business and Investment Info Databank - www.ibpus.com

LAOS

TAX GUIDE

VOLUME 1
STRATEGIC INFORMATION AND REGULATIONS

TABLE OF CONTENTS

For additional analytical, business and investment opportunities information,
please contact Global Investment & Business Center, USA
at (703) 370-8082. Fax: (703) 370-8083. E-mail: ibpusa3@gmail.com
Global Business and Investment Info Databank - www.ibpus.com

For additional analytical, business and investment opportunities information,
please contact Global Investment & Business Center, USA
at (703) 370-8082. Fax: (703) 370-8083. E-mail: ibpusa3@gmail.com
Global Business and Investment Info Databank - www.ibpus.com

**For additional analytical, business and investment opportunities information,
please contact Global Investment & Business Center, USA
at (703) 370-8082. Fax: (703) 370-8083. E-mail: ibpusa3@gmail.com
Global Business and Investment Info Databank - www.ibpus.com**

**For additional analytical, business and investment opportunities information,
please contact Global Investment & Business Center, USA
at (703) 370-8082. Fax: (703) 370-8083. E-mail: ibpusa3@gmail.com
Global Business and Investment Info Databank - www.ibpus.com**

**For additional analytical, business and investment opportunities information,
please contact Global Investment & Business Center, USA
at (703) 370-8082. Fax: (703) 370-8083. E-mail: ibpusa3@gmail.com
Global Business and Investment Info Databank - www.ibpus.com**

For additional analytical, business and investment opportunities information, please contact Global Investment & Business Center, USA at (703) 370-8082. Fax: (703) 370-8083. E-mail: ibpusa3@gmail.com Global Business and Investment Info Databank - www.ibpus.com

For additional analytical, business and investment opportunities information,
please contact Global Investment & Business Center, USA
at (703) 370-8082. Fax: (703) 370-8083. E-mail: ibpusa3@gmail.com
Global Business and Investment Info Databank - www.ibpus.com

LAOS STRATEGIC AND DEVELOPMENT PROFILES

STRATEGIC PROFILE

Capital and largest city	Vientiane 17°58′N 102°36′E
Official languages	Lao
Spoken languages	Lao Hmong Khmu
Ethnic groups (2005[1])	55% Lao 11% Khmu 8% Hmong 26% othera
Religion	Buddhism
Demonym	Laotian Lao
Government	Marxist–Leninistone-party socialist state
• **General Secretary and President**	Bounnhang Vorachith
• **Prime Minister**	Thongloun Sisoulith
• **Vice President**	Phankham Viphavanh
Legislature	National Assembly
Formation	
• **Kingdom of Lan Xang**	1354–1707
• **Luang Phrabang, Vientiane and Champasak**	1707–1778
• **Vassal of Thonburi and Siam**	1778–1893
• **War of Succession**	1826–8
• **French Indochina**	1893–1949
• **Independence from France**	19 July 1949
• **Declared Independence**	22 October 1953
• **Laotian civil war**	9 November 1953 – 2 December 1975
• **Lao Monarchy abolished**	2 December 1975
• **Current constitution**	14 August 1991
Area	
• **Total**	237,955 km2 (84th) 91,428.991 sq mi

• **Water (%)**	2
Population	
• **2014 (Jul) estimate**	6,803,699[2](104th)
• **2015 census**	6,492,228[3]
• **Density**	26.7/km2 (177th)
	69.2/sq mi
GDP (PPP)	2014 estimate
• **Total**	US$34.400 billion[4]
• **Per capita**	US$4,986[4]
GDP (nominal)	2014 estimate
• **Total**	US$11.676 billion[4]
• **Per capita**	US$1,692[4]
Gini (2008)	36.7[5]
	medium
HDI (2014)	0.575[6]
	medium · 141st
Currency	Kip (LAK)
Time zone	ICT
Date format	dd/mm/yyyy
Drives on the	right
Calling code	+856
ISO 3166 code	LA
Internet TLD	.la

Laos, officially the **Lao People's Democratic Republic**, is a landlocked socialist republic communist state in southeast Asia, bordered by Myanmar (Burma) and the People's Republic of China to the northwest, Vietnam to the east, Cambodia to the south, and Thailand to the west. Laos traces its history to the Kingdom of Lan Xang or *Land of a Million Elephants*, which existed from the 14th to the 18th century. After a period as a French colony, it gained independence in 1949. A long civil war ended when the communist Pathet Lao came to power in 1975.

Private enterprise has increased since the mid-1980s, but development has been hampered by poor communications in the heavily forested and mountainous landscape. 80%[1] of those employed practice subsistence agriculture; this is coupled with widespread starvation due to the many failures of communism and the state's command economy. The country's ethnic make-up is extremely diverse, with only around 60% belonging to the largest ethnic group, the Lao.

In 1975 the communist Pathet Lao took control of the government, ending a six-century-old monarchy. Initial closer ties to Vietnam and socialization were replaced with a gradual return to private enterprise, an easing of foreign investment laws, and the admission into ASEAN in 1997.

GEOGRAPHY

Location: Southeastern Asia, northeast of Thailand, west of Vietnam
Geographic coordinates: 18 00 N, 105 00 E

Map references: Southeast Asia
Area:
total: 236,800 sq km
land: 230,800 sq km
water: 6,000 sq km

Area - comparative: slightly larger than Utah

Land boundaries:
total: 5,083 km
border countries: Burma 235 km, Cambodia 541 km, China 423 km, Thailand 1,754 km, Vietnam 2,130 km

Coastline: 0 km (landlocked)
Maritime claims: none (landlocked)
Climate: tropical monsoon; rainy season (May to November); dry season (December to April)
Terrain: mostly rugged mountains; some plains and plateaus

Elevation extremes:
lowest point: Mekong River 70 m
highest point: Phou Bia 2,817 m

Natural resources: timber, hydropower, gypsum, tin, gold, gemstones

Land use:
arable land: 3%
permanent crops: 0%
permanent pastures: 3%
forests and woodland: 54%
other: 40%

Irrigated land: 1,250 sq km
note: rainy season irrigation - 2,169 sq km; dry season irrigation - 750 sq km (1998 est.)
Natural hazards: floods, droughts, and blight

Environment - current issues: unexploded ordnance; deforestation; soil erosion; a majority of the population does not have access to potable water

---

Environment - international agreements:
party to: Biodiversity, Climate Change, Desertification, Environmental Modification, Law of the Sea, Nuclear Test Ban, Ozone Layer Protection
signed, but not ratified: none of the selected agreements

Geography - note: landlocked

PEOPLE

Population: 5,497,459

Age structure:
0-14 years: 43% (male 1,191,608; female 1,173,144)
15-64 years: 54% (male 1,447,788; female 1,500,016)
65 years and over: 3% (male 85,028; female 99,875)

Population growth rate: 2.5%
Birth rate: 38.29 births/1,000 population
Death rate: 13.35 deaths/1,000 population
Net migration rate: 0 migrant(s)/1,000 population

Sex ratio:
at birth: 1.05 male(s)/female
under 15 years: 1.02 male(s)/female
15-64 years: 0.97 male(s)/female
65 years and over: 0.85 male(s)/female
total population: 0.98 male(s)/female

Infant mortality rate: 94.8 deaths/1,000 live births

Life expectancy at birth:
total population: 53.09 years
male: 51.22 years
female: 55.02 years

Total fertility rate: 5.21 children born/woman

Nationality:
noun: Lao(s) or Laotian(s)
adjective: Lao or Laotian

Ethnic groups: Lao Loum (lowland) 68%, Lao Theung (upland) 22%, Lao Soung (highland) including the Hmong ("Meo") and the Yao (Mien) 9%, ethnic Vietnamese/Chinese 1%
Religions: Buddhist 60% (in October 1999, the regime proposed a constitutional amendment making Buddhism the state religion; the National Assembly is expected to vote on the amendment sometime in 2000), animist and other 40%
Languages: Lao (official), French, English, and various ethnic languages

Literacy:
definition: age 15 and over can read and write
total population: 57%
male: 70%
female: 44%

GOVERNMENT

Country name:
conventional long form: Lao People's Democratic Republic
conventional short form: Laos
local long form: Sathalanalat Paxathipatai Paxaxon Lao
local short form: none

Data code: LA
Government type: Communist state
Capital: Vientiane

Administrative divisions: 16 provinces (khoueng, singular and plural), 1 municipality* (kampheng nakhon, singular and plural), and 1 special zone** (khetphiset, singular and plural); Attapu, Bokeo, Bolikhamxai, Champasak, Houaphan, Khammouan, Louangnamtha, Louangphabang, Oudomxai, Phongsali, Salavan, Savannakhet, Viangchan*, Viangchan, Xaignabouli, Xaisomboun**, Xekong, Xiangkhoang

Independence: 19 July 1949 (from France)
National holiday: National Day, 2 December (1975) (proclamation of the Lao People's Democratic Republic)
Constitution: promulgated 14 August 1991

Legal system: based on traditional customs, French legal norms and procedures, and Socialist practice

Suffrage: 18 years of age; universal

Executive branch:

chief of state: President BOUNNYANG Vorachit (since 20 April 2016); Vice President PHANKHAM Viphavan (since 20 April 2016)

head of government: Prime Minister THONGLOUN Sisoulit (since 20 April 2016); Deputy Prime Ministers BOUNTHONG Chitmani, SONXAI Siphandon, SOMDI Douangdi (since 20 April 2016)

cabinet: Council of Ministers appointed by the president, approved by the National Assembly

elections/appointments: president and vice president indirectly elected by the National Assembly for a 5-year term (no term limits); election last held on 20 April

2016 (next to be held in 2021); prime minister nominated by the president, elected by the National Assembly for 5-year term

election results: BOUNNYANG Vorachit (LPRP) elected president; PHANKHAM Viphavan (LPRP) elected vice president; percent of National Assembly vote - NA; THONGLOUN Sisoulit (LPRP) elected prime minister; percent of National Assembly vote - NA

Legislative branch:

description: unicameral National Assembly or Sapha Heng Xat (132 seats; members directly elected in multi-seat constituencies by simple majority vote from candidate lists provided by the Lao People's Revolutionary Party; members serve 5-year terms)

elections: last held on 20 April 2016 (next to be held in 2021)

election results: percent of vote by party - NA; seats by party - LPRP 128, independent 4

Judicial branch:

highest court(s): People's Supreme Court (consists of the court president and organized into criminal, civil, administrative, commercial, family, and juvenile chambers, each with a vice president and several judges)

judge selection and term of office: president of People's Supreme Court appointed by National Assembly on recommendation of the president of the republic for a 5-year term; vice presidents of People's Supreme Court appointed by the president of the republic on recommendation of the National Assembly; appointment of chamber judges NA; tenure of court vice-presidents and chamber judges NA

subordinate courts: appellate courts; provincial, municipal, district, and military courts

Political parties and leaders: Lao People's Revolutionary Party or LPRP [KHAMTAI Siphandon, party president]; other parties proscribed

Political pressure groups and leaders: noncommunist political groups proscribed; most opposition leaders fled the country in 1975

International organization participation: ACCT, AsDB, ASEAN, CP, ESCAP, FAO, G-77, IBRD, ICAO, ICRM, IDA, IFAD, IFC, IFRCS, ILO, IMF, Intelsat (nonsignatory user), Interpol, IOC, ITU, NAM, OPCW, PCA, UN, UNCTAD, UNESCO, UNIDO, UPU, WFTU, WHO, WIPO, WMO, WToO, WTrO (observer)

Diplomatic representation in the US:
chief of mission: Ambassador VANG Rattanavong

chancery: 2222 S Street NW, Washington, DC 20008
telephone: [1] (202) 332-6416
FAX: [1] (202) 332-4923

Diplomatic representation from the US:
chief of mission: Ambassador Wendy Jean CHAMBERLIN
embassy: Rue Bartholonie, B. P. 114, Vientiane
mailing address: American Embassy, Box V, APO AP 96546
telephone: [856] (21) 212581, 212582, 212585
FAX: [856] (21) 212584

Flag description: three horizontal bands of red (top), blue (double width), and red with a large white disk centered in the blue band

ECONOMY

The government of Laos, one of the few remaining one-party communist states, began decentralizing control and encouraging private enterprise in 1986. The results, starting from an extremely low base, were striking - growth averaged 6% per year from 1988-2008 except during the short-lived drop caused by the Asian financial crisis that began in 1997. Laos' growth exceeded 7% per year during 2008-13. Despite this high growth rate, Laos remains a country with an underdeveloped infrastructure, particularly in rural areas. It has a basic, but improving, road system, and limited external and internal land-line telecommunications. Electricity is available in 83 % of the country.

Laos' economy is heavily dependent on capital-intensive natural resource exports. The labor force, however, still relies on agriculture, dominated by rice cultivation in lowland areas, which accounts for about 25% of GDP and 73% of total employment. Economic growth has reduced official poverty rates from 46% in 1992 to 26% in 2010. The economy also has benefited from high-profile foreign direct investment in hydropower, copper and gold mining, logging, and construction though some projects in these industries have drawn criticism for their environmental impacts. Laos gained Normal Trade Relations status with the US in 2004 and applied for Generalized System of Preferences trade benefits in 2013 after being admitted to the World Trade Organization earlier in the year. Laos is in the process of implementing a value-added tax system. Simplified investment procedures and expanded bank credits for small farmers and small entrepreneurs will improve Laos' economic prospects. The government appears committed to raising the country's profile among investors, but suffered through a fiscal crisis in 2013 brought about by public sector wage increases, fiscal mismanagement, and revenue shortfalls. The World Bank has declared that Laos' goal of graduating from the UN Development Program's list of least-developed countries by 2020 is achievable, and the country is preparing to enter the ASEAN Economic Community in 2015.

GDP (purchasing power parity):
$20.78 billion (2013 est.)
country comparison to the world: 132

$19.18 billion (2014 est.)
$17.78 billion (2011 est.)
note:data are in 2013 US dollars

GDP (official exchange rate):
$10.1 billion (2013 est.)

GDP - real growth rate:
8.3% (2013 est.)
country comparison to the world: 9
7.9% (2014 est.)
8% (2011 est.)

GDP - per capita (PPP):
$3,100 (2013 est.)
country comparison to the world: 176
$2,900 (2014 est.)
$2,700 (2011 est.)
note:data are in 2013 US dollars

Gross national saving:
27.4% of GDP (2013 est.)
country comparison to the world: 38
26.2% of GDP (2014 est.)
25.2% of GDP (2011 est.)

GDP - composition, by end use:
household consumption:
66.9%
government consumption:
9.8%
investment in fixed capital:
31.7%
investment in inventories:
-1.3%
exports of goods and services:
40%
imports of goods and services:
-48.4%
(2013 est.)

GDP - composition, by sector of origin:
agriculture:
24.8%
industry:
32%
services:

For additional analytical, business and investment opportunities information,
please contact Global Investment & Business Center, USA
at (703) 370-8082. Fax: (703) 370-8083. E-mail: ibpusa3@gmail.com
Global Business and Investment Info Databank - www.ibpus.com

37.5% (2013 est.)

Agriculture - products:
sweet potatoes, vegetables, corn, coffee, sugarcane, tobacco, cotton, tea, peanuts, rice; cassava (manioc, tapioca), water buffalo, pigs, cattle, poultry

Industries:
mining (copper, tin, gold, gypsum); timber, electric power, agricultural processing, rubber, construction, garments, cement, tourism

Industrial production growth rate:
11% (2013 est.)
country comparison to the world: 12

Labor force:
3.373 million (2013 est.)
country comparison to the world: 100

Labor force - by occupation:
agriculture:
73.1%
industry:
6.1%
services:
20.6% (2014 est.)

Unemployment rate:
1.9% (2010 est.)
country comparison to the world: 11
2.5% (2009 est.)

Population below poverty line:
22% (2013 est.)

Household income or consumption by percentage share:
lowest 10%:
3.3%
highest 10%:
30.3%

Distribution of family income - Gini index:
36.7
country comparison to the world: 83
34.6 (2002)

Budget:

revenues:
$2.481 billion
expenditures:
$2.642 billion (2013 est.)

Taxes and other revenues:
24.6% of GDP (2013 est.)
country comparison to the world: 135

Budget surplus (+) or deficit (-):
-1.6% of GDP (2013 est.)
country comparison to the world: 77

Public debt:
46.3% of GDP (2013 est.)
country comparison to the world: 77
49.1% of GDP (2014 est.)

Fiscal year:
1 October - 30 September

Inflation rate (consumer prices):
6.5% (2013 est.)
country comparison to the world: 183
4.3% (2014 est.)

Central bank discount rate:
4.3% (31 December 2010)
country comparison to the world: 94
4% (31 December 2009)

Commercial bank prime lending rate:
23.2% (31 December 2013 est.)
country comparison to the world: 14
22.3% (31 December 2014 est.)

Stock of narrow money:
$1.389 billion (31 December 2013 est.)
country comparison to the world: 141
$1.154 billion (31 December 2014 est.)

Stock of broad money:
$4.071 billion (31 December 2013 est.)
country comparison to the world: 136
$3.673 billion (31 December 2014 est.)

For additional analytical, business and investment opportunities information,
please contact Global Investment & Business Center, USA
at (703) 370-8082. Fax: (703) 370-8083. E-mail: ibpusa3@gmail.com
Global Business and Investment Info Databank - www.ibpus.com

Stock of domestic credit:
$4.716 billion (31 December 2013 est.)
country comparison to the world: 114
$4.034 billion (31 December 2014 est.)

Market value of publicly traded shares:
$1.012 billion (2014 est.)
$NA

Current account balance:
-$484.3 million (2013 est.)
country comparison to the world: 98
-$315.5 million (2014 est.)

Exports:
$2.313 billion (2013 est.)
country comparison to the world: 141
$1.984 billion (2014 est.)

Exports - commodities:
wood products, coffee, electricity, tin, copper, gold, cassava

Exports - partners:
Thailand 34%, China 21.5%, Vietnam 12.2%

Imports:
$3.238 billion (2013 est.)
country comparison to the world: 145
$2.744 billion (2014 est.)

Imports - commodities:
machinery and equipment, vehicles, fuel, consumer goods

Imports - partners:
Thailand 62.1%, China 16.2%, Vietnam 7.3%

Reserves of foreign exchange and gold:
$845.4 million (31 December 2013 est.)
country comparison to the world: 141
$796.9 million (31 December 2014 est.)

Debt - external:
$6.69 billion (31 December 2013 est.)
country comparison to the world: 110
$6.288 billion (31 December 2014 est.)

For additional analytical, business and investment opportunities information,
please contact Global Investment & Business Center, USA
at (703) 370-8082. Fax: (703) 370-8083. E-mail: ibpusa3@gmail.com
Global Business and Investment Info Databank - www.ibpus.com

Stock of direct foreign investment - at home:
$15.14 billion (31 December 2014 est.)
country comparison to the world: 81
$12.44 billion (31 December 2011 est.)

Exchange rates:
kips (LAK) per US dollar -
7,875.9 (2013 est.)
8,007.3 (2014 est.)
8,258.8 (2010 est.)
8,516.04
8,760.69

ENERGY

Electricity - production:
3.629 billion kWh
country comparison to the world: 127

Electricity - consumption:
2.4 billion kWh
country comparison to the world: 136

Electricity - exports:
2.537 billion kWh
country comparison to the world: 41

Electricity - imports:
1 billion kWh
country comparison to the world: 65

Electricity - installed generating capacity:
3.217 million kW
country comparison to the world: 87

Electricity - from fossil fuels:
2.6% of total installed capacity
country comparison to the world: 201

Electricity - from nuclear fuels:
0% of total installed capacity
country comparison to the world: 122

Electricity - from hydroelectric

For additional analytical, business and investment opportunities information,
please contact Global Investment & Business Center, USA
at (703) 370-8082. Fax: (703) 370-8083. E-mail: ibpusa3@gmail.com
Global Business and Investment Info Databank - www.ibpus.com

plants:
97.4% of total installed capacity
country comparison to the world: 9

Electricity - from other renewable sources:
0% of total installed capacity
country comparison to the world: 191

Crude oil - production:
0 bbl/day
country comparison to the world: 186

Crude oil - exports:
0 bbl/day
country comparison to the world: 140

Crude oil - imports:
0 bbl/day
country comparison to the world: 206

Crude oil - proved reserves:
0 bbl
country comparison to the world: 152

Refined petroleum products - production:
0 bbl/day
country comparison to the world: 161

Refined petroleum products - consumption:
3,391 bbl/day
country comparison to the world: 177

Refined petroleum products - exports:
0 bbl/day
country comparison to the world: 191

Refined petroleum products - imports:
3,160 bbl/day
country comparison to the world: 170

Natural gas - production:

For additional analytical, business and investment opportunities information,
please contact Global Investment & Business Center, USA
at (703) 370-8082. Fax: (703) 370-8083. E-mail: ibpusa3@gmail.com
Global Business and Investment Info Databank - www.ibpus.com

0 cu m
country comparison to the world: 151

Natural gas - consumption:
0 cu m
country comparison to the world: 163

Natural gas - exports:
0 cu m
country comparison to the world: 132

Natural gas - imports:
0 cu m
country comparison to the world: 86

Natural gas - proved reserves:
0 cu m
country comparison to the world: 156

COMMUNICATIONS

Telephones - main lines in use:
112,000
country comparison to the world: 143

Telephones - mobile cellular:
6.492 million
country comparison to the world: 99

Telephone system:
general assessment:
service to general public is improving; the government relies on a radiotelephone network to communicate with remote areas
domestic:
4 service providers with mobile cellular usage growing very rapidly
international:
country code - 856; satellite earth station - 1 Intersputnik (Indian Ocean region) and a second to be developed by China

Broadcast media:
6 TV stations operating out of Vientiane - 3 government-operated and the others commercial; 17 provincial stations operating with nearly all programming relayed via satellite from the government-operated stations in Vientiane; Chinese and Vietnamese programming relayed via satellite from Lao National TV; broadcasts available from stations in Thailand and Vietnam in border areas; multi-channel satellite and cable TV systems provide access to a wide range of foreign stations; state-controlled radio with state-operated Lao National Radio (LNR) broadcasting on 5 frequencies - 1 AM, 1 SW, and 3 FM; LNR's AM and FM programs are relayed via satellite constituting a large part of the programming schedules of the provincial radio stations; Thai radio broadcasts available in border areas and transmissions of multiple international broadcasters are

also accessible

Internet country code:
.la

Internet hosts:
1,532
country comparison to the world: 166

Internet users:
300,000
country comparison to the world: 130

TRANSPORTATION

Airports:
41

country comparison to the world: 103

Airports - with paved runways:
total: 8
2,438 to 3,047 m: 3
1,524 to 2,437 m: 4
914 to 1,523 m: 1 (2013)

Airports - with unpaved runways:
total: 33
1,524 to 2,437 m: 2
914 to 1,523 m: 9
under 914 m:
22

Pipelines:
refined products 540 km (2013)

Roadways:
total: 39,568 km

country comparison to the world: 89
paved: 530 km
unpaved: 39,038 km

Waterways:
4,600 km (primarily on the Mekong River and its tributaries; 2,900 additional km are intermittently navigable by craft drawing less than 0.5 m)
country comparison to the world: 24

MILITARY

For additional analytical, business and investment opportunities information, please contact Global Investment & Business Center, USA at (703) 370-8082. Fax: (703) 370-8083. E-mail: ibpusa3@gmail.com
Global Business and Investment Info Databank - www.ibpus.com

Military branches:
Lao People's Armed Forces (LPAF): Lao People's Army (LPA; includes Riverine Force), Air Force

Military service age and obligation:
18 years of age for compulsory or voluntary military service; conscript service obligation - minimum 18-months

Manpower available for military service:
males age 16-49: 1,574,362
females age 16-49: 1,607,856 (2010 est.)
Manpower fit for military service:
males age 16-49: 1,111,629
females age 16-49: 1,190,035 (2010 est.)

Manpower reaching militarily significant age annually:
male: 71,400
female: 73,038 (2010 est.)

Military expenditures:
0.23% of GDP

Military - note:
serving one of the world's least developed countries, the Lao People's Armed Forces (LPAF) is small, poorly funded, and ineffectively resourced; its mission focus is border and internal security, primarily in countering ethnic Hmong insurgent groups; together with the Lao People's Revolutionary Party and the government, the Lao People's Army (LPA) is the third pillar of state machinery, and as such is expected to suppress political and civil unrest and similar national emergencies, but the LPA also has upgraded skills to respond to avian influenza outbreaks; there is no perceived external threat to the state and the LPA maintains strong ties with the neighboring Vietnamese military

TRANSNATIONAL ISSUES

Disputes - international:
southeast Asian states have enhanced border surveillance to check the spread of avian flu; talks continue on completion of demarcation with Thailand but disputes remain over islands in the Mekong River; concern among Mekong River Commission members that China's construction of dams on the Mekong River and its tributaries will affect water levels; Cambodia and Vietnam are concerned about Laos' extensive upstream dam construction

Illicit drugs:
estimated opium poppy cultivation in 2008 was 1,900 hectares, about a 73% increase from 2007; estimated potential opium production in 2008 more than tripled to 17 metric tons; unsubstantiated reports of domestic methamphetamine production; growing domestic methamphetamine problem

IMPORTANT INFORMATION FOR UNDERSTANDING LAOS1

Official Name: Lao People's Democratic Republic

PROFILE

GEOGRAPHY

Area: 236,800 sq. km. (91,430 sq. mi.); area comparable to Oregon.
Capital--Vientiane (est. 569,000). *Other principal towns*--Savannakhet, Luang Prabang, Pakse, Thakhek.
Terrain: rugged mountains, plateaus, alluvial plains.
Climate: tropical monsoon; rainy season (May to November); dry season (November to April).

PEOPLE

Nationality: *Noun and adjective*--Lao (sing. and pl.).
Population : 5.4 million.
Annual growth rate: 2.7%.
Ethnic groups: Lao Loum 53%; other lowland Lao 13% (Thai Dam, Phouane); Lao Theung (midslope) 23%; Lao Sung (highland), including Hmong, Akha, and the Yao (Mien) 10%; ethnic Vietnamese/Chinese 1%.
Religions: Principally Buddhism, with animism among highland groups.
Languages: Lao (official), French, various highland ethnic, English.
Education: *Literacy*--60%.
Health : *Infant mortality rate*--89.32/1,000. *Life expectancy*--55.87 years for women, 52.63 years for men.
Work force (2.6 million, 1999): *Agriculture*--85%; *industry and services*--15%.

GOVERNMENT

Branches: *Executive*--president (head of state); Chairman, Council of Ministers (prime minister and head of government); nine-member Politburo; 49-member Central Committee. *Legislative*--99-seat National Assembly. *Judicial*--district, provincial, and a national Supreme Court.
Political parties: Lao People's Revolutionary Party (LPRP)--only legal party.
Administrative subdivisions: 16 provinces, one special region, and Vientiane prefecture.
Flag: A red band at the top and bottom with a larger blue band between them; a large white circle is centered.

ECONOMY

Natural resources: Hydroelectric power, timber, minerals.
Agriculture (51% of GDP): *Primary products*--glutinous rice, coffee, corn, sugarcane, vegetables, tobacco, ginger, water buffalo, pigs, cattle, and poultry.
Industry (22% of GDP, 1999): *Primary types*--garment manufacturing, electricity

---

[1] **U.S. Department of State, *Bureau of East Asian and Pacific Affairs***

production, gypsum and tin mining, wood and wood processing, cement manufacturing, agricultural processing.
Industrial growth rate --7.5%.
Services --27% of GDP.
Trade: *Exports* --$370 million: garments, electricity, wood and wood products, coffee, rattan. Major markets--France, U.K., Germany, Holland, Thailand, Belgium, U.S., Italy, Japan, Vietnam. *Imports* --$570 million. *Major imports*--fuel, food, consumer, goods, machinery and equipment, vehicles and spare parts. *Major suppliers*--Thailand, Singapore, Japan, Vietnam, China.

GEOGRAPHY, TOPOGRAPHY AND CLIMATE

The Lao People's Democratic Republic (Lao PDR) has a land area of 236,800 square kilometers, stretching more than 1,700 km from the north to south and between 100 km and 400 km from the east to west. The Lao PDR has an eastern border of 1,957 km with the Socialist Republic of Vietnam, a western border of 1,730 km with the, Kingdom of Thailand, a southern border of 492 kin with t he Kingdom of Combodia, and northern borders of 416 kin with the People's Republic of China and 230 km with the Union of Myamar.

Although the Lao PDR has no direct access to the sea, it has an abundance of rivers, including a 1,865 km stretch of the Mekong (Nam Kong), defining its border with Myanmar and a major part of the border with Thailand. Ma'or stretches of the Mekong and its tributaries are navigable and provide alluvial deposits for some. of the fertile plains. About two thirds of the country is mountainous, with ranges from 200 to the 2,820 meters high. The mountains pose difficulties for transportation and communication and complicate development, but together with the rivers they produce vast potential for hydro power.

The Lao PDR is a tropical country, whose climate is affected by monsoon rains from May to September. In Vientiane, the average temperatures range from a minimum of C 16.4 degrees in January to a maximum of C 13 degrees in April.

WATER RESOURCES

Its abundant water resources is probably the most important natural resource endowment of the country. There are only three hydroelectric plants in operation so far, of which Nam Ngum I is the biggest. These three plants with a combined capacity of 200 MW, reportedly realizes only less than five percent of the country's hydroelectric potential. About 90% of hydroelectric power production is exported to Thailand, constituting one of the leading exports of the Lao PDR. Plans are underway to construct a number of new hydroelectric power facilities, which are described in greater detail in Section B.

FOREST RESOURCES

Forests cover about 47% of the country, comprising a wide variety of commercial tree species suitable for production of saw timber, plywood, parquet, furniture, etc.... The most important high value species are hardwoods belonging to the Diterocarpaceae

For additional analytical, business and investment opportunities information,
please contact Global Investment & Business Center, USA
at (703) 370-8082. Fax: (703) 370-8083. E-mail: ibpusa3@gmail.com
Global Business and Investment Info Databank - www.ibpus.com

family and rosewoods belonging to the Genera Pterocarpus, Dalbergia and Afzelia. Pines and other coniferous species are also available but in comparatively small quantities. Eighty percent of domestic energy consumption is based on fuel wood, and an estimated 300,000 hectares of forest are lost annually largely due to shifting cultivation and logging activities. In the effort to protect forest resources from unsustainable felling of trees, the total annual allowable cut (AC) has been set by the Tropical Forest Action Plan (1991) to 280,000 cubic meters per annum, exportation of logs was temporarily restricted to restructure forest management, and protective measures have been implemented to prevent depletion of forests due to shifting fanning practices.

MINERAL RESOURCES

Sizeable deposits of gemstones such as sapphire, zircon, amethyst, gold, iron are and tin are know to exist in the country. Gemstones, gold, coal and tin are estimated to have a high economic value. More geologic surveys are needed to identify location of mineral deposits that would allow their exploitation in commercial quantities. Meanwhile, exploration of potential petroleum deposits are underway. Economic exploitation of mineral resources will depend on development of the required physical infrastructures.

ADMINISTRATIVE STRUCTURE OF LAOS

ATTAPEU PROVINCE

Attapeu Province is best known for the Bolaven Plateau, which also extends into Champassak, Salavan and Sekong provinces. The Bolaven Plateau is covered in the Champassak section -The plateau is best accessed from Pakse, in Champassak province.

Attapeu province is rugged,wild and very scenic, but transportation is very difficult, especially by land in the rainy season.

The town of Samakhi Xai (Attapeu) is situated in a large picturesque valley. The population of the province is more Lao Loum than the neighbouring provinces.

Parts of the Ho Chi Minh Trail can be explored from Attapeu, although using a local guide is essential.

BOKEO PROVINCE

Bokeo province is the smallest province in the country and borders Thailand and Myanmar. This is the Lao side of the 'Golden Triangle'. The province has 34 ethnic groups, the second most ethnically diverse province in Laos. The photo shows a group of Akha (Ikaw or Kaw) people from the Golden Triangle area taken in 1900.

Huay Xai is the border town with Thailand, the city is busy and prosperous.

For additional analytical, business and investment opportunities information, please contact Global Investment & Business Center, USA at (703) 370-8082. Fax: (703) 370-8083. E-mail: ibpusa3@gmail.com Global Business and Investment Info Databank - www.ibpus.com

Located in the center of Huay Xay is Chomkao Manilat temple. The view from the the temple hill over Houy Xay city,the Mekong river and surrounding mountains is a definite reward for making it up the many steps.

BOLIKHAMSAI PROVINCE

Bolikhamsai province contains part of the wilderness area known as the Nakai - Nam Theun National Biodiversity Conservation Area the largest conservation area in the country at 3700 sq km. The area is home to over a dozen threatened species including Asiatic black bear, clouded leopard, elephant, giant muntjac, guar, Malayan sun bear, and tiger.

The saola (spindlehorn) or Vu Quang Ox - *Pseudoryx nghetinhensis* was discovered in neighbouring Vietnam in 1992 and sighted since then in Laos in the conservation area. Only two other land mammals have been classified with their own genus this century. The first live saola was captured in neighbouring Khammouane province in 1996.

The capital of Bolikhamsai is Paxxan, which can be reached from Vietntiane by bus in about three hours.

CHAMPASSAK PROVINCE - PAKSE

The province of Champassak is home to one of Asia's great, but least visited temples, Wat Phu. Pakse, the capital is situated at the confluence of the Se river and the Mekong (Pakse means 'mouth of the Se') and is a busy trading town. The province also houses much of the Bolaven Plateau, an area that is home to a number of ethnic minorities. To the south is Si Pan Don (four thousand islands), where the Mekong reaches up to 14km wide during the rainy season and the Khone Phapeng Falls.

Pakse has a number of comfortable places to stay and is a good base from which to explore the surrounding area. The town has one of the largest markets in the region. Within Pakse is the Champassak Museum where trader can see relics from Wat Phu as well as from the Bolaven Plateau.

HOUA PHAN

Houa Phan province is situated in the northeast of Laos and was the base of the Lao People's Revolutionary Army activities. There are over 100 caves in the Vieng Xai district of Houa Phanh many of which were used as hideouts and bunkers during the Indochina war.

Lao Aviation flies daily to the capital Xam Neua from Vientiane - The most famous caves in the area are:

Tham Than Souphanouvong: formerly known as Tham Phapount. In 1964, Prince Souphanouvong set up his residence in this cave. Tham Than Kaysone: formerly known as Tham Yonesong, was established for the residence of Mr. Kaysone Phomvihane.

For additional analytical, business and investment opportunities information, please contact Global Investment & Business Center, USA at (703) 370-8082. Fax: (703) 370-8083. E-mail: ibpusa3@gmail.com Global Business and Investment Info Databank - www.ibpus.com

Tham Than Khamtay: was the residence of Mr. Khamtay Siphandone, consisting of many area, such as a meeting room, reception room and research room.

Other attractions include Keo Nong Vay Temple located in Xam Neua district.

Hot springs in Xam Tay district are located about 154 km away from Xam Neua the waters reach a temperature of around 40 degrees Celcius. Xam Tay waterfall is located Xam Tay district.

Saleu and Nasala villages, well known for their weaving activities, located in Xieng Kor district on the road No: 6 to Xieng Khouang province 125 km away from Xam Neua.

KHAMMOUANE PROVINCE

Khammouane province contains two vast wilderness areas known as the Khammuane Limestone National Biodiversity Conservation Area and the Nakai - Nam Theun National Biodiversity Conservation Area.

The Kahmmuane Limestone is a maze of limestone karst peaks forming a stone forest of caves, rivers and pristine jungle. For most of the wet season, the area is not accessible by road - most 'roads' being tracks with log bridges across deeps streams. These tracks are often routes across rice paddies near the river banks - during the rainy season, the only way to get around is by boat.

The National Tourism Authority of Lao PDR is currently investigating ecotourism projects in this beautiful region. The capital of Khammouane province is Tha Kek, situated across the Mekong from Nakorn Phanom in Thailand.

LUANG PRABANG

Luang Prabang is the jewel of Indochina, and a UNESCO World Heritage Site since 1995. The ancient royal city is surrounded by mountains at the junction of the Mekong and its tributary, the Khan river. In the centre of the city is Mount Phousi with stunning views of the surrounding temples and hills. Luang Prabang is a city where time seems to stand still. As part of the UNESCO plan, new buildings have been limited and development must be in keeping with this magical place.

Minority village in Luang Namtha

Luang Prabang is small, and just about everywhere can be reached by foot. Walking and travelling by bicycle is the best way to see this tiny city.

LUANG NAMTHA PROVINCE

Located in the northern part of Laos, Luang Namtha shares its northwestern border with Myanmar and its northeastern border with China. The province is mountainous, home to large numbers of minorities. The Nam Ha National Biodiversity Conservation Area is located in the southwest of Luang Namtha - a pristine habitat of dense tropical rainforest covering almost all of the protected area.

UNESCO are funding a ecotourism project in Luang Namtha that will be capable of sustaining sustainable development in the province. The concept of the project is to provide education, conservation, management and sustainable economic benefits for the local population. The province is home to a 39 minorities the largest number in the country.

OUDOMXAI

Located in the northern part of Laos. This mountainous province has 23 ethnic groups each with it own distinct culture, religion, language and colorful style of dress. The provincial capital , Muang Xay lies between two strings of Hmong villages.

Lao Aviation flies to Oudomxai from Vientiane

Oudomxai can be reached overland from Luang Prabang. Oudomxay is also accessible from Bokeo and Luang Namtha Provinces. Oudomxay is an ideal base for excursions and trekking to varied sights and attractions as well as destination in its own right. Muang Xai, has one of the best produce markets in the area.

Near Muang Xai, there is a waterfall, Lak Sip – Et (located at km No 11) and hot springs near Muang La.

PHONGSALI PROVINCE

Phongsali province the most remote in northern Laos is surrounded on three sides by China and Vietnam.   The Phu Den Din National Biodiversity Conservation Area along the Vietnamese border with mountains as high as 1950m with over 70% forest cover is home to the asiatic black bear, bantang, clouded leopard, elephant, guar and tiger.

The capital Phongsali, can be reached from Muang Xai with buses leaving once a day. Phongsali has a year round cool climate with temperatures as low as 5 degrees Celcius at night. Rain can be heavy - bring a jacket and warm clothes.

Muang Khoa is a small town situated on the junction of Route 4 and the Nam Ou river. The journey to Muang Khoa along route 4 from Udomxai takes about four hours. It is possible to travel up river to Phongsali from here, or down to Luang Prabang.

SALAVAN PROVINCE

Salavan Province is best known for the Bolaven Plateau, which also extends into Attapeu, Champassak and Sekong provinces. The Bolaven Plateau is covered in the Champassak section.. The plateau is best accessed from Pakse, in Champassak province.

Salavan province is home to the Phu Xieng Thong National Biodiversity Conservation Area, covering nearly 1,000 sq km in the western part of the province next to the Mekong river. It is thought that asiatic black bear, banteng, clouded leopard, Douc langur, elephant, gibbon, guar, Siamese crocodile and tiger and inhabit this area.

SEKONG PROVINCE

Sekong Province is best known for the Bolaven Plateau, which also extends into Attapeu, Champassak and Salavan and provinces. The Bolaven Plateau is covered in the Champassak section. The plateau is best accessed from Pakse, in Champassak province. Sekong province is rugged,wild and very scenic, but transportation is very difficult, especially by land in the rainy season.

SAYABOURI PROVINCE

Sayabouri province is quite close to Vientiane, but being quite mountainous is quite remote.   The province shares its borders with six Thai provinces. The capital of the province, Sayabouri is on the banks of the Nam Hung, a tributary of the Mekong.

The province houses the Nam Phoun National Biodiversity Conservation Area which is 1150 sq km of forested hills that contain Asiatic black bear, dhole, elephant, guar, gibbon, Malayan sun bear and Sumatran rhino.

The southern part of the province has many scenic waterfalls, but getting around this part of the province is very difficult.

SAVANNAKHET

Savannakhet town is situated on the banks of the   Mekong river opposite Mukdahan in Thailand. The province bridges the country between Thailand and Vietnam and the town is a very active junction for trade between the two countries. The town itself can be easily explored by foot and has a number of interesting temples, including Vietnamese temple and school and a large Catholic church. Much of the town's architecture is French Colonial.

VIENTIANE

Vientiane, capital of Laos is Asia's biggest village. Busy and hectic in comparison to the rest of the country, it is quiet compared with any other city in Asia. Vientiane, as all of Lao's major cities, is situated on the Mekong river which forms the lifeline of the country. Vientiane is the hub for all travel in the country. The city has a population of 450,000, about 10% of the country.

Vientiane is a city full of surprises. Here trader can find fields of rice and vegetables, agriculture hidden behind tree lined avenues. French Colonial architecture sits next to gilded temples. Freshly baked French bread is served next to shops selling noodle soup.

There is little modern in Vientiane. Old French colonial houses are being restored as offices and as restaurants and hotels. There are only a handful of modern buildings which sometimes look remarkably out of place in this quiet capital.

XIENG KHOUANG PROVINCE

Xieng Khouang province is situated in the north of Laos, a province of green montains and karst limestone. Much of the province was heavily bombed during the Vietnam war and old war scrap is used in building houses throughout the province. The capital of Xieng Khouang is Phonsavan. Situated at an altitude of 1,200m is an excellent climate. Decmber and January can be chilly so bring a light jacket or fleece for cool evenings and mornings.

PEOPLE

Laos' population was estimated at about 5.4 million in 1999, dispersed unevenly across the country. Most people live in valleys of the Mekong River and its tributaries. Vientiane prefecture, the capital and largest city, had about 569,000 residents in 1999. The country's population density is 23.4/sq. km.

About half the country's people are ethnic Lao, the principal lowland inhabitants and politically and culturally dominant group. The Lao are descended from the Tai people who began migrating southward from China in the first millennium A.D. Mountain tribes of Miao-Yao, Austro-Asiatic, Tibeto-Burman--Hmong, Yao, Akha, and Lahu--and Tai ethnolinguistic heritage are found in northern Laos. Collectively, they are known as Lao Sung or highland Lao. In the central and southern mountains, Mon-Khmer tribes, known as Lao Theung or midslope Lao, predominate. Some Vietnamese and Chinese minorities remain, particularly in the towns, but many left in two waves--after independence in the late 1940s and again after 1975.

The predominant religion is Theravada Buddhism. Animism is common among the mountain tribes. Buddhism and spirit worship coexist easily. There also is a small number of Christians and Muslims.

The official and dominant language is Lao, a tonal language of the Tai linguistic group. Midslope and highland Lao speak an assortment of tribal languages. French, once common in government and commerce, has declined in usage, while knowledge of English--the language of the Association of Southeast Asian Nations (ASEAN)--has increased in recent years.

HISTORY

Laos traces its first recorded history and its origins as a unified state to the emergence of the Kingdom of Lan Xang (literally, "million elephants") in 1353. Under the rule of King Fa Ngum, the wealthy and mighty kingdom covered much of what today is Thailand and Laos. His successors, especially King Setthathirat in the 16th century, helped establish Buddhism as the predominant religion of the country.

For additional analytical, business and investment opportunities information, please contact Global Investment & Business Center, USA at (703) 370-8082. Fax: (703) 370-8083. E-mail: ibpusa3@gmail.com Global Business and Investment Info Databank - www.ibpus.com

By the 17th century, the kingdom of Lan Xang entered a period of decline marked by dynastic struggle and conflicts with its neighbors. In the late 18th century, the Siamese (Thai) established hegemony over much of what is now Laos. The region was divided into principalities centered on Luang Prabang in the north, Vientiane in the center, and Champassak in the south. Following its colonization of Vietnam, the French supplanted the Siamese and began to integrate all of Laos into the French empire. The Franco-Siamese treaty of 1907 defined the present Lao boundary with Thailand.

During World War II, the Japanese occupied French Indochina, including Laos. King Sisavang Vong of Luang Prabang was induced to declare independence from France in 1945, just prior to Japan's surrender. During this period, nationalist sentiment grew. In September 1945, Vientiane and Champassak united with Luang Prabang to form an independent government under the Free Laos (Lao Issara) banner. The movement, however, was shortlived. By early 1946, French troops reoccupied the country and conferred limited autonomy on Laos following elections for a constituent assembly.

Amidst the first Indochina war between France and the communist movement in Vietnam, Prince Souphanouvong formed the Pathet Lao (Land of Laos) resistance organization committed to the communist struggle against colonialism. Laos was not granted full sovereignty until the French defeat by the Vietnamese and the subsequent Geneva peace conference in 1954. Elections were held in 1955, and the first coalition government, led by Prince Souvanna Phouma, was formed in 1957. The coalition government collapsed in 1958, amidst increased polarization of the political process. Rightist forces took over the government.

In 1960, Kong Le, a paratroop captain, seized Vientiane in a coup and demanded formation of a neutralist government to end the fighting. The neutralist government, once again led by Souvanna Phouma, was not successful in holding power. Rightist forces under Gen. Phoumi Nosavan drove out the neutralist government from power later that same year. Subsequently, the neutralists allied themselves with the communist insurgents and began to receive support from the Soviet Union. Phoumi Nosavan's rightist regime received support from the U.S.

A second Geneva conference, held in 1961-62, provided for the independence and neutrality of Laos. Soon after accord was reached, the signatories accused each other of violating the terms of the agreement, and with superpower support on both sides, the civil war soon resumed. Although the country was to be neutral, a growing American and North Vietnamese military presence in the country increasingly drew Laos into the second Indochina war (1954-75). For nearly a decade, Laos was subjected to the heaviest bombing in the history of warfare, as the U.S. sought to destroy the Ho Chi Minh Trail that passed through eastern Laos.

In 1972, the communist People's Party renamed itself the Lao People's Revolutionary Party (LPRP). It joined a new coalition government in Laos soon after the Vientiane cease-fire agreement in 1973. Nonetheless, the political struggle between communists, neutralists, and rightists continued. The fall of Saigon and Phnom Penh to communist forces in April 1975 hastened the decline of the coalition in Laos. Months after these communist victories, the Pathet Lao entered Vientiane. On December 2, 1975, the king abdicated his throne in the constitutional monarchy, and the communist Lao People's Democratic Republic (LPDR) was established.

The new communist government imposed centralized economic decisionmaking and broad security measures, including control of the media and the arrest and incarceration of many members of the previous government and military in "re-education camps". These draconian policies and deteriorating economic conditions, along with government efforts to enforce political control, prompted an exodus of lowland Lao and ethnic Hmong from Laos. About 10% of the Lao population sought refugee status after 1975. Many have since been resettled in third countries, including more than 250,000 who have come to the United States.

The situation of Lao refugees is nearing its final chapter. Over time, the Lao Government closed the re-education camps and released most political prisoners. From 1975 to 1996, the U.S. resettled some 250,000 Lao refugees from Thailand, including 130,000 Hmong. By the end of 1999, more than 28,900 Hmong and lowland Lao had repatriated to Laos--3,500 from China, the rest from Thailand. Through the Office of the United Nations High Commissioner for Refugees (UNHCR), the International Organization for Migration (IOM), and non-governmental organizations, the U.S. has supported a variety of reintegration assistance programs throughout Laos. UNHCR monitors returnees and reports no evidence of systemic persecution or discrimination to date. As of December 1999, about 115 Hmong and lowland Lao remained in Ban Napho camp in Thailand awaiting third-country resettlement by the UNHCR.

GOVERNMENT AND POLITICAL CONDITIONS

The only legal political party is the Lao People's Revolutionary Party (LPRP). The head of state is President Khamtay Siphandone. The head of government is Prime Minister Sisavath Keobounphanh, who also is Chairman of the LPRP. Government policies are determined by the party through the all-powerful nine-member Politburo and the 49-member Central Committee. Important government decisions are vetted by the Council of Ministers.

Laos adopted a constitution in 1991. The following year, elections were held for a new 85-seat National Assembly with members elected by secret ballot to 5-year terms. This National Assembly, expanded in 1997 elections to 99 members, approves all new laws, although the executive branch retains authority to issue binding decrees. The most recent elections took place in December 1997. The FY 2000 central government budget plan calls for revenue of $180 million and expenditures of $289 million, including capital expenditures of $202 million.

PRINCIPAL GOVERNMENT OFFICIALS NEW CABINET MEMBERS APPROVED

The National Assembly, the country's top legislature on 15 June approved the appointment of Mr. Thongsing Thammavong as Prime Minister and four deputy prime ministers and cabinet members.

The First Plenary Session of the 7 th NA approved the proposed list of four deputy prime ministers are Mr. Asang Laoly, Dr. Thongloun Sisoulith, Mr. Duangchay Phichit and Mr. Somsavat Lengsavad. Four of them are members of Politburo under the Lao People's Revolutionary Party Central Committee.

Under the approval, Dr. Thongloun Sisoulith is responsible for Ministry of Foreign Affairs and Mr. Duangchay Phitchit takes the post the Minister of National Defence.

The NA also approved the appointment of government members accordingly,

Mr. Bounthong Chitmany serves as President of State Inspection Committee and Head of Anti-Corruption Agency;

Mr. Phankham Viphavanh, Minister of Education and Sports;

Mr. Thongbanh Seng-aphone, Minister Public Security; Mrs Onchanh Thammavong, Minister of Labour and Social-Welfare;

Mr. Chaleune Yiabaoher, Minister of Justice;

Mr. Soulivong Daravong, Minister of Energy and Mining;

Mrs Bounpheng Mouphosay, Minister for Government's Office;

Mr. Vilayvanh Phomkhe, Minister of Agriculture and Forestry;

Mr. Sinlavong Khouphaythoune, Minister and Head of Government's Office;

Mr. Nam Viyaket, Minister of Industry and Commerce;

Mr. Sommad Pholsena, Minister of Public Works and Transport;

Mr. Somdy Duangdy, Minister of Planning and Investment;

Mr. Phouphet Khamphounvong, Minister of Finance;

Prof Dr. Bosengkham Vongdara, Minister of Information, Culture and Tourism;

Prof Dr. Eksavang Vongvichit, Minister of Public Health;

Mr. Bounheuang Duangphachanh, Minister for Government's Office;

Mr. Khampane Philavong, Minister of Interior;

Prof Dr. Bountiem Phitsamay, Minister for Government's Office;

Dr. Douangsavad Souphanouvong, Minister for Government's Office;

Mrs Khempheng Pholsena, Minister for Government's Office;

Prof Dr. Boviengkham Vongdara, Minister of Science and Technology;

Mr. Noulin Sinbandith, Minister of Natural Resources and Environment;

Mr. Hiem Phommachanh, Minister of Post, Telecommunication and Communication;

Mr. Sompao Phaysith, Governor of the State Bank of Laos;

Mr. Khamphanh Sitthidampha, President of People's Supreme Court and

Mr. Khamsan Souvong, Head of General Prosecutor's Office.

Laos maintains an embassy in the United States at 2222 S Street NW, Washington, D.C. 20009 (tel: 202-332-6416).

ECONOMY

Currency	Lao Kip
Fiscal year	1 October - 30 September
Trade organisations	ASEAN, WTO
	Statistics
GDP	$17.66 billion (PPP; est.)
GDP growth	8.3% (2014 est.)
GDP per capita	$2,700 (PPP; est.)
GDP by sector	services (42.6%), industry (20.2%), agriculture (37.4%) (est.)
Inflation (CPI)	7.6% (est.)
Population below poverty line	26% (est.)
Labour force	3.69 million (est.)
Labour force by occupation	agriculture (75.1%), industry (n/a), services (n/a) (est.)
Unemployment	2.5% (est.)
Main industries	copper, tin, gold, and gypsum mining; timber, electric power, agricultural processing, construction, garments, cement, tourism
Ease of doing business rank	165th
	External
Exports	$2.131 billion (est.)
Export goods	wood products, garments, electricity, coffee, tin, copper, gold
Main export partners	Thailand 32.8% China 20.7% Vietnam 14.0% (est.)
Imports	2.336 billion (est.)
Import goods	machinery and equipment, vehicles, fuel, consumer goods
Main import partners	Thailand 63.2% China 16.5%

	Vietnam 5.6% (est.)
Gross external debt	$5.953 billion (31 December 2011 est)
	Public finances
Public debt	$3.179 billion
Revenues	$1.76 billion
Expenses	$1.957 billion (est.)
Economic aid	$345 million (est.)
Foreign reserves	$773.5 (31 December est.)

The **economy of the Lao Peoples' Democratic Republic** is rapidly growing, as the government began to decentralise control and encourage private enterprise in 1986. Currently, the economy grows at 8% a year, and the government is pursuing poverty reduction and education for all children as key goals. The country opened a stock exchange, the Lao Securities Exchange in 2011, and has become a rising regional player in its role as a hydroelectric power supplier to neighbors such as China, Vietnam and Thailand. Laos remains one of the poorest countries in Southeast Asia, but may transition from being a low middle-income country to an upper-middle income one by 2020. A landlocked country, it has inadequate infrastructure and a largely unskilled work force. The country's per capita income in 2009 was estimated to be $2,700 on a purchasing power parity-basis.

The Lao economy depends heavily on investment and trade with its neighbours, Thailand, Vietnam, and, especially in the north, China. Pakxe has also experienced growth based on cross-border trade with Thailand and Vietnam. In 2009, despite the fact that the government is still officially communist, the Obama administration in the US declared Laos was no longer a marxist-lenninist state and lifted bans on Laotian companies receiving financing from the U.S. Export Import Bank. In 2011, the Lao Securities Exchange began trading. In 2014, the government initiated the creation of the Laos Trade Portal, a website incorporating all information traders need to import and export goods into the country.

Subsistence agriculture still accounts for half of the GDP and provides 80% of employment. Only 4.01% of the country is arable land, and a mere 0.34% used as permanent crop land, the lowest percentage in the Greater Mekong Subregion. Rice dominates agriculture, with about 80% of the arable land area used for growing rice. Approximately 77% of Lao farm households are self-sufficient in rice.

Through the development, release and widespread adoption of improved rice varieties, and through economic reforms, production has increased by an annual rate of 5% between 1990 and 2005, and Lao PDR achieved a net balance of rice imports and exports for the first time in 1999. Lao PDR may have the greatest number of rice varieties in the Greater Mekong Subregion. Since 1995 the Lao government has been working with the International Rice Research Institute of the Philippines to collect seed samples of each of the thousands of rice varieties found in Laos.

The economy receives development aid from the IMF, ADB, and other international sources; and also foreign direct investment for development of the society, industry, hydropower and mining (most notably of copper and gold). Tourism is the fastest-growing industry in the country. Economic development in Laos has been hampered by brain drain, with a skilled emigration rate of 37.4% in 2000.

Laos is rich in mineral resources and imports petroleum and gas. Metallurgy is an important industry, and the government hopes to attract foreign investment to develop the substantial deposits of coal, gold, bauxite, tin, copper, and other valuable metals. In addition, the country's plentiful water resources and mountainous terrain enable it to produce and export large quantities of hydroelectric energy. Of the potential capacity of approximately 18,000 megawatts, around 8,000 megawatts have been committed for exporting to Thailand and Vietnam.

The country's most widely recognised product may well be Beerlao which is exported to a number of countries including neighbours Cambodia and Vietnam. It is produced by the Lao Brewery Company.

FOREIGN RELATIONS

The new government that assumed power in December 1975 aligned itself with the Soviet bloc and adopted a hostile posture toward the West. In ensuing decades, Laos maintained close ties with the former Soviet Union and its eastern bloc allies and depended heavily on the Soviets for most of its foreign assistance. Laos also maintained a "special relationship" with Vietnam and formalized a 1977 treaty of friendship and cooperation that created tensions with China.

With the collapse of the Soviet Union and with Vietnam's decreased ability to provide assistance, Laos has sought to improve relations with its regional neighbors. The Lao Government has focused its efforts on Thailand, Laos' principal means of access to the sea and its primary trading partner. Within a year of serious border clashes in 1987, Lao and Thai leaders signed a communiquŽ, signaling their intention to improve relations. Since then, they have made slow but steady progress, notably the construction and opening of the Friendship Bridge between the two countries.

Relations with China have improved over the years. Although the two were allies during the Vietnam War, the China-Vietnam conflict in 1979 led to a sharp deterioration in Sino-Lao relations. These relations began to improve in the late 1980s. In 1989 Sino-Lao relations were normalized.

Laos' emergence from international isolation has been marked through improved and expanded relations with other nations such as Australia, France, Japan, Sweden, and India. Laos was admitted into the Association of Southeast Asian Nations (ASEAN) in July 1997 and applied to join WTO in 1998.

Laos is a member of the following international organizations: Agency for Cultural and Technical Cooperation (ACCT), Association of Southeast Asian Nations (ASEAN), ASEAN Free Trade Area (AFTA), ASEAN Regional Forum, Asian Development Bank, Colombo Plan, Economic and Social Commission for Asia and Pacific (ESCAP), Food and Agriculture Organization (FAO), G-77, International Bank for Reconstruction and Development (World Bank), International Civil Aviation Organization (ICAO),

International Development Association (IDA), International Fund for Agricultural Development (IFAD), International Finance Corporation (IFC), International Federation of Red Cross and Red Crescent Societies, International Labor Organization (ILO), International Monetary Fund (IMF), Intelsat (nonsignatory user), Interpol, International Olympic Commission (IOC), International Telecommunications Union (ITU), Mekong Group, Non-Aligned Movement (NAM), Permanent Court of Arbitration (PCA), UN, United Nations Convention on Trade and Development (UNCTAD), United Nations Educational, Social and Cultural Organization (UNESCO), United Nations Industrial Development Organization (UNIDO), Universal Postal Union (UPU), World Federation of Trade Unions, World Health Organization (WHO), World Intellectual Property Organization (WIPO), World Meteorological Organization (WMO), World Tourism Organization, World Trade Organization (observer).

U.S.-LAO RELATIONS

The United States opened a legation in Laos in 1950. Although diplomatic relations were never severed, U.S.-Lao relations deteriorated badly in the post-Indochina War period. The relationship remained cool until 1982 when efforts at improvement began. For the United States, progress in accounting for Americans missing in Laos from the Vietnam War is a principal measure of improving relations. Counternarcotics activities also have become an important part of the bilateral relationship as the Lao Government has stepped up its efforts to combat cultivation; production; and transshipment of opium, heroin, and marijuana.

Since the late 1980s, progress in these areas has steadily increased. Joint U.S. and Lao teams have conducted a series of joint excavations and investigations of sites related to cases of Americans missing in Laos. In counternarcotics activities, the U.S. and Laos are involved in a multimillion-dollar crop substitution/integrated rural development program. Laos also has formed its own national committee on narcotics, developed a long-range strategy for counternarcotics activities, participated in U.S.-sponsored narcotics training programs, and strengthened law enforcement measures to combat the narcotics problem.

U.S. Government foreign assistance to Laos covers a broad range of efforts. Such aid includes support for Laos' efforts to suppress opium production; training and equipment for a program to clear and dispose of unexploded ordnance; school and hospital construction; public education about the dangers of unexploded ordnance and about HIV/AIDS; support for medical research on hepatitis. Economic relations also are expanding. In August 1997, Laos and the United States initialed a Bilateral Trade Agreement and a Bilateral Investment Treaty.

Principal U.S. Embassy Officials

Ambassador-- Rena Bitter

Ambassador Rena Bitter is a career Senior Foreign Service Officer with more than 20 years of experience in Washington and overseas. Most recently, Ambassador Bitter served as Consul General at the U.S. Consulate General in Ho Chi Minh City, Vietnam. Prior to that, she served as the Director of the State Department Operations Center, the Department's 24/7 Briefing and

Crisis Management Center. In Washington, she served on the Secretary of State's Executive Staff and as a Special Assistant to Secretary Colin Powell. Her overseas tours include Amman, London, Mexico City and Bogota. Ambassador Bitter grew up in Dallas.

Deputy Chief of Mission--Susan M. Sutton

The American Embassy in Laos is on Rue Bartholonie, B.P. 114, Vientiane, tel: 212-581/582/585; fax: 212-584: country code: (856): city code (21).

Information on the embassy, its work in Laos, and U.S.-Lao relations is available on the Internet at http://www.usembassy.state.gov/laos.

TRAVEL AND BUSINESS INFORMATION

The U.S. Department of State's Consular Information Program provides Consular Information Sheets, Travel Warnings, and Public Announcements. **Consular Information Sheets** exist for all countries and include information on entry requirements, currency regulations, health conditions, areas of instability, crime and security, political disturbances, and the addresses of the U.S. posts in the country. **Travel Warnings** are issued when the State Department recommends that Americans avoid travel to a certain country. **Public Announcements** are issued as a means to disseminate information quickly about terrorist threats and other relatively short-term conditions overseas which pose significant risks to the security of American travelers. Free copies of this information are available by calling the Bureau of Consular Affairs at 202-647-5225 or via the fax-on-demand system: 202-647-3000.

Consular Information Sheets and Travel Warnings also are available on the Consular Affairs Internet home page: http://travel.state.gov. Consular Affairs Tips for Travelers publication series, which contain information on obtaining passports and planning a safe trip abroad are on the internet and hard copies can be purchased from the Superintendent of Documents, U.S. Government Printing Office, telephone: 202-512-1800; fax 202-512-2250.

Emergency information concerning Americans traveling abroad may be obtained from the Office of Overseas Citizens Services at (202) 647-5225. For after-hours emergencies, Sundays and holidays, call 202-647-4000.

Passport information can be obtained by calling the National Passport Information Center's automated system ($.35 per minute) or live operators 8 a.m. to 8 p.m. (EST) Monday-Friday ($1.05 per minute). The number is 1-900-225-5674 (TDD: 1-900-225-7778). Major credit card users (for a flat rate of $4.95) may call 1-888-362-8668 (TDD: 1-888-498-3648). It also is available on the internet.

Travelers can check the latest health information with the U.S. Centers for Disease Control and Prevention in Atlanta, Georgia. A hotline at 877-FYI-TRIP (877-394-8747) and a web site at http://www.cdc.gov/travel/index.htm give the most recent health advisories, immunization recommendations or requirements, and advice on food and drinking water safety for regions and countries. A booklet entitled Health Information for

International Travel (HHS publication number CDC-95-8280) is available from the U.S. Government Printing Office, Washington, DC 20402, tel. (202) 512-1800.

Information on travel conditions, visa requirements, currency and customs regulations, legal holidays, and other items of interest to travelers also may be obtained before your departure from a country's embassy and/or consulates in the U.S. (for this country, see "Principal Government Officials" listing in this publication).

U.S. citizens who are long-term visitors or traveling in dangerous areas are encouraged to register at the U.S. embassy upon arrival in a country (see "Principal U.S. Embassy Officials" listing in this publication). This may help family members contact you in case of an emergency.

For additional analytical, business and investment opportunities information, please contact Global Investment & Business Center, USA at (703) 370-8082. Fax: (703) 370-8083. E-mail: ibpusa3@gmail.com Global Business and Investment Info Databank - www.ibpus.com

TAXATION SYSTEM IN LAOS: STRATEGIC INFORMATION

Tax or mandatory contribution	Payments (number)	Time (hours)	Statutory tax rate	Tax base	Total tax rate (% profit)	Notes on TTR
Corporate income tax	4	138	35.0%	taxable profit	25.2	
Social Security contributions	12	42	5.0%	gross salaries	5.6	
Property transfer tax (stamp duty)	1		3% or 4%	sale price	2.4	
Fuel tax	1			included in the price of fuel	0.4	
Land tax	1		80 to 180 kip	per square meter	0	
Vehicle tax	1		Kip 40,000	type of vehicle	0	
Tax on insurance contracts	1		0.2%	insurance premium	0	
Stamp duty on general contracts	1		Kip 10,000	per contract		small amount
Business turnover tax on sales (VAT)	12	182	5% and 10%	value added		not included
Totals:	34	362			33.7	

CORPORATE TAX RATES

Profits tax applies to the profits of business operations and professional service providers. For businesses operated by Lao nationals, the profits tax rate is 35 percent. However, this rate falls to 20 percent where the entity is licensed under the Foreign Investment Law (FIL). Companies in certain industries (e.g. mining) are taxed at different rates, depending on their agreement with the Government of The Lao PDR. Further concessionary rates are available under the FIL, dependant upon the nature and location of activity. Additionally, the tax law provides for a Minimum Tax, which is a flat rate tax equal to between a quarter percent for all types of domestic manufacturing activities and one percent for trade and services (including for freelancers) of the turnover. This tax can be offset against any profits tax liability.

PERSONAL TAX RATES

Where a foreigner is employed by an entity falling under the FIL the foreigner will be subject to income tax at a flat rate of 10 percent. For Lao nationals, their income is subject to progressive rates of up to 25 percent. Additionally, other income (both for locals and foreigners) is subject to income tax at the following rates:

Income	Income tax rates (%)
Income from houses, land or other assets Income	15
Income from dividends, profits from the sale of shares, interest from loans, security fees of individuals or legal entities	10
Income from non-commercial operations of the Lao Front for National Construction, mass organizations ocial organizations	10
Income from patents, copyright, trademarks, and other intellectual property of individuals or legal entities	5

Statutory reference: Lao Tax Law (No. 04/NA, dated 25 May 2005) article 60. **Currency** 1 US Dollar = approximately 8,469 Lao Kip 1 Lao Kip (LAK) = 0.000118 US Dollar (USD) *Source: Banque Pour Le Commerce Exterieur Lao on January 13, 2009)*

The Lao People's Democratic Republic (Lao PDR) Government is actively promoting inbound investment and there are a number of forms of investment available. The Law on the Promotion and Management of Foreign Investment (The Foreign Investment Law [FIL]) was adopted in March 1994, which was promulgated by a Presidential Decree in October 1995 and established a legal framework for foreign investment.

The FIL was subsequently amended in 2004, promulgated by a Presidential Decree on November 15, 2004. The key areas of investment encouraged by The Lao PDR Government are hydroelectric power, mining, manufacturing, infrastructure, tourism and telecommunications. Taxation in The Lao PDR is governed by legislation that was issued in late 1995 and early 1996 (Tax Law).

The Tax Law was amended by legislation that was promulgated by Presidential Decree on May 25, 2005, with the amendments effective from that date. In line with the Government's commitment to attracting inward investment, the taxation system for foreign investors was simplified under the FIL. The Lao PDR government is seeking to encourage more foreign investment and maintains lower business tax rates for foreign companies than those applicable to domestic companies. The current system of taxation in Laos remains one of the more liberal systems in the Asia-Pacific region.

However, it is still being developed and can be unclear at times. The Lao PDR taxes all Lao PDR resident individuals and companies1 on their worldwide income. Companies or branches established under the Foreign Investment Law, are only taxed in The Lao PDR on income earned in The Lao PDR. The Government imposes taxes on all persons or legal entities consuming goods or services, conducting business, performing independent professions and generating income in The Lao PDR.

There are 8 broad categories of tax outlined in the Tax Law, as follows:

• **VAT**

- **Turnover Tax**

- **Excise Tax**

- **Charges and Service Fees**

- **Personal Income Tax (PIT)**

- **Profit Tax and Income Tax**

- **Social Security**

- **Minimum Tax.**

Only juristic entities and individuals are recognized under the tax law, and are subject to "Profit Tax". There are no specific provisions in relation to the taxation of pass-through entities. The tax year in Laos is the calendar year, i.e. January 1 to December 31. ***Introduction of VAT*** Companies operating in Laos need to consider the implications of the new VAT regime (whether it applies to them directly now, or is expected to in the future) with regard to: Tax administration, including changes which may need to be made to invoice templates, training and awareness of the new regime among their finance staff, accounting, billing and financial systems, record keeping and reporting requirements. Refer to section 9.2 for more details

TAXATION OF COMPANIES

Companies registered under Lao PDR law are subject to profit tax on their worldwide income. Companies registered under the FIL and carrying on business in Laos are taxed on their net profits arising from their business activities in Laos. **2.2 Residence** There is no definition of residence for tax purposes in Lao PDR. All companies (including all forms of legal entity) that are registered under Lao PDR law, or that are incorporated under foreign law and carrying on business in Laos, are subject to Lao PDR profit tax (or minimum tax, if applicable).

TAXABLE INCOME

For the purpose of profits tax, taxable income includes the following:

- Income from industrial and handicraft production

- Income from the exploitation of natural resources

- Income from import/export businesses

- Income from wholesale or retail trade businesses

- Income from general service provision

For additional analytical, business and investment opportunities information,
please contact Global Investment & Business Center, USA
at (703) 370-8082. Fax: (703) 370-8083. E-mail: ibpusa3@gmail.com
Global Business and Investment Info Databank - www.ibpus.com

• Income of independent professionals.

CAPITAL GAINS TAX

There is no separate capital gains tax in Laos. Capital gains are taxed in the same manner as other operating profits.

DIVIDENDS

Dividends are subject to profit tax at the rate of 10 percent of the gross dividend received.

EXEMPT INCOME

Companies (both for local and foreign companies) that have received approval from the Government to invest in projects in priority areas in Laos may receive tax exemptions or discounted tax rates.

Discounted rates:

• Urban area (zone 3) - income tax rate from year 1 to year 2 is 0 percent, years 3 and to 4th is "10 percent" and year **5t**h onward is 20 percent

• Rural and lowland area (zone 2) - income tax rate from year 1 to year 5 is 0 percent, years 6 to 8 is 7.5 percent and year 9 onwards is 15 percent

• Mountains and remote area (zone 1) - income tax rate from year 1 to year 7 is 0 percent, and thereafter 10 percent

Statutory reference: Law on the Promotion of Foreign Investment in The Lao PDR (No.11/NA, dated October 22, 2004) article 17-18

DEDUCTIONS

Profit tax is calculated on the difference between the total income and total deductible expenses for the accounting year.

Certain expenses are allowable deductions in determining the annual profit, which is subject to profit tax, as follows:

• General expenses of the business; including utility costs, advertising, salaries, lease costs, and insurance.

• Certain expenses such as travel and entertaining costs relating to guests can be deducted up to 0.40 percent of the annual income (turnover), for each type of expense

- Depreciation can be claimed on a straight line or cost reduction method. In the year of acquisition or disposal, depreciation can be claimed for the portion of the year that the asset was owned

- Pre-operating expenses (amortized over two years)

- Reserves (provisions) made for risks relating to items such as inventory or receivables.

- Business Turnover Tax which is not permitted to be offset and other fees related to Business Turnover Tax **Specifically disallowed**

There are certain expenses that are specifically not allowable, including profits tax, minimum tax, income tax on salaries paid to partners in partnerships, luxury expenses such as golfing, dancing, sports, and other entertainment, interest payments to shareholders, all types of fines, donations, support payment, gifts and prizes.

The tax authorities will disallow other items of expenditure that are considered commercially unreasonable or cannot be supported by appropriate documentation. **2.8 Losses** Businesses and independent professionals who suffer annual losses acknowledged by the tax authorities may carry forward these losses for deduction from future taxable profits arising within the following three years. Upon expiration of this period, any remaining loss would be written off and no longer carried forward.

CONSOLIDATION

There are no grouping provisions in Laos PDR. **2.10 Tax Depreciation/Capital Allowances** Depreciation can be claimed on a straight line basis at varying rates ranging from 2.5 percent to 50 percent per annum, depending on the nature of the assets and the period of use. In the year of acquisition or disposal, depreciation can be claimed for the portion of the year in which the asset was owned.

AMORTIZATION

Amortization of expenditure is not provided for in the existing tax laws. **2.12 Interest** For profit tax purposes, interest is deductible on an accruals basis i.e. following the accounting treatment of interest. However, all interest payments must be supported by relevant documentation showing that the payments are commercially reasonable; otherwise, the tax authorities may seek to disallow an element of the interest expense. Payment of interest is subject to withholding tax at the rate of 10 percent.

Tax Rates

Profits tax applies to the profits of business operations and professional service providers. For businesses operated by Lao nationals, the profits tax rate is 35 percent. However, this rate falls to 20 percent where the entity is licensed under the FIL. Companies in certain industries (e.g. mining) may have an agreement with the

Government to be taxed at different rates. Further concessionary rates are available under the FIL, dependant upon the nature and location of the business activity.

Additionally, the tax law provides for a minimum tax (Minimum Tax), which is a flat rate tax equal to between a quarter percent for all types of domestic manufacturing activities and one percent for trade and services (including freelancers) of the business turnover. This tax can be offset against any profits tax liability.

Tax Administration

Profits tax is determined on a calendar year basis and is generally payable quarterly in advance with finalization carried out after the year-end. The first three payments are due on the April 10, July 10 and October 10 of the year in question, with a final payment due on March 10 following the year-end. The quarterly payments are based on the previous year's profit tax payments (or the profit projected in the plan for the accounting year) and the actual liability for the final March payment. Any residual profits tax payment can be carried forward for deduction against future profits tax liabilities.

SETTING UP BUSINESS AND TAXES

The FIL which was initially passed in 1994 and subsequently updated in 2004 outlines the procedures for foreign investment into The Lao PDR. The FIL is designed to attract capitalist-style enterprise and contains liberal provisions for repatriation of profits and the involvement of foreign equity in Lao businesses. It outlines the areas in which investment is encouraged and those areas where investment is not permitted. Prohibited areas include activities that affect national security, or those deemed detrimental to the environment, public health or national culture.

The law prescribes the forms of acceptable foreign investment and the rights, benefits and obligations that come with such investment. It also explains the responsibilities of the Committee for Promotion and Management of Investment (CPMI), formerly known as the Committee for Investment and Cooperation (CIC), the government body that deals with inward investment. Specific exemptions to tax rates and other requirements are set out in foreign business licenses. All applications for foreign investment go through the CPMI, which offers a one-stop service for investors. The process is legislated to take a maximum of 90 days, although in the majority of instances the process takes longer. The Enterprise Registry Office (ERO) is part of the Internal Trade Department and has a vertical line to the provinces, Vientiane Capital or districts or municipality. Its roles are to provide services for enterprise registration and to monitor and record the business unit's compliance with the Enterprise Law.

A person or juristic person shall apply for an enterprise name registration with the ERO at Vientiane Capital only in order to obtain the permit for name reservation and name certificate. An applicant outside of the Vientiane capital system may apply through the ERO at the provincial level where the enterprise is located. An enterprise name reservation permit is required before a name certificate can be issued and before submitting an application form to the CPMI. In the application phase, the investor deals principally with the CPMI and any appointed advisers. As the application progresses, it is referred to the relevant ministry. It is therefore desirable that officials at the specific

Ministries be informed of the application in advance. The investor is required to complete and submit a standard application to the CPMI in compliance with the one stop service mechanism, accompanied by certain documents depending on the legal form of the business venture. These documents are as follows: ● A standard application form for a foreign investment ● A feasibility study of the project/investment ● Articles of association

● Identification of the investor – a certificate of registration for a company, or identification such as a passport for an individual

● Memorandum of understanding, joint venture agreement, etc. for joint ventures

● Any other documentation as deemed necessary on a case-by-case basis

● Enterprise Name Certificate. The procedure for issuance of the licenses after the CPMI receives a complete investment application is as follows:

● Within two working days the CPMI shall submit the application to the relevant sectoral representative for examination and to seek directives from their leadership levels.

● After obtaining an Investment License from the CPMI, the agency for the commercial sector shall issue the Business license corresponding to the Investment license within 2 working days, In practice it may take longer than this.

The enterprise is required to notify its intention to further extend its Business license in October of each year. ● Subsequently, the agency for the financial sector shall issue the Tax registration license (temporary copy) within 2 working days. This temporary tax registration license has a term of 60 working days.

After the investor has fulfilled the condition for the importation of his capital, then the CPMI shall coordinate with the agency for the financial sector in order to issue a permanent Tax registration license to the investor within a further 2 working days. Business and Tax Registration licenses must be renewed annually. The scope of each license is limited, e.g. a company may need a separate import/export license in addition to its business license.

Foreign investors are permitted to incorporate wholly owned subsidiaries in The Lao PDR or enter into joint ventures with local and/or foreign partners. In any joint-venture arrangement, foreign investors must contribute at least 30 percent of the total equity capital. In some industries, such as wood production, only joint ventures are allowed. Banks have the choice of a joint venture or a wholly owned branch. Investors may also establish branches, however, as the law is unclear, few investors, apart from the banks, have chosen this form of business structure.

The government provides tax incentives to encourage investors to reinvest in The Lao PDR. An investor may reinvest profits in The Lao PDR without incurring any additional tax liability. If the enterprise suffers losses in the initial tax exemption period of two to four years, it may be permitted to carry the losses forward. The losses may then be deducted from taxes levied on profits in the following year, or be spread over a period of up to three years.

4 Foreign Exchange Controls The LAK is not a freely convertible currency. Investors should investigate the foreign currency implications when formulating investment plans and economic feasibility studies. Foreign investors and personnel may repatriate their earnings through a Lao bank or foreign bank established in The Lao PDR. As mentioned in 3.0 above, the FIL contains liberal provisions for repatriation of profits.

5 Tax Incentives The FIL provides special tax incentives for foreign investors in The Lao PDR. These incentives are summarized below: • Reduced tax rates for foreign companies and personnel where the investment is registered under the FIL • Certain investment incentives may be made available to investors where the relevant project relates to encouraging specific sectors or is located in certain regions • If a foreign enterprise is granted an initial tax exemption period of two to four years and suffers losses in that period, it may be permitted to carry the losses forward. The losses may then be deducted from taxes levied on profits in the following year, or be spread over a period of up to three years • Raw materials and intermediate components that are imported in order to achieve import substitution are eligible for special duty reductions.

INTERNATIONAL TAX

DOUBLE TAX RELIEF

Relief from international double taxation is provided by DTAs that The Lao PDR has negotiated with Thailand, China, North Korea, South Korea, Brunei, Kuwait, Russia and Vietnam. Treaties with Myanmar and Singapore are currently under negotiation. As there is limited outward investment from Laos, the DTA provisions for relief tend to follow the approach taken by the other country that is party to the DTA. 6.2 Withholding Taxes Certain payments are subject to withholding tax at the following rates:

Payments	Rates (%)
Dividends	10
Interest	10
Royalties	5

Statutory reference: Lao Tax Law (No. 04/NA, dated 19 May 2005), article 60. **6.3 Double Tax Agreements** In addition to Lao PDR's domestic arrangements that provide relief from international double taxation, Lao PDR has signed DTAs with Thailand, China, North Korea, South Korea, Brunei, Kuwait, Russia and Vietnam The following withholding tax rates apply to recipient countries that do not have a PE or fixed base in Lao.

Country of recipient	Dividends (%)	Interest) (%	Royalties (%)
China	5	5	5
Korea (Rep.)	5/10(1)	10	5
Russia	10	10	0

Thailand	10	10	5
Vietnam	10	10	5
North Korea	10	10	5
Brunei	5/10(2)	10	10
Kuwait	0	0	10

Note: 1. Dividend: - 5 percent of the gross amount of the dividends if the beneficial owner is a company (other than a

partnership) which holds directly at least 10 per cent of the capital of the company paying the dividends; - 10 percent of the gross amount of the dividends in all other cases. 2. Interest: - 10 percent of the gross amount of the interest if it is received by any financial institution (including an insurance company). - 15 percent of the gross amount of the interest in the other cases.

ANTI-AVOIDANCE RULES

There are no specific anti-avoidance provisions in either the 2005 Tax Law or the Foreign Investment Law. There are no transfer pricing rules in The Lao PDR.

There are no specific PE provisions under the Laos Tax Law. Notwithstanding, any individual or juristic body, resident or non-resident, is subject to profit tax on Laos source income. Lao PDR has signed DTAs with Thailand, Vietnam, North Korea, South Korea, Russia, Brunei, Kuwait and China. The typical wording of the term PE in those DTAs follows the OECD Model. There are no thin capitalization rules in The Lao PDR. There are no CFC provisions in The Lao PDR.

TAXATION OF INDIVIDUALS

Resident individuals deriving income generated in The Lao PDR are subject to Laos income tax on their worldwide income. Non-residents are subject to tax on their Laos sourced income.

RESIDENCE

An individual's residence is determined by the period of their stay in The Lao PDR. Individuals are regarded as resident in The Lao PDR if they are present for more than 180 days in any given tax year.

TAXABLE INCOME

Income typically subject to tax includes employment remuneration, returns on investment transactions and amounts received for the use of intellectual or real property. Employment remuneration includes bonuses and most benefits-in-kind, including the costs of accommodation provided.

CAPITAL GAINS TAX

There is no separate capital gains tax in Laos. Capital gains are taxed the same as other income. **8.5 Dividends** Dividends are taxed at a rate of 10 percent of the gross dividend declared. However, dividends that have been subject to withholding tax are excluded from the calculation of taxable income.

EMPLOYMENT INCOME

Taxable income includes income from salaries, such as wages, bonuses, position bonuses, and other material benefits, including benefits in kind.

EXEMPT INCOME

Certain types of income are exempted from tax in Laos, as follows: • Income of foreign experts implementing aid projects in The Lao PDR, as provided for in an agreement between the Lao government and the relevant party • Income earned from agricultural produce of family farming units

• Income of diplomats and employees of other international organizations located in The Lao PDR

• Income in the form of contributions to certain employment and welfare funds

• Income in bank deposit and bond related interest

• Income from certain awards and lottery wins

• Certain types of allowances which have been approved within the scope of the Labour Law

• One time allowances, pensions, and per diems

• Income from artistic activities, sports, charity or other public activities which have been properly authorized

• Prizes received for achievements in relation to scientific research and invention

• Social security • Allowances which are rewards or prizes paid by an official authority to those with a good record of monitoring, seeking out, defending against, combating against and preventing wrongful acts that violate the laws and regulations of the country.

TAX ADMINISTRATION

Salary tax is deducted at source by the employer on a monthly basis. Payment of salary tax to the tax authorities is made on a monthly basis, on or before the 15th day of the following month.

INDIRECT AND OTHER TAXES

Social Security Taxes The Social Security Decree came into force in June 2001 and is being introduced gradually. It will apply to: ● Employees of state-owned enterprises, private enterprises and joint enterprises ● Enterprises that employ 10 or more employees

● An enterprise that has less than 10 employees, but is a branch of a larger enterprise. The decree requires a deduction from gross salary as follows: ● Five percent to be paid by the employer ● Four and a half percent to be paid by the employee. Salaries above LAK 1,500,000 per month will be ignored for Social Security. As a result, the maximum charge will be LAK 75,000 per month from employers, and LAK 67,500 per month from employees. **9.2 VAT** From January 1, 2009 The Lao PDR introduced VAT.

The rate of VAT is 10%. Initially, the VAT is to apply to a limited range of locally produced and imported products including: Electricity, water, fuel and all imported products unless they receive an exemption from the Lao government. The Government's intention is to expand the scope of this new VAT, replacing the current Business Turnover Tax,. However it is acknowledged that companies in The Lao PDR need time to adapt their systems to cater for this regime and so the scope of the regime is only expected to be broadened slowly.

Those business operators subject to the new regime are required to register for the VAT regime with the tax authority. They will be required to file VAT returns from the day they are registered in the VAT system on a monthly basis. All companies which may now or in future be subject to the VAT regime in The Lao PDR need to be taking steps to prepare for the introduction of VAT; considering the implications for their financial systems and processes, staff training, record keeping and transaction documentation such as the content and layout of invoices.

TURNOVER TAX

Turnover tax is a form of goods and services tax. It is collected on imports and the sale of imported and locally produced goods. In addition, general services, constituting the supply of labor to others in return for a service fee, are also subject to turnover tax. The current applicable rates of turnover tax are five percent and ten percent. Payment of turnover tax is made to the tax authorities on a monthly basis, on or before the 15th day of the following month.

Taxpayers who have paid turnover tax at the point of origin may deduct the amount already paid from the amount of tax payable monthly. If the tax paid at the point of origin is in excess of the tax payable, the excess may be carried forward for offset in the following month. Importers of goods for re-export to third countries, export oriented producers or providers of services that have been subjected to turnover tax at the port of entry are entitled to deduct these payments from the taxes payable on the next import of goods, raw materials etc. As at 9.2 above, the Government is currently phasing in a VAT regime, from January 1, 2009, which is ultimately expected to replace the Business Turnover Tax regime, which consequently would be phased out. The full timetable for

For additional analytical, business and investment opportunities information, please contact Global Investment & Business Center, USA
at (703) 370-8082. Fax: (703) 370-8083. E-mail: ibpusa3@gmail.com
Global Business and Investment Info Databank - www.ibpus.com

this transition to VAT is not yet known and so currently both systems are operating in parallel.

CUSTOMS DUTY

Duties are levied on all types of imported and exported commodities at varying rates from five percent to 40 percent. Administrative fees are levied at five percent ad valorem on equipment and materials.

EXCISE DUTY

Excise tax is collected on certain types of goods, including fuel (five to 25 percent), alcohol (50 to 70 percent), carbonated drinks and invigorating drinks (10 to 30 percent), tobacco products (55 percent) and cosmetics (30 percent). Imports of equipment, means of production, spare parts and other materials used in the operation of foreign investors' projects or in their productive enterprises are taxed at a uniform flat rate of one percent of the imported value.

Raw materials and intermediate components, imported for the purpose of processing and then exported, are exempt from such import duties. For imported goods, excise tax is payable at the time of import; taxes must be remitted in full before goods leave the customs post. For domestic production, producers must produce a monthly excise tax return every month before the 15th day of the following month. **9.6 Stamp Duty** Stamp duty is imposed at LAK 50,000 per contract. All contracts in the Lao PDR need to be stamped.

PROPERTY TAXES

Land taxes vary depending on the location and the type of the land (e.g. land for construction, land for agriculture, etc). The calculation of land tax is based on both the location and the size of the land and is levied at annual rates per square meter. Land tax is payable in the first quarter of the relevant calendar year. **9.8 Payroll Tax** Salary tax is imposed at progressive rates of up to 25 percent on the gross income of Lao personnel as follows. Table 1: For a person with gross income not exceeding LAK 1,500,000 in a given month

Salary tax on earnings of foreign personnel is levied at a flat rate of 10 percent on gross income, including most benefits in kind. It is withheld at payment and paid over on a monthly basis to the tax authority. **9.9 Inheritance Tax** There is no inheritance tax in the Laos PDR. **9.10 Gift Tax** There is no gift tax in the Laos PDR.

TAXES ON NATURAL RESOURCES

Natural resources tax applies to the oil and gas industry and businesses involved in the exploitation of rare and precious resources, including oil shale/petroleum and natural gas, metallic/non-metallic minerals, construction materials, peat, anthracite, hydro-electric power and land concessions. The applicable rates vary from two to 20 percent of the sale or export price or are based on a tax per cubic meter. For wood, the taxes vary

For additional analytical, business and investment opportunities information,
please contact Global Investment & Business Center, USA
at (703) 370-8082. Fax: (703) 370-8083. E-mail: ibpusa3@gmail.com
Global Business and Investment Info Databank - www.ibpus.com

depending upon the type of wood. Tobacco, coffee, tea and flower seeds are also subject to natural resources tax.

CHARGES AND SERVICE FEES

Under the Tax law, Government sectors can collect fees for the issuance of enterprise registration licenses, tax registration licenses, business licenses, permits, certificates or other official documents, the use of roads, the entry into and exit from the country, the issuance of visas to enter and exit the country, residency in Laos, the use of radio and television satellite receivers, the affixing of advertising signs, shop signs, and other services in The Lao PDR. The charges and service fee rates are set periodically by Presidential Decree in order to meet the actual socio-economic conditions from time to time. *Import Duty on Motor Vehicles* The standard rate of import duty on motor vehicles ranges from 50 to 150 percent. However, for the time being, companies and joint ventures with operating licenses (including branches but excluding representative offices) are able to import vehicles for use in production and direct services such as: trucks, bulldozers, goods transportation trucks and buses (for transportation business of 35 seats and above) shall be granted importation with exemption from duty, use tax, and business turnover tax. The number of vehicles that are receiving approval for importation with custom duty, use tax and business turnover tax exemption must be consistent with the volume of work based on the economic-technical feasibility study and the actual demand of each project adopted by the relevant sector agencies.

Other taxes include:

● Document registration fees at variable ad valorem rates on the registration of legal documents

● Annual tax registration fees at variable rates, based on turnover or estimated turnover

● Annual road taxes at variable rates on all vehicles to be used in the Lao PDR

BASIC TAX RATES IN LAOS

PROFIT TAX

Description	Rates
Standard rate	24%
Tobacco companies	26%
Freelancers & sole-trader enterprises	Progressive rates of 0% to 24%

EMPLOYEE INCOME TAX

Annual turnover	Lump-sum tax rates		
(LAK)	Manufacturing	Trading	Services
Less than 12,000,000	Exempt	Exempt	Exempt
12,000,001 – 50,000,000	Fixed amount – but not exceeding LAK600,000 per year		

Level	Taxable Salary at Each Level (LAK)	Basis of Calculation (LAK)	Tax Rate	Income Tax at Each Level (LAK)	Cumulative Income Tax (LAK)
	50,000,001 – 120,000,000	3%		4%	5%
	120,000,001 – 240,000,000	4%		5%	6%
	240,000,001 – 400,000,000	5%		6%	7%
1	1,000,000 and below	1,000,000	0%	0	0
2	1,000,001 – 3,000,000	2,000,000	5%	100,000	100,000
3	3,000,001 – 6,000,000	3,000,000	10%	300,000	400,000
4	6,000,001 – 12,000,000	6,000,000	12%	720,000	1,120,000
5	12,000,001 – 24,000,000	12,000,000	15%	1,800,000	2,920,000
6	24,000,001 – 40,000,000	16,000,000	20%	3,200,000	6,120,000
7	Above 40,000,000		24%		

NON-RESIDENTS & COMPULSORY PROFIT WITHHOLDING TAX

Income source	Gross profit rates	Profit tax deemed rates
Production activity (agricultural and industrial products)	3%	0.72%
Commercial activity	5%	1.2%
Services:		
1. Goods and passenger transportation	5%	1.2%
2. Construction and repairs	10%	2.4%
3. Exploitation and trading of trees, wood, minerals and other forest products	20%	4.8%
4. Tree plantation and exploitation	5%	1.2%
5. Black and red soil, sand and rock extraction, land filling activities	15%	3.6%
6. Entertainment activities	25%	6%
7. Legal, engineering, architecture and other consultancy activities	10%	2.4%
8. Brokers and agents	20%	4.8%
9. Development of lands and buildings for sale	20%	4.8%
Other services	10%	2.4%

OTHER INCOME TAXES

Type of income	Rates
Dividends, interest, commissions	10%
Sales of shares	2% or 10%
Rental of real estate, vehicles, machinery, goods	10%
Royalties from intellectual property	5%
Transfer of land-use, building-use rights	2% or 10%

VALUE ADDED TAX

Type of supply	Rates
Import of goods Local production of goods and supply of services Export of unprocessed natural resources	10%
Export of goods Export of processed natural resources	0%

EXCISE TAX

Type of goods	Rates for 20162017	Rates for 20182019	Rates for 2020 and after
Fuel: -Gasoline (super) -Gasoline (normal) -Diesel -Jet fuel -Lubricants, hydraulic oil, grease, and brake oil	35% 30% 20% 10% 5%	39% 34% 24% 14% 9%	
Compressed natural gas for vehicles	10%		
Liquor or alcoholic drinks: -Liquor or drinks with alcoholic content of 20 percent and over -Liquor, wine and other drinks with alcoholic content under 20 percent	30% 25%	50% 45%	70% 60%
Beer	50%		
Type of goods	Rates for 20162017	Rates for 20182019	Rates for 2020 and after
Ready-made drinks: -Soft drinks, sodas, mineral water, fruit juices and other similar drinks -Stimulant drinks	5% 10%		
Cigarettes: -Cigars -Cigarettes in packages -Tobacco -Others	30% 30% 15% 30%	45% 45% 25% 45%	60% 60% 35% 60%
Crystal items or crystal adornments		20%	
Carpets with a value of LAK1 million or more		15%	

For additional analytical, business and investment opportunities information, please contact Global Investment & Business Center, USA at (703) 370-8082. Fax: (703) 370-8083. E-mail: ibpusa3@gmail.com Global Business and Investment Info Databank - www.ibpus.com

Type of goods	Rates for 2016-2017	Rates for 2018-2019	Rates for 2020 and after
Furniture sets (sofas) with a value of LAK10 million or more		15%	
Perfumes and cosmetics		20%	
Playing cards and gambling materials if authorized by the relevant sectors		90%	
Traditional rockets, fireworks, firecrackers if authorized by the relevant sectors		80%	
Vehicles: 1. Motorcycles:			
-With engine volume of 110 cc and lower		20%	
-With engine volume of 111-150 cc		30%	
-With engine volume of 151-250 cc		40%	
-With engine volume of 251-500 cc		60%	
-With engine volume of 501 cc or more		80%	
-That use clean energy		5%	
-Motorbike spare parts 2. Transport vehicles: 2.1. Vehicles using fuel:		5%	
-With engine volume of 1,000 cc and lower		25%	
-With engine volume of 1,001-1,600 cc		30%	
-With engine volume of 1,601-2,000 cc		35%	
-With engine volume of 2,001-2,500 cc		40%	
-With engine volume of 2,501-3,000 cc		45%	
-With engine volume of 3,001-4,000 cc		70%	
-With engine volume of 4,001-5,000 cc		80%	
-With engine volume of 5,001 cc or more		90%	
2.2. Vehicles using clean energy 2.3. Small transport vehicles (2-		10%	

door pick-ups, trucks):	
-using fuel	10%
-using clean energy 2.4. Medium transport vehicles:	5%
-using fuel	8%
-using clean energy 2.5. Large transport vehicles:	5%
-using fuel	5%
-using clean energy	3%
3. Vehicle spare parts	5%

Type of goods	Rates for 2016-2017	Rates for 2018-2019	Rates for 2020 and after
Accessories for vehicles		20%	
Speedboats, yachts, motorboats, including their spare parts and accessories		20%	
Satellite television signal receivers, audio-video players, cameras, telephones, audio-video recorders, musical instruments, including their components and accessories		20%	
Electrical appliances, including air conditioners, washing machines, vacuum cleaners		20%	
Billiard tables, snooker tables, bowling equipment, football playing tables		30%	
All kinds of game players		35%	
Type of services	Rates for 2016-2017	Rates for 2018-2019	Rates for 2020 and after
Entertainment: Nightclubs, discotheques, karaoke	10%	20%	35%
Bowling services		10%	
Beauty services		10%	
Use of services for mobile phones, digital television, cable television, internet		10%	
Golfing services		10%	
Lottery services		25%	
Casino services, poker machines		35%	

For additional analytical, business and investment opportunities information,
please contact Global Investment & Business Center, USA
at (703) 370-8082. Fax: (703) 370-8083. E-mail: ibpusa3@gmail.com
Global Business and Investment Info Databank - www.ibpus.com

TAXATION LAWS AND REGULATIONS IN LAOS

TAX AND DUTY INCENTIVES

The government of Laos, one of the few remaining official Communist states, began decentralizing control and encouraging private enterprise in 1986. The results, starting from an extremely low base, were striking - growth averaged 6% per year in 1988-2006 except during the short-lived drop caused by the Asian financial crisis beginning in 1997. Despite this high growth rate, Laos remains a country with a primitive infrastructure. It has no railroads, a rudimentary road system, and limited external and internal telecommunications, though the government is sponsoring major improvements in the road system with possible support from Japan. Electricity is available in only a few urban areas. Subsistence agriculture, dominated by rice, accounts for about half of GDP and provides 80% of total employment. The economy will continue to benefit from aid by the IMF and other international sources and from new foreign investment in hydropower and mining.

Construction will be another strong economic driver, especially as hydroelectric dam and road projects gain steam. Several policy changes since 2004 may help spur growth. In late 2004, Laos gained Normal Trade Relations status with the US, allowing Laos-based producers to benefit from lower tariffs on exports. Laos is taking steps to join the World Trade Organization in the next few years; the resulting trade policy reforms will improve the business environment. On the fiscal side, a value-added tax (VAT) regime, slated to begin in 2008, will streamline the government's inefficient tax system.

The DDFI automatically awards all approved foreign investors an incentive tax rate of 20 percent, compared to the general tax rate of 35%. Unlike most other countries, this 20 percent rate applies to foreign investment in all sectors of the economy and does not depend on company or performance. Foreign investors must pay a 10 % dividend withholding tax. Foreign investors and expatriate personnel pay a flat 10 % personal income tax.

There is a minimum tax on all companies (unless tax holidays are granted) of 1% of turnover, i.e., foreign-owned companies pay either 20 % tax on profits or 1 % tax on turnover, whichever is greater. In special cases, primarily for hydroelectric projects or resource-based development projects, tax holidays can be negotiated.

As an incentive to all foreign investors, a duty of only 1 % is charged for imports of capital equipment, spare parts, and other means of production. No duties or import turnover taxes are payable on any imported inputs for export production. Foreign investors whose products substitute for imports can negotiate incentive duties and turnover taxes on imported inputs on case by case basis.

At present, an administrative ruling of the Minister of Finance allows all imports subject to incentive duty rates to be free of turnover tax and excise tax. Producers, whose output is sold on both the domestic and export markets, pay no duty on the inputs for export production and a negotiated rate on inputs for import substituting production. This simple

For additional analytical, business and investment opportunities information,
please contact Global Investment & Business Center, USA
at (703) 370-8082. Fax: (703) 370-8083. E-mail: ibpusa3@gmail.com
Global Business and Investment Info Databank - www.ibpus.com

system obviates the necessity of instituting cumbersome duty drawback systems or creating free trade or export processing zones.

In the future, however, the government may move to a system in which foreign investors face the same tax and tariff incentives as do domestic investors. Under this system, investment in "promoted industries" would receive tax and duty reduction incentives, but investment in other sectors would pay the normal corporate profit tax, turnover tax and duty rates.

NON-TAX INCENTIVES

The government provides the following incentives to all foreign investors:

  a. Permission to bring in foreign nationals to undertake investment feasibility studies.
  b. Permission to bring in foreign technicians, experts, and managers if qualified Lao nationals are not available to work on investment projects.
  c. Permission to lease land for up to 20 years from a Lao national and up to 50 years from the government.
  d. Permission to own all improvements and structures on the leased land, transfer leases to other entities, and permission to sell or remove improvements or structures.
  e. Facilitation of entry and exit visa facilities and work permits for expatriate personnel.

The government also offers guarantees against nationalization, expropriation, or requisition without compensation.
Under the FI Law, the government does not offer incentives of import protection (in the form of increasing duties or banning imports) for import substituting investments and it does not provide measures to restrict further entry to reduce competition for current investors. The policy of not reducing market competition as an incentive for investors is not a feature of the foreign investment systems of most other countries, such as Thailand and Vietnam, in the region.

PDR improved the business climate for local firms in 2009/2010 by modernizing its business tax system, according to Doing Business 2011: Making a Difference for Entrepreneurs, the eighth in a series of annual reports published by IFC and the World Bank. Lao PDR introduced a value added tax to replace its outdated turnover tax regime. A value added tax is more efficient, broad-based and offers lower tax liability to firms than under the turnover tax, where there is tax on tax.

For the first time in eight years, the economies of East Asia and the Pacific were among the most active reformers. Eighteen of 24 reformed business regulations and institutions in the past year—more than in any other region.

Lao PDR still has opportunities to catch up with its Asian neighbors, such as by reducing the time it takes to obtain a company seal which currently takes up to 45 days. In the overall ease of doing business ranking Lao PDR stands at 171 out of 183 economies.

For additional analytical, business and investment opportunities information,
please contact Global Investment & Business Center, USA
at (703) 370-8082. Fax: (703) 370-8083. E-mail: ibpusa3@gmail.com
Global Business and Investment Info Databank - www.ibpus.com

Singapore, Hong Kong SAR China, and New Zealand lead the world in the ease of doing business for local firms. In East Asia, emerging-market economies such as Indonesia, Malaysia, and Vietnam took the lead, easing business start-up, permitting, and property registration, and improving credit information sharing. Malaysia reduced the time and cost to transfer property by introducing more online services. Vietnam earned a spot among the 10 most-improved economies and moved up 10 places in the global rankings on the ease of doing business, to 78 among 183 economies.

New information technologies simplified business start-up, international trade, and property registration in Brunei Darussalam, Malaysia, the Philippines, and Samoa.

"New technology underpins regulatory best practice around the world," said **Janamitra Devan, Vice President for Financial and Private Sector Development at the World Bank Group**. "Technology makes compliance easier, less costly, and more transparent."

Since 2005, about 85 percent of the world's economies have made it easier for local firms to operate, through 1,511 improvements to business regulation. China was among the 15 most-improved economies, having introduced in the past several years 14 regulatory changes that make it easier to do business—affecting nine areas covered by Doing Business.

Globally, doing business remains easiest in OECD high-income economies and most difficult in Sub-Saharan Africa and South Asia. But developing economies are increasingly active. In the past year 66 percent of developing economies reformed business regulation; six years before, only 34 percent did.

TAX LAW

PART I GENERAL PROVISIONS

Article 1 :Tasks of the Tax Law

The present law is proposed to determine the tax system aimed at

facilitating all economic sectors, social and public organizations, Lao

citizens, immigrants, foreigners, non-citizenship persons who have businesses or earn their living in the Lao PDR, to contribute to the implementation of the national tasks, and promote business activities in every economic sector and accelerate the circulation/distribution of goods, stabilize the currencies and market prices, rationalize fairly the incomes between various strata of the society, ensure acquiring incomes to the state budget and the developing the national economy continuously.

Article 2 :Tax

Tax is a duty of every person who deals in business activities or earns their living in the Lao PDR. to contribute to the defence and development of the country.

Article 3 Tax system

The tax system of the Lao P.D.R consists of direct and indirect tax.

The indirect tax :

- Turnover tax

- Excise tax

The direct tax:

- Profit tax

- Income tax

- Minimum tax

- Fees/charges

Article 4 :Utilization of the Tax Law

The Tax Law shall, be applied to individuals or entities who consume goods or services, and have a business, or liberal professions and generating incomes within the Lao PDR territory.

PART II - TURNOVER TAX

CHAPTER I Turnover Tax Regulations

Article 5 :Turnover tax

The turnover tax is an indirect tax to be paid by consumers of goods and services through business conductors as stated in the Article 7 of the present law.

Article 6 :Territory of turnover tax

The turnover tax is collected from imports, sales of goods and general

services which take place in the Lao PDR.

Article 7 :Work-activities subject to turnover tax payments

The work activities subject to turnover tax payment are as follows:

1-Import of goods to the Lao PDR;

2-The first-time sale of import goods or domestic products by importers or domestic manufacturers is the first-time transfer of the property to other people by importers or domestic producers who will, in return, receive compensation in money or other types of benefits, and such deal shall be made in a manner of wholesale of retail sales, in cash or by credit, on commission or commodity exchange.

3-The general service is an economic activity which deals with supplies of labor power to other people but not import, production or sales of goods, and shall be compensated in a manner of service changes. The general service includes : transport, post, communications, construction,repair, market management by subcontract, land development and leasing activities, hotel and tourist businesses, drinking bars, concerts, sport and other entertainment activities, medical service, agent/commission or dealers' activities and so on.

Article 8 :Persons who shall pay turnover tax

Individuals or entities providing activities as stated in the Article No. 7 of the present law, shall pay turnover tax despite of that, their activities would be either on continual or interval, commercial or non-commercial basis .

Article 9 :Activities exempted from turnover tax

The activities which shall be exempted from turnover tax include:

- Import of crop seeds, animal breeds and insecticides;

- Import of materials, instruments and chemical components for research purposes;

- Import of gold for the notes issuing institution;

- Import of bank notes or coins;

- Import or activity relating to tax or post stamps;

- Import planes and instruments for international air transportation;

- Import of goods or accessories for components of international air transportation;

- Import of goods for selling to diplomats and international organizations in the Lao PDR according to permissions of Ministry of Foreign Affairs;

- Import of goods with tax exemption or temporary import;

- Import and sales of animal treating medicines;

- Sales of self-produced agricultural products by peasants;

- Forestation activities, industrial trees and fruits planting;

- Sales of agricultural and handicraft products by Government employees or cooperative members on a family basis or limit;

- Export of goods and services;

- Sales of allowed text books, newspapers and magazines;

- International transportation and relevant services;

(International transportation-transportation of passengers or cargos from abroad or to abroad by land, air and sea/river);

- Transportation by manpower, animals and boats without engines;

- Provision of leasing immovable properties, such as land, houses and others by persons who do not have business activities;

- Export services;

- Independent job-occupation by one's own labor;

- Educational activities: child schools, primary schools, secondary and high schools, universities and professional technical schools;

- Activities for public benefits held by Government authorities and International Organizations;

- Banking and insurance activities.

CHAPTER II Time and basis for calculation and collection of turnover tax

Article 10 : Time and basis for turnover tax calculation

The tax calculation time and principles have been determined as follows.

1-The tax on import goods shall be calculated during declarations and payments for customs duty. The calculation shall be based on the declared amount of import goods plus customs duty excise tax (if exist) and other fees;

The declared amount shall include cost of goods, insurance and freight to the destined import border.

2-In case of the first-time sales of goods imported or manufactured inside the country, the tax shall be calculated during its selling or delivery by importers or domestic manufacturers. The calculation shall be based on the actual sales amounts without turnover tax;

3-The tax on services shall be calculated after full or partial completion of the work. The calculation shall be based on the actual service charges without turnover tax.

Article 11 : Self-utilization and temporary import

Goods imported or produced inside the country, any of constructed or services used by businessmen themselves, shall be imposed to turnover tax according to the general principles except those stated in Article 9 of the present law. The calculation shall be based on the actual prices of goods or services applied therein and at that time.

Import goods exempted from import duties shall be levied on turnover tax during its selling. The calculation shall be based on the actual sales prices.

CHAPTER III Rates of Turnover Tax

Article 12 :Rates of turnover tax

The rates of turnover tax shall be as follows:

a)The rate of 3% for

1-Import or sales of:

- Agricultural products : rice, bran, rice flour, manioc and maize flour;

- Foodstuff;

- Raw materials, semi-products, chemical products for agricultural, industrial and handicraft production;

- Fertilizer, animal foods;

- Machines, tools and instruments for cultivation, cattle-breeding and production (industrial, agricultural and craft);

- Machines or vehicles for land development, transport, mining including petroleum and gas, construction of infrastructure (bridges-roads, railway, irrigation, dams, ports and airports) and spare parts;

- Ore: iron, tin, zinc, red copper and others;

- Glue-stone, lignite, coal, gas and others;

- Water supply;

- Medicaments, medical instruments and education materials;

- Ambulance, fire-fighting vehicles and other special service cars;

- Bicycle and tricycle;

- Cotton thread, silk thread and other yam;

- Art and craft products

- Toys and other play-games for children;

- Instruments for sport and physical training.

2-Services:

Agricultural services with machines;

Analysis of agricultural, forest and construction soils, and ores;

Municipal sanitation;

Slaughter-house and general animal killings;

Hairdressing salon (barber's shop);

Medical treatment for human and animal;

Concert, art play, opera, sport (football, volleyball, basketball, boxing, tennis and physical training;

Massage (treatment) activity;

Golden and silver hand-made products making;

Diamond, jewel and glass processing;

b) The rate of 5% for:

1-Import or sales of:

- Electric power, electrical tools and instruments;

- any type of fuel;

- Wooden coal and fire-wood;

For additional analytical, business and investment opportunities information,
please contact Global Investment & Business Center, USA
at (703) 370-8082. Fax: (703) 370-8083. E-mail: ibpusa3@gmail.com
Global Business and Investment Info Databank - www.ibpus.com

- General construction materials and instruments including gravel and sand;

- Wood and rattan products;

- Tea and coffee products;

- Pure water, lump-ice, ice-cream;

- Soft-drinks and other non-alcoholic drinks;

- General office supplies: typewriter, duplicating machine, photocopier, calculator, computer and others including instruments;

- Communications instruments;

- House furniture: sofa, table, chair, shelf, bed, mattress, pillow and others;

- Electrical products: fridge, electric cooker, electrical iron, water-cooler, rice-cooker, kettle, fen, radio, vacuum cleaner, washing machine, meat and fruits scraping machine and others;

- Fabrics, clothes, hat, shoes, belt and umbrella;

- Suitcase, travel bags, handbag and other similar products;

- Watch, glasses;

- General sewing machines;

- Motorcycle, took-took and jumbo, passenger truck, transport truck, bus, mini-bus, fuel-tank truck;

- Any car instruments, spare parts and batteries;

- Fishing tools and instruments;

- Ship and motor-boat for domestic transportation including spare parts and accessories;

- Sport motor-boat;

- Plane for domestic transportation including tools and spare parts;

- Product for body cleansing;

- Perfume and cosmetics;

- Precious metal and glass: silver, gold, diamond, jewel and other similar products;

For additional analytical, business and investment opportunities information,
please contact Global Investment & Business Center, USA
at (703) 370-8082. Fax: (703) 370-8083. E-mail: ibpusa3@gmail.com
Global Business and Investment Info Databank - www.ibpus.com

- Air-pressured gun;

- Unrecorded cassette;

- Recorded cassette with Lao songs;

- Musical instruments and accessories;

- Other items excluded in the 3 , 10 and 15 percent rates;

2 -Services :

- Soil and sand loading services, development of land for cultivation, cattle-breading and construction purpose;

- Post, telecommunications and transport services;

- Construction, installation and general repairs;

- Bridge-road, irrigation, dam, port and airport services;

- Tailoring and dresser's salons, capitonage, photos, shoes sewing shops;

- Printing or publication activity;

- Wood-sawing mills, wood and rattan manufacturing plants;

- Tobacco-leaves drying mills;

- Development of land for sales (utilization rights) and construction of houses for sale;

- Market management service by subcontract;

- Such activities as advertising, study, planning, analysis of

data-information, accounting, and laws consultancy, engineering and architectural consultancy;

- Other services excluded in the 3, 10 and 15 percent rates;

c) The rate of 10% for:

1- Import or sales of:

- TV, radio, tape-recorder, sound-recording equipments, amplifier, camera, movie-camera, video. player and video camera, recording discs, photo-making equipment, cinema- film, unrecorded film, film for camera, video cassette, tape cassette of foreign songs, long-sight scope, other similar products, accessories and spare parts;

- Sport gun;

- Cooling and heating equipment;

- Passenger car, pick-up, jeep;

- Plane, ship, motor-boat for tourism;

- Decorating products made of silver, gold, diamond, jewel, glass, pearl and other precious metals:

2-Services:

- Hotel, resort, tourism and drinking bars;

- Broker and dealer activities;

- Film and video shows, video photographing, video and tape recording, video or video cassette renting;

- Golf activity;

- Horse and car racing activity;

d) The rate of 15% for :

1- Import or sales of:

- Alcohol and any other drinks containing alcohol;

- Cigarettes including packed and unpacked, and cigars;

- Any hunting guns;

- Billiard and snooker tables, football table and other games;

- Salute and other similar products;

- Play cards and other similar plays;

2-Services :

- Entertainment activity : night club, discotheque, karaoke;

- Snooker, billiard and balling activity;

- Lottery activity.

CHAPTER IV Declaration and taxation system of turnover tax

Article 13 : Persons who shall declare and pay turnover tax

Persons who should pay turnover tax as determined in Article No. 8 of the present law, shall declare and pay turnover tax according to the following cases :

1-Any import of goods: importers shall produce the declaration

document to customs offices at the import customs checkpoints for tax payments. The tax shall be fully paid before removing the goods out of the customs checkpoint area;

2-For the first-time sales of goods imported or produced inside the country and services, the importers, producers and servers shall submit declaration sheets on their business incomes to the tax authority concerned before the 15-day of the next month in order to pay turnover tax for the current month.

The tax-payers using the forfeit system (contract system), shall pay tax duties according to the terms and conditions of the contract.

CHAPTER V Deduction of the turnover tax paid initially

Article 14 : Persons who shall have a right to obtain the deduction of

initial turnover tax paid

Importers, producers or servers who operate sales or services inside the country and have paid the initial tax (at customs checkpoints) as determined in Article No. 9 of the present law, shall have the right to get the deduction of initially paid turnover tax from a monthly tax amount due to payment. If amount of the initial tax paid exceeds the monthly tax volume, the difference shall be transferred to the next month deduction until its completion .

Those who are able to obtain the initial tax deduction, shall have the tax registration with the tax authority and hold a legal accounting system as well as providing a full set of tax payment certificates, such as import documents on tax declaration (D10), tax-payment receipts and invoices stating a certain turnover tax amount.

Article 15 : Limits of initial turnover tax deduction

The initial turnover tax deduction shall be implemented within the following limits:

1-Importers : The deduction of the initial turnover tax shall be made from import goods proposed for further sales or further transforming;

2-Producers : The initial turnover tax shall be deducted from purchases of raw materials, production instruments, trucks and other production materials;

3-Servers : The deduction shall be made from purchases of transport vehicles, spare parts or other service materials.

The initial turnover tax deduction shall not be allowed for the following, except the above items 1, 2 and 3:

- Service charge

- Purchase of transport vehicles including accessories and spare parts which are not used directly by the companies.

- Purchase of consumer goods for personal utilization by the company management staff or workers.

Article 16 : Re-export

Re-exporter, export producers and servers who have paid the initial turnover tax as determined in Article No. 13 of the present law, shall have the right to obtain the deduction during the next import of goods, raw materials and other products.

The deduction shall be operated in conformity with the conditions stated in Article No. 15 of the present law, and with presentation of the re-export documents.

Article 17 : Reimbursement of the initial turnover tax paid

In the event when the sales or service operations have been liquidated for some reasons, the initial turnover tax paid shall be deducted from the amount subject to tax payment in the amount of the liquidation, or in the next month until it has been fully deducted.

PART III - EXCISE TAX

CHAPTER I Limit of Excise Tax, Goods due to Tax Payment or Exemption

Article 18 : Excise tax

The excise tax is an indirect tax collected from some consumers goods.

Article 19 : Limit of excise tax

The excise tax shall be collected from some products imported or manufactured by domestic producers for sales inside the country.

Article 20 :Goods due to excise tax payment

Some products that be imported or supplied for sales by local factories, such as fuel, alcohol or the alcoholic drinks, soft drinks and others, packed and unpacked cigarettes, cigars, perfumes and cosmetic, shall be imposed at the rates determined in Article 23 of the present law.

Article 21 : Tax-exempted goods

In order to promote export and health activities and to implement the international principles, the following goods shall be exempted from the excise tax.

- Some products as determined in Article No. 20 of the present law that shall be export according to the confirmation of the concerned authority of the Lao PDR;

- kerosene;

- Alcohol (90) for medical purposes;

- Some products sold to the Embassies and International Organization in the Lao PDR according to the confirmation of

Ministry of Foreign Affairs,

CHAPTER II Calculation basis, Rates, Declaration and Payment of excise tax

Article 22 : Basis for calculation of excise tax

The excise tax calculation shall be based on the import cost for import goods or factory cost for domestic products.

The import cost includes the import amount declared plus import duty and other fees (if exist).

The factory cost includes the production cost plus other fees (if exist).

Article 23 : Rates of excise tax

The rates of excise tax shall be as follows:

1-Fuel:

- Gasoline (super) 23 percent

- Gasoline (Normal) 20 percent

- Diesel 10 percent

- Aviation gasoline 10 percent

- Lubricant, hydraulic oil, grease, brake oil 2 percent

2-Alcohol or other alcoholic drinks:

- Alcohol or alcoholic drinks (above 15 degree) .... 40 percent

- Beer, wine and other drinks (below 15 degree) .... 30 percent

3-Bottled soft drinks and other vitamin drinks .... .20 percent

4-Packed and unpacked cigarettes, cigars .... 30 percent

5-Perfume and cosmetic .... 10 percent

6-Play-cards and other similar items.......................... 50 percent

Article 24 :Declaration and payment of utilization tax

Imports, or producers of some products as stated in Article No. 20 of

the present law, shall declare and pay excise tax as follows:

- For import: the importers shall produce the customs declaring documents to the customs offices at the import customs checkpoints in order to pay tax. The tax shall be fully paid before removing the goods out of the customs checkpoint.

- For domestic production: the domestic manufacturers shall produce the tax declaring sheets to the concerned tax authority monthly before the l5-day of the next month for payment of excise tax for current month.

PART IV - PROFIT AND INCOME TAX

CHAPTER I Tax limits, taxable profits and incomes, and

persons who shall pay the tax

Article 25 :Profit and income tax

The profit and income tax is a direct tax paid by businessmen or independent jobbers, or those who obtain incomes from salary or wages, movable or immovable property, intellectual property right and other licenses.

Article 26 : Limit of profit and income tax

The profit and income tax shall be collected from annual profits or incomes of those persons who have profits or income in the Lao PDR including that stated in Article No.

29 of the present law. The profits or incomes gainers can be an individual or entity who have a permanent residence in the Lao PDR or abroad.

Article 27 : Profit tax

The profits which shall be imposed, are as follows:

1-The business profit is a type of profits gained from such business activities as agriculture-forestry, industry and handicrafts including natural resources mining, import-export operations, wholesale and retail sales, and general services, such as transport, post, telecommunications, construction, repairs, development of land for leasing purposes, auctions on market management and construction of projects funded by the Government budget, foreign aids or loans on bilateral or multilateral basis, banking and insurance operations, hotel and tourist activities, drinking bars, lottery, concerts, sport, agent or dealer business;

2-The profit made from the independent type of jobs or professions, such as doctors, advocates, law and accounting consultants, engineering and sculpturing consultants.

Article 28 : Income tax

The taxable incomes shall be as follows:

1- The income made from salaries, such as labor charges, bonus, careers allowances, and other material benefits obtained according to the contracts by any of the Government or private parties;

2- The income made from movable capital informs of share dividends or other benefits shared between shareholders, lending interest rates, warranty

fees obtained according to the contracts' or other obligations unless otherwise agreed between the Government of Lao PDR and concerned parties,

The profits shared or other taxable benefits shall include such profits as may be applied to any forms of utilization including direct spending, unless it shall be saved to the accumulation funds or included to the companies' capital assets, bonuses, meeting per diems, benefits arisen by increase or reduction of capital assets of companies, concentration of' enterprises, transfer of shares, values added from the companies bankruptcy or debt liquidation;

3-The income made from rents of the immovable property, such as rentals or other benefits gained according to the contract, or renting obligations on the land, houses or other property;

4-The income from the copyright. or other rights, such as intellectual property, know-how, trade-mark, compositions and novels.

Article 29 : Persons who shall pay the profit and income tax

For additional analytical, business and investment opportunities information, please contact Global Investment & Business Center, USA at (703) 370-8082. Fax: (703) 370-8083. E-mail: ibpusa3@gmail.com Global Business and Investment Info Databank - www.ibpus.com

Lao Individuals or entities, immigrants or foreigners including non-citizenship persons who, have the profitable activities in the Lao PDR as determined in the Article No. 27-28 of the present law, shall pay the profit or income tax to the state budget.

If the Government officials appointed to reside or work with International Organizations abroad have been exempted from paying the income tax there, they shall declare and pay that duty in the Lao PDR.

If foreign workers who come to work and stay in the Lao PDR more than 180 days within the fiscal year and receive salaries abroad, shall pay the income tax in the Lao PDR unless otherwise agreed with the Lao Government.

CHAPTER II Tax-Exempted Incomes, Tax Exemption or

Payment of Profit Tax at a Discount Rate

Article 30 : Tax-exempted incomes

The tax-exemption incomes shall include :

Income made from agricultural production by peasants themselves;

Income obtained from concert performance, sport and others;

Salary of foreign consultants or experts who provide a project assistance in the Lao PDR, and such exemption should be stated in the agreement between the Lao Government and concerned parties;

Salary of the Diplomatic and International Organizations official to the Lao PDR;

Allowances permitted within the limits of the Labor Law;

Deducted funds for pensions or other welfare matters, family allowances;

7-Single allowance, pension, per diems;

8-Lending interests; bond or shares interests;

9-Social security funds;

10-   Lottery prizes;

11-   Bonus or premium given by the Government to those people who have achievements in preventing the violation of the laws;

12-   Scientific premiums

Article 31 : Tax exemption or payment of profit tax at a discount rate Persons who have been permitted by the Government to invest projects or other priority zones in the Lao PDR, shall be exemption, or depending on each case, shall pay the profit tax at the discount rates within the duration determined by the concerned committees.

In order to obtain such privileges the above mentioned persons shall hold an accounting system conformed to the principles set by the Accounting Law.

CHAPTER III Place of the Profit and Income Tax Payment

Article 32 : Place of the profit and income tax payment

-Businessmen and independent workers shall declare and pay the profit tax in the tax office where they have been registered.

Those who obtain incomes by providing their immovable property for leasing (land, houses and other property) shall declare and pay profit tax to the tax office which controls that property.

The companies branches or representatives operating in the local provinces, shall pay profit tax in those places directly.

CHAPTER IV Basis for the Calculation of the Profit and Income Tax

Article 33 : Basis for the profit tax calculation

The calculation of the taxable profit made from business operations or professional services shall be based on the net annual profit of the accounting year completed.

The end-year net profit is a difference between gross incomes and expenditures in the fiscal-accounting years.

Article 34 : Expenses that can be deducted from the annual profit

The expenses that can ve deducted from the annual profit, include the following:

1-General expenses :

- Electric power, water, telephone, advertisement, and repair charges;

- Travel and guest's reception expenses which shall not exceed 0.20 percent of the annual business income, or not more than 6,000,000 Kip for each item per year;

- Salaries and wages, welfare and social-security spending;

- Services, lending interest rates, transport charges;

- Rents of premises;

- Insurance of company assets or property;

- Non-deductible turnover tax and other fees;

- Gifts, allowances, presents and prizes which shall not exceed 0.15 percent of the annual business income, and not more than 4,000,000 Kip per year.

2-Amortization

The amortization shall be made from the capital assets depreciated from time-to-time of its utilization, or technical changes in order to reserve funds for renewals of the capital assets in the future.

The amortization shall be calculated according to the following rates:

Company capital assets (immovable)

Duration of Amortization   utilization rate (%)

- Expenses for the establishment   2 years 50

- Industrial premises   20 years

05 - Trade premises and dwelling houses:

+ permanent basis 20 years 05+ temporary basis (or medium-term basis) 10 years 10

- Machines and equipments for industrial, agricultural, craft and other activities 5 years 20

- Land transport facilities (vehicles) 5 years 20

- Instruments and tools sets 5 years 20

- Office instruments and other supplies 10 years 10

- Installation, improvement and decoration 10 years 10

- Vessels and passenger planes 20 years 05

Article 35 :Expenses non-deductible from the annual profit

The expenses which can not be deducted from the annual profit, shall include:

For additional analytical, business and investment opportunities information,
please contact Global Investment & Business Center, USA
at (703) 370-8082. Fax: (703) 370-8083. E-mail: ibpusa3@gmail.com
Global Business and Investment Info Databank - www.ibpus.com

-The expenditures considered as luxuries: expenses relating to golf-play, dancing, sport and other entertainments;

-Profit tax and enterprise minimum tax;

-Income tax collected from salary and wages;

-Salary paid to share-holders or employers by themselves;

-Interest paid to the share-holders;

-Any type of penalties;

-Reimbursement of credits.

The amortization can be made with parallel or downwards methods based on the cost of the capital assets. The calculated amount of amortization shall be showed in the accounting book during close of the accounting at end of the year. The annual or partial amortization funds that have not been included or written in the book-keeping, shall not be confirmed as expenditures deducted from the annual profit. In event of selling a property, the annual or partial depreciation of the asset subject to the sale, shall be deducted from its cost in order to assess the excess or reduced value of that property,

3-Funds for reasonable emergent expenses and certain risks, amortization fund, stock reserves and receivable debt amounts.

Unused reserves or used for other purpose shall be transferred to the taxable annual profit.

The independent workers shall not be permitted to establish any type or reserve funds deductible from the annual profit.

Article 36 : Transfer of the annual losses to another forth-coming year.

Businessmen or independent workers who pay the profit tax based on the ordinary or extended counting system audited and confirmed by the tax officials, shall have the right to transfer the financial losses to another forth-coming year for further deduction from the annual profit with a cooperation of three years, and thereafter such transfer shall not be allowed.

Article 37 :Basis for calculation of the income tax

The basis for calculation of the income tax by each type shall be as follows :

1-Income from salary/wages:

- Salary amount plus other allowances received according to the contract;

2-Income from movable capitals:

- Profit or other benefits shared to share-controllers or share-holders according to the by-law of companies or decisions of the share-controllers or share-holders meetings;

- Interests from providing credits, guarantee fees gained according to the contract or other commitments;

3-Income from providing rent of the immovable property: renting charges or other material benefits obtained according to the contract or commitments;

4-Income from licenses or other intellectual property rights: gross income obtained according to the contract or other commitments.

CHAPTER V Rates of Profit and Income Tax

Article 38 :Rates of annual profit and income tax

The rates of annual profit and income tax applied to individuals and entities shall consist of general and discount rates:

1-The general rate:

- The net business profit of entities 35 percent

- The net profit obtained by individuals from business operations, independent job, and providing land, houses and other properties for rent, shall be imposed on the progressive rate basis:

Table No. I

The income from salary shall be imposed as follows :

Table No. II

- Dividends, lending interests, guarantee fees of individual entities or 10 percent

- Receipts from licences or other intellectual property rights of individual or entities 05 percent

- Rents of land. houses, and other property, incomes from non- business activities of public organizations or other social associations 10 percent

2-The discount rate

The net profits made by entities from the business activities which have been promoted by the Government, shall be imposed according to the following positions of location:

For additional analytical, business and investment opportunities information,
please contact Global Investment & Business Center, USA
at (703) 370-8082. Fax: (703) 370-8083. E-mail: ibpusa3@gmail.com
Global Business and Investment Info Databank - www.ibpus.com

- Urban area 20 percent
- Rural and low land areas 15 percent
- Mountains and remote areas 10 percent

CHAPTER VI Calculation of Profit and Income Tax

Article 39 : Calculation of profit and income tax
The profit and income tax shall be paid annually based on the total profit or income obtained within the year. Before tax calculation, any profits or incomes in foreign currencies shall be converted into Kip at the exchange rates of the Bank of Lao PDR applied in each period

The profit and income tax shall be calculated as follows:

1-Entities: The tax shall be made from the net annual profit or income at the fixed rate as stated in Article No. 38 of the present law, and minus the amount of profit or income tax paid in advance within the year;
2-Individuals: Before calculating the tax for those persons who have profits from the business, independent jobs, or obtain incomes from the rent of land, house or other property, the annual discount sum of 360,000 Kip shall be deducted from the total annual taxable income.

If a tax-payer has various incomes as mentioned above, a summary of the incomes shall be made first, and thereafter to make deduction of the annual basic discount. The remaining shall be the net annual income subject to be imposed according to the "Table 1" of Article No. 38 of the present law.

A monthly basic discount amount of 30,000 Kip for the tax-payers who have incomes from salaries, should be also deducted before tax calculation which should be based on "Table II" of the above Article No. 38. The basis discount amount is an essential sum for living which should be deducted from taxation.

The advance tax payment made within `the year, should be also deducted from the real taxable profit or income.

CHAPTER VII Systems of the Profit and Income Taxation, Submission of the Profit and Income Tax Declaration

Article 40 : Taxation of profits made from business operations or independent jobs.

Enterprises (entities), individuals who deal in business or independent work, shall pay the profit tax according to holding the extended, ordinary or primary accounting system.

Article 41 : Profit tax systematization
1-Those who pay the profit tax based on holding an extended accounting system, shall be enterprises with an entity status and independently working individuals who have the annual business income more than 240,000,000 Kip.

2-Those who pay the profit tax based on holding an ordinary or common accounting system, shall be any business individuals or independent jobbers who have the annual business income from 24,000,001 Kip to 240,000,000 Kip.

3-Those who pay the profit tax according to holding a primary accounting system, shall be individuals who have a small business, or independent workers who have the annual business income less than 24,000,000 Kip.

Such simple system of tax payment shall associate turnover tax and profit tax into one payment.

The simple system of tax payment requires an agreement between the tax authority and the tax-payer. The agreement shall be effective within one year. In order to cancel the agreement, the tax payer shall inform the tax

authority sixty days before expiration of the contract. The tax authority may cancel the agreement in any time when finding out that the tax-payer has violated the limits of business operations stated in the contract.

Rates for the simple system of tax payment have been determined as follows :
Estimated annual income
Less than 2,000,000 Kip
2,000,001 - 4,000,000
4,000,001 - 8,000,000
8,000,001 - 12,000,000
12,000,001 - 16,000,000
16,000,001 - 20,000,000
20,000,001 - 24,000,000

Article 42 : Selection of the tax payment systems
Those who pay or have conditions to pay the tax on a contract basis (simple method of tax payment), may apply to the tax office where they have been registered if they want to pay the tax according to the regime of holding an ordinary accounting system, and their proposals shall be approved.

In order to change the system of tax payment, those who implement the tax payment based on a contract basis, shall apply to the tax office within sixty days before expiration of the contract:

Article 43 : Close of Accounting
The businessmen or independent jobbers who pay the profit tax based on holding an extended or ordinary accounting system, shall close their accounting on December 3 1 of each year except when the business has been stopped, sold or transferred to another owner during the year.

Article 44 :
Liquidation sale or transfer of a business activity

For additional analytical, business and investment opportunities information,
please contact Global Investment & Business Center, USA
at (703) 370-8082. Fax: (703) 370-8083. E-mail: ibpusa3@gmail.com
Global Business and Investment Info Databank - www.ibpus.com

In event of business stopping, sale or transfer of a business activity (partially or fully) to another person, the businessmen or independent workers shall close their accounting and submit it to the tax office concerned for tax clearance within 10 days after the liquidation, sale or transfer of the activity. Besides, if the activity has been sold or transferred to another person, the full name and address of the new owner shall be also informed to the tax office.

In event of the owner's death, the heir shall prepare the necessary income data to the tax office concerned within ninety days after the death in order to clear the unpaid tax duty of the previous owner. The responsibility in the tax payment shall be within a limit of the property value received.

Article 45 : Income from salary

The salary tax shall be paid monthly by deducting from the salary amount during its pay. The calculation of salary tax shall be made according to the principles stated in Item No. 2, Article No. 39 of the present law. If a tax-payer receives the salary from different sources or declares the income under its volume, the tax shall be recalculated at end of the year.

Article 46 :
Incomes from the rent of immovable property

The income tax on the rent of immovable property shall be paid every time upon receipts. The tax calculation shall be operated according to the principles stated in Item No.2, Article No. 39 of the present law.

If the tax-payers receive the rents in advance for some years, the tax shall be calculated on the annual basis, and then multiplied with number of the rented years.

Article 47 : Incomes from movable capitals, licenses and other intellectual property rights

The tax on dividends, lending interests, guarantee fees, incomes from licenses and other intellectual property rights, shall be paid upon every receipt by deducting the tax amount from the income during the pay. If the lending interests and guarantee fees of an enterprise which regularly pays profit tax, have been included into the annual income, it shall not be re-imposed. In event if the income has been imposed earlier, it should be deducted from the annual taxable profit. If the tax amount imposed earlier is more than the annual tax value, the non-deducted sum shall be transferred to a next year for further deduction.

Article 48 :
Submission of the profit and income tax declaration

Those who pay the profit tax according to the extended or ordinary accounting system shall pay, the annual profit tax quarterly (each face shall include three months) based on the profit of the previous year or the estimated profit of the fiscal accounting year. The real annual tax amount shall be recalculated in the last face of the tax payment during closing the accounting at end of the year.

Duration of the profit-tax declaration shall be as follows:

- First phase
: before April 10 of the year
- Second phase   : before July 10 of the year
- Third phase: before October 10 of the year

- Forth phase: before March 10 of the next year
If the total amount of tax paid quarterly is more than the actual annual tax volume, the difference shall be transferred to a next year for further
deduction.

The inventory report and other accounting documents shall be submitted to the tax office concerned before March 1 of every year. The report of meeting between the share-holders or board's members shall be submitted to the tax office within 10 days after the meeting. The company group which consists of a number of enterprises with a joint capital, shall report the property, results of all activities and other benefits to the tax office concerned within the duration stated above. Those who pay the tax on the contract basis or based on holding the primary accounting system, shall fulfill their tax duties according to the terms and conditions of the contract.

Article 49 : Income from salary and wages
Organizations, enterprises, or individuals who pay salary or wages to their staff, workers and other persons according to the contract, shall deduct the income tax amount from the salary/wags monthly, and make a list of the tax collected and send to the tax office concerned within 10 days after the pay.

Article 50 : Income from rent of the immovable property
Those who have income from rent of the immovable property, shall
submit the tax declaration to the tax office where registered within 10 days after receipt of the rentals for the calculation and issue of tax invoice. In the rate of rent declared or according to the contract was too low, the tax officials may make re-verification or recalculation of the tax in conformity with the general market average rate in that place.

In event of providing land, houses or other properties for the utilizationof another person without any rent, the user who makes benefits from thosefacilities, shall be responsible for the income tax payment instead of theowner of the property. The tax shall be calculated and paid according to asuitable market rate applied to the same conditions of the property.

If the owner does not require rents for a definite period of time because the renter has paid for development of the land, construction or repair of the premises rented, the material benefits gained by the owner shall be also imposed. The annual income tax shall be calculated by sharing the total expenditure for the development, construction or rehabilitation with the number of years excluded from the rents.

In the tax duty had not been paid in time, the tax-payer who had the rentals, shall be made to pay the tax in accordance with Article No. 85 of the present law.

Article 51 :
Income from movable capitals, licenses and other intellectual property rights

Organizations, enterprises or individuals who pay dividends lending interests, guarantee fees, charges of license and other property rights to the recipients, shall deduct the tax amount and submit the list of tax collected to the tax office concerned within 10 days after the payment in order to calculate and issue the tax invoice.

CHAPTER VIII Minimum tax

Article 52 : Minimum tax

The minimum tax is a minimum duty of the businessmen or independent workers who pay the profit tax according to holding the extended or ordinary accounting system as stated in Article No. 41 of the present law.

Article 53 :Minimum-tax payers

The businessmen and independent workers, such as individuals, entities, Lao citizens, immigrants and foreigners who operate a business in Lao PDR and hold the extended or common accounting system, shall pay the minimum tax.

Article 54 : Minimum-tax exemption

Those who may be exempted from the minimum tax, shall include :

- Foreign investors who are in a period of the annual profit tax
exemption according to the conditions of the Law on the promotion and management of foreign investment in the Lao PDE No. 07/SNA of April 19, 1998 and No. 01/94 of March 14, 1994;

- Local investors who are in a period of the annual profit tax
exemption based on Article, No. 70 of the Decree of the Council of Ministers No. 47/SNA dated June 26, 1989, and the Law on the promotion of domestic investment.
- Those who pay the profit tax on the contract basis as stated in Article No. 41 of the present law.

Article 55 :
Rate of the minimum tax
The rate of the minimum tax shall be at 0.5 percent of the annual business income without the turnover tax, for the businessmen, or of the total annual income, for the independent workers.

Article 56 :
Calculation and payment of the minimum tax
The minimum tax shall be paid annually based on the annual business income or the total annual income of the preceding year at the rate stated in Article No. 55 of the present law.

For additional analytical, business and investment opportunities information, please contact Global Investment & Business Center, USA at (703) 370-8082. Fax: (703) 370-8083. E-mail: ibpusa3@gmail.com
Global Business and Investment Info Databank - www.ibpus.com

The minimum-tax payers shall submit the tax declaration sheets to the tax office where registered before March 01 of every year for the calculation and issue of tax invoices.

Article 57 :
Deduction of the minimum tax
The annual profit paid in advance quarterly within the preceding year shall be deducted from the minimum tax due to payment. The minimum tax paid shall be deducted from the actual annual taxable profit. If the minimum tax paid is more than the annual profit tax amount, the minimum tax paid or the difference shall be reimbursed.
35

PART V OTHER FEES OR ROYALTIES

Article 58 : Collection of fees and service charges

The Government work-sections shall collect fees from the issue of tax registrations, business permissions, approvals, certificates and other official documents, and from using the transport roads, the country's entry or exit travel, issue of entry-exit visa, stay in the Lao PDR, utilization of satellite system of tele-antenna, TV utilization, installation of advertising posters or boards and name-plates of stores as well as of other services in the Lao PDR.

Article 59 : Determination of the rates of fees or service changes
The rates of fees and service charges applied in each work-section shall be determined by the President's Provision in conformity with the real social-economic situation of the country in each period.

Article 60 : Transfer of the fees and services charges
All incomes made from the fees and service charges shall be transferred to the state budget.

PART VI GENERAL PRINCIPLES ON THE TAX AND VARIOUS FEES

Article 61 : Accounting holding
Those who pay the profit tax on holding the extended or common accounting as stated in Item No. 1 and 2, Article 41 of the present law, shall hold a full legal accounting which conforms to the principles set by the Law on enterprise accounting of the Lao PDR. The enterprise accounting shall be made in details and clearly without omission, spacing, errors, deletion, overwriting and so on.

Before utilization the accounting books shall be registered with numbering, sealed and signed by the competent tax authority. All book-keeping documents already used shall be kept within 10 years and ready to be presented to the audit of tax officials at any time.

Article 62 : Issuance of payment receipts for the sales goods or services
Those who deal in such business as production, trade and services, or have an independent job-occupation any pay the profit tax on the system of accounting holding as stated in Article 41 of the present law as well as providing the sales of goods and services, shall issue the bills of payment receipt to the buyers or clients served.

The bill of payment receipt shall consist of the following contents: - Name and location of the shop selling goods, commodities or providing services; - Name and address of the buyer of clients receiving serves;

CUSTOMS LAW

PART 1 GENERAL PRINCLPLES

Chapter 1 General Provisions

Article 1. the taxation law provides rules and principles on the import, export and circulation of commodities within the Lao People's Democratic Republic in view of protecting, encouraging the local production of commodities and services, promoting the local production of commodities and services, promoting investments and exothermal cooperation, promoting export, ensuring state budget revenues and contributing to the national economic development'

Article 2. within the customs territory which covers the total territorial integrity of the Lao People's Democratic Republic, all persons, organizations and economic sectors without differentiation of nationality, shall strictly comply with the Lao customs laws and regulations, including the international customs treaties entered by or acknowledged by the Government of the Lao People's Democratic Republic.

Article 3. Universal duties shall be paid for goods exported out of or imported into the Lao People's Democratic Republic according to the rules and principles as provided in the tariff code adopted by the National Assembly, except in case of goods categorized under the regime of duty suspension or exemption; The provided tax rates may not be increased or reduced in any way.

All types of exported, imported or circulated goods within the country shall be controlled by customs officers, except in cases provided in Articles 57 and 59 of this Law.

Article 4. In necessary and urgent cases for the preservation of the interest and in conformity with the periodical national economic conditions, the President of the Republic may issue decrees on duty rates for certain categories of goods or modify ad values duties as provided in the Tariff Code into a definite duty rate and determine an area as duty free zone.

Article 5. Each issued customs provision and regulation shall be binding thirty days from the day it is published in the official Gazette.

Chapter 2 Types of Goods and Country of Origin

Article 6. All type of export or import goods shall be declared according to the code number and type of goods provided in the Tariff code.

Article 7. Regarding certain types of import or export goods, the President of the Republic will issue a decree on special duty rates for countries with which there is reciprocity. The determination of a special duty rates could be could be vested on the goods' country of origin. The country of goods is the country harvesting, exploiting or producing such goods.

CHAPTER 3 VALUE OF GOODS, PROHIBITED GOODS

Article 8. The declared export value is the actual value of goods delivered to the customs border station at the point export exclusive of customs duties.

Article 9. The declared import value is the actual value of delivered goods to the Lao border inclusive of the goods' value and others costs, such as : insurance and transport costs at which buyers and sellers have agreed to transact.

Article 10. Prohibited goods are goods prohibited by the State from export or import, or goods categorized in limited quantity, under regulations on quality, packaging or other specific regulations.

PART II DECLARATION OF GOODS

Article 12. Export goods shall be accompanied with a bill of lading, a detailed customs declaration form and shall be controlled by customs officers.

Article 13. Goods imported through land border shall be transported along routes determined be the authorities and declared to the nearest customs office of station. It is forbidden to use other routes, to store goods in a building or to run though the station. Any violation will considered as voluntary tax cession.

At the arrival to the customs station, importers shall present bills of lading as temporary declarations to customs officers for the registration of warehouse entry and proceed to detailed customs declarations according to Article 16 of this Law.

Article 14. Goods transported by air shall be accompanied with airway bills certified by airline officers. At the landing to the point of entry airport, airline officers shall present such airway bills to the airport customs for registration of warehouse entry and detailed customs declarations.
Aircrafts flying international routes shall land in airports specified by the authorities, except in of emergency.

Article 15. All types of import commodities by boat on international rivers shall be accompanied with shipping documents, Such documents shall be certified by the ship's owner and shall contain all information as required in the forms. Crafts sailing on international rivers, whether transporting shipments or not, shall only stop at ports where customs stations are established. The crafts' owners shall immediately declare the shipment to the customs officers after the crafts' arrival or before its departure.

PART III DETAILED CUSTOMS DECLARATIONS AND PAYMENT OF CUSTOMS DUTIES

CHAPTER 1 DETAILED CUSTOMS DECLARATION

Article 16. All type of export or import goods shall be declared in detail and according to the tariff code even it duty exempted

Article 17. Detailed declarations shall be handed over to the customs station within ten days from the registration of warehouse entry exclusive of public holidays. If such period is exceeded, the goods will fall under specific customs supervision. In case of deteriorated or perishable goods, goods difficult or inadequate for storage, the customs authorities shall sell such commodities through tenders and preserve the proceed pending payment.

Article 18. Both import and export commodities shall be declared in details by their owners or representatives in possession of a power of attorney in writing or by the customs declaration servicing party.
Detailed declarations shall mention each packing unit, and several packing units may not be grouped as one.
In case the customs declarer ignores the goods' details to be filled in a detailed declaration form, the customs declarer shall be authorized to inspect the goods be forehand.

Article 19. The customs declaration servicing party conducts the business of performing detailed tax declarations on behalf of the goods' owners or transporters.
The Ministry of Finance shall issue detailed regulations on customs declaration services.

Article 20. Detailed customs declarations shall be made in writing and clearly mention all data necessary for the implementation of the customs regulations and statistics gathering.

Detailed customs declarations shall be signed by the decelerates.
Article 21. Detailed customs declarations which customs officers, register shall not change.

CHAPTER 2 INSPECTION OF GOODS, COMPUTATION, PAYMENT OF CUSTOMS DUTIES, AND REMOVAL OF GOODS FROM THE CUSTOM-HOUSE

article 22. As the detailed customs declarations are registered, customs officers shall proceed to the inspection of the goods in totality or in part as seen appropriate.

In case of differences on the result of partial inspection o goods, declarers may request customs officers to inspect the goods in totality.

Inspection of goods at the custom-house shall take place at the warehouse or in the warehouse compound or in other premises as specified by the customs authorities.

Transportation, handing and other necessary costs according to the laws and regulations incurred for the inspection of goods shall be long by the declarers.

Article 23. Inspection of goods shall always take place in the presence of the declarers.

In case of difference between customs officers and declarers on information provided in detailed customs declarations, such as on the type, code number, country of origin of goods,... customs officers shall forward the matter of difference to the investigation committee appointed by specific regulations for decision.

In case of difference regarding prices, and if the investigation committee has determined the commodities prices, but the declarers still refuses to comply, the customs authorities any purchase such goods at the declared price with an additional compensation of fifteen percent of the declared value. At the purchase of the goods, the difference will be resolved.

Article 24. Customs duties shall be computed at the applicable rate on the day the detailed customs declarations are registered at absolute numbers. Customs duties shall be paid in cash for which receipts shall be given to the customs duty payer.

Article 25. After proper inspection, goods may authorize to remove certain types and inspected goods from the warehouse before payment of customs duties, but a guarantee shall be made for the payment of customs duty in due time as specified by the customs officers which shall not exceeding seven days.
Import goods, for which authorization has been given for removal shall be removed immediately.

Article 26. Export goods, at the presentation of proper documentation and inspection by customs officers, shall be immediately exported.

Article 27. Detailed customs declarations are subject to review by customs authorities within three years from the day of their registration. If irregularities are observed in the customs declaration. To the actual facts as supported by evidence in the possession of customs officers, the declarer shall be liable for the offence as provided in this Law on the charge of voluntarily impacting on customs duties.

PART IV GUARANTEE, CUSTOMS DUTY SUSPENSION, TEMPORARY IMPORT AND EXPORT AND SPECIFIC REGIMES FOR CERTAIN TYPES OF GOODS

Chapter 1
Removal of Guaranteed Goods

Article 28. The transportation of customs controlled goods by and water and air from one place to another within the customs territory shall be accompanied by guaranteed goods removal permits. The removal of such goods may be guaranteed by a deposit of equal value to the customs duties or may be guaranteed by a reliable financial institution or legal entity or individual. The removal of prohibited goods shall be accompanied by specific permits issued by the authoritative state agencies.

Article 29. Importers or transporters shall strictly comply to all wordings contained in the guaranteed goods removal permits.
Transporters shall present such removal permits to the customs officers along used routes.

Article 30. As goods are delivered to the specified point of destination, transporters shall immediately present removal permits and guaranteed goods to the customs office for detailed customs declaration according to the customs regime. Inspection of goods shall proceed according to the rules and principles applicable at the point of destination. if the customs duty remains payable, the customs duty in totality and proceed similarly to import goods for local consumption, except if such goods are categorized under other customs regimes.

Article 31. As customs officers certify that the specified conditions have been fully and properly implemented, the agreement contained in the guaranteed goods removal permits shall expire. In case of cash guarantee, such guarantee shall be reimbursed to the owner.

Chapter 2
Transportation though Foreign Territory
and Goods in Transit

Article 32. In necessary cases, locally produced goods and import duty paid goods according to the rules and principles may be removed from one place to another within the Lao People's Democratic Republic through foreign territory. Such goods will be exempted from export duty, and from exit and entry restriction rules.

The transportation of such goods shall be accompanied with guaranteed goods circulation permits. If such goods do not belong to the category of goods prohibited from export or exempted from export duty, their transportation may be authorized by normal circulation permits.

Article 33. Transported commodities from abroad under the transit regime through the Lao People's Democratic Republic to a third country shall be accompanied with guaranteed transit goods permits issued by the customs at the point of departure and will be exempted form customs duties according to specific regulations. Owners or transporters of transit goods shall present guaranteed transit goods transport permits to customs officers along used routes and the border customs at the point of export.

The guarantee agreement contained in the guaranteed transit goods transport documents shall expire only when certified by border customs officers at the point of export that such goods have exited from the Lao People's Democratic Republic. Guarantee
Agreements shall be terminated specifically for the actual quantities and types of goods exported from the Lao territory only.

CHAPTER WAREHOUSE SYSTEM

Article 34. The warehouse regime is a regime for the storage of locally produced or import goods which are to be exported by business operators or locally consumed, for a definite period of time with customs duty suspension and under the control of the customs authorities pending the implementation of the customs regime.

For additional analytical, business and investment opportunities information,
please contact Global Investment & Business Center, USA
at (703) 370-8082. Fax: (703) 370-8083. E-mail: ibpusa3@gmail.com
Global Business and Investment Info Databank - www.ibpus.com

Warehouses included in the warehouse regime includes 4 categories:
- Real warehouse;
- Special warehouse;
- Fictive warehouse;
- Industrial warehouse;
-

Businessmen shall be authorized to use the warehouse regime according to conditions outlined by Government.

The Minister of Finance shall authorize the establishment of warehouse regime, and outline regulations on warehouse construction sites, their organization, the use, the supervision and the determination of the storage period for each type of goods.

Article 35. Real warehouses store general goods pending their removal from the warehouse according to the customs regime and under the supervision of the customs authorities.

Article 36. Special warehouses store the following types of goods
- Live animals;
- Goods under restriction of entry or under special supervision;
- Goods hazardous to health, lacking sanitation or hazardous to the environment.
In addition to the above mentioned goods, the Minister of Finance will determine separately other types of goods.

Article 37. Fictive warehouses are duty free shops under contract for sale of goods to outgoing travelers and according to specific regulations.
Article 38. Industrial warehouses store goods imported by enterprises for assembly, improvement, processing or repair and then re-exported within a definite period of time.

Article 38. Industrial warehouses store goods imported by enterprises for assembly, improvement, processing or repair and then re-exported within a definite period of time

Article 39. Goods restricted from entry and transit through the Lao People's Democratic Republic may be stored in any above warehouse but shall be exported within a definite period of time.

Customs authorities are entitled to prohibit the storage of certain goods in warehoused if such commodities are seen as detrimental to health, the environment and warehouse operations.

Article 40. Customs officers are entitled to control the inventory and goods in warehouses at any time if deemed necessary.

In case it is proven by custom officers that stored goods are missing or do not confirm to the initial declaration, the warehouse owner shall be responsible for the payment of duty at the applicable rate on the day the loss is observed and for other liabilities according to the laws and regulations.

Article 41. The removal of goods from one warehouse to another, to the custom-house or re-exported shall be accompanied with a guaranteed goods removal permit.

Article 42. In case it is required to remove goods stored in warehouse under duty holiday regime for domestic consumption, the owner of such goods shall pay duties at the applicable rate on the day the detailed duty declaration for consumption is registered.

CHAPTER 4 TEMPORARY IMPORTATION AND EXPORTATION

Article 43. Goods classified under the regime of temporary importation include:

- Imported goods for any purpose then re-exported in the original quantity and condition;
- Imported goods for processing, assembly into finished products, improvement and repair, then re-exported;
- Goods classified under the temporary import regime will be exempted from duty at their importation and re-exportation according to outlined regulations and principles.

Article 44. For the temporary importation of goods, importers shall sign a contract in the temporary import declaration whereas such goods shall be re-exported or entered in the warehouse system or in the duty free zone pending their re-export and shall fully comply to the conditions provided by the law and regulations on temporary importation.

Article 45. Customs duty shall be paid for remains from processing, improved or finished products not corresponding to the required conditions for re-export which shall be used or sold within the country.

Article 46. The customs authorities shall outline conditions for temporary export of goods for improvement or addition. At the re-import, customs duty shall be paid on the basis of the improvement's value.

CHAPTER 5 TEMPORARY IMPORT AND EXPORT OF PERSONAL BELONGINGS

Article 47. The people temporarily entering the Lao People's Democratic Republic with non-prohibited personal belongings shall be exempted from customs duties provided such goods are re-exported within the authorized period of stay in the Lao People's Democratic Republic as provided in guaranteed declarations. Details will be separately provided.

Article 48. The people temporarily exiting from the Lao People's Democratic Republic may temporarily take their personal belongings without paying customs duties.
For temporary export, exporters shall declare such personal belongings in forms provided by the customs authorities.

For additional analytical, business and investment opportunities information,
please contact Global Investment & Business Center, USA
at (703) 370-8082. Fax: (703) 370-8083. E-mail: ibpusa3@gmail.com
Global Business and Investment Info Databank - www.ibpus.com

Article 49. Regarding certain prohibited personal belongings, exporters shall be authorized to export before their departure only when approved by the authoritative state agencies and as a third person guarantees that such belongings shall return in their original number and conditions.

In case exported belongings are not re-imported, exporters or guarantors shall be liable the laws.
Chapter 6 Specific Regime for Certain Types of Goods

Article 50. The customs radius is the customs officers' control area which covers up to thirty kilometers from the border into the customs territory. However, in view of ensuring control and the restriction of illicit trafficking, the customs radius may be extended as approved by the Government.

Any circulation of goods within the customs radius shall be accompanied with goods circulation permits issued by the customs authorities.

Article 51. Within the customs radius, as well within the customs territory, no family shall be allowed to store, retain or possess goods in excess to the family's need, except if a family id in possession of documents certifying their lawful acquisition.

PART V RETENTION OF GOODS UNDER THE CUSTOMS' SPECIFIC MANAGEMENT

CHAPTER 1 GOODS KEPT UNDER THE CUSTOMS' SPECIFIC MANAGEMENT

Article 52. Goods to be kept under the customs' specific management:
- Goods which have not been decreed in details in due time as provided under Article 17 of this Law;
- Goods remaining in warehouses for other reasons.

The above-mentioned goods shall be recorded in a specific customs register. Warehouse fees, deterioration and loss shall remain under the responsibility of the commodities' owners.

Customs officers are entitled to open containers subject to the customs' specific management in the presence of their owners or of three witnesses who do not belong to the customs authorities. If such goods do not have any sale value, the customs authorities may destroy them according to the regulations.

Article 53. As goods are recorded in specific customs registers, their owners are entitled to claim them back within four months, but shall:

- Pay fined as provided in Article 90 of this Law in the case of goods intended for exportation, entry in the warehouse system or in the duty free zone.
- Pay duties and fines as provided in Article 90 of this Law for import goods intended for local consumption.

CHAPTER 2 CONFISCATION OF GOODS PLACED UNDER THE CUSTOMS' SPECIFIC MANAGEMENT

Article 54. Goods placed under the customs' specific management which are degraded, rapidly deteriorable, causing storage difficulties or inappropriate for storage may be immediately sold according to Article 17. Fines according to Article 90 of this Law, as well as duties and other expenses shall be deducted from the proceed of such sale. The remaining sum shall be preserved by the customs authorities for the commodities' owner for a period of four months from the day the goods are entered in the customs' specific register. If such period is exceeded, the sum shall be remitted to the state budget.

Article 55. Goods kept under the customs' specific management in excess of four months without any claim from their owners shall be confiscated by the customs authorities as state property and sold according to regulations provided in Article 17 of this Law. Such sold goods shall not include duties. The sales proceed after deduction of lawful expenses shall be to the state budget.

PART VI IMPORT DUTY EXEPTION AND DIPLOMATIC PRIVILEGES

Article 56. Imported materials or belongings exempted from import duty include:
- Certain types of food for travelers;
- Certain family implements when changing residence;
- Certain type of materials obtained from inheritance;
- Belongings and presents of governmental delegations returning from abroad.
- Certain types and quantity of personal belongings of Lao students, pupils, civil servants and diplomats imported after termination of students, training or civil service abroad;
- Necessary devices for education and materials imported for noncommercial experimental production;
- Fuel remaining in tanks of motored vehicles;
- Fuel for international flights by Lao and foreign airplanes on the basis of agreement or mutual compensation;
- Non-salable samples;
- Presents, assistance materials, loans or debt serving by the Government.
- Humanitarian assistance materials;
- Specific defense and police equipment;
- Certain types of necessary religious items based on the concerned state agency's approval;

Article 57. Personal belongings of foreign diplomats and staffs of international organizations enjoying diplomatic privileges; belongings of embassies and international organizations appointed to the Lao People's Democratic Republic on the basis of approval from, the Lao Ministry of Foreign Affairs; accompanying items of high level foreign delegations invited by the Government shall be duty exempted or suspended on the basis of mutual compensation. In case of firm suspicion, customs officers many inspect such goods in the presence of their owners or authorized representatives, representatives from the Ministry of Foreign Affairs and representatives of the concerned state.

Personal belongings of foreign governmental agencies, international organizations and foreign non governmental organizations shall comply with the agreements signed between the Lao Government and the concerned organizations.

Article 58. Types in case of goods to be duty exempted or suspended shall be governed by separate regulations.

Article 59. In case of reliable information and if it may be firmly certified that diplomatic pouches contain prohibited items, statements shall be immediately sent back in coordination with representatives of the Ministry of Foreign Affairs and the relevant embassy staffs.

PART VII DUTY FREE ZONE

Article 60. A duty free zone is an area where goods shall be suspended from customs duty and are not subject to regular control from customs authorities.
The creation of duty free zones shall be approved by the National Assembly on the Government's proposal. Regulations on duty free zones shall be outlined by the Government.

PART VIII THE USE OF BOATS FOR THE TRANSPORTATION OF PASSENGERS OF SHIPMENTS ALONG BORDER RIVERS.

Article 61. Any craft which owner resides in Laos and conducts the business of transporting passengers or shipments along border Rivers shall be properly registered according to the laws and regulations.

Such crafts shall stop at ports with customs or where the customs are located, except in case of emergency; before loading or unloading the commodities, the craft owner shall present the ship log and shipping documents to the customs officers for control.

Before departing or after accosting the port or in case of and inspection on board, the ship log and shipping documents shall be presented to customs officers for control whether containing shipments or not.

In case of sale, transfer, cession of the craft, or in case of change to the features of the craft or cessation of navigation, the craft's owner shall notify customs officers and relevant agencies where the craft is registered within twenty days from such change.

PART IX PROSECUTION

Chapter 1 Ascertainment of Customs Regulations Violation

For additional analytical, business and investment opportunities information,
please contact Global Investment & Business Center, USA
at (703) 370-8082. Fax: (703) 370-8083. E-mail: ibpusa3@gmail.com
Global Business and Investment Info Databank - www.ibpus.com

Article 62. As violations to the customs law and regulations are ascertained, customs officers are entitled to seize goods and vehicles, including relevant documents as evidence for prosecution, and other officers and all citizens have the obligation to cooperate with customs officers.

In case of flagrant offence, customs officers are entitled to incarcerate the offender, while other officers and all citizens are entitled to seize goods and arrest offenders shall comply to with the conditions provided in the Law on Criminal Procedures.

Seize goods, vehicles and documents, together with the incarcerated individuals, shall be immediately sent to the closest customs office for the establishment of an official statement and prosecution. After investigation and the establishment of a statement, of the offender is guilty of a criminal action, the customs authorities shall hand over the offender to the police for prosecution. Customs authorities shall conduct procedures in relation with goods according to the customs law.

In case goods are seized on board of a ship, the statement may be made at such place.

If seized goods and vehicles may not be immediately handed over to the customs office, the shall be left with the local administrative authorities or local armed forces, but statements shall have been made as evidence.

Article 63. Statements shall be immediately established by at least two customs officers.

Such statements shall clearly mention the name, surname, grade, position, duty and assignment posts of customs officers and persons ascertaining the offence, including the name, surname, age, nationality, occupation, address of the offenders, the date, time and place the offence has been ascertained and reason for arrest. Regarding seized goods and documents, their types, quantity, weight, quality and other necessary details shall be clearly mentioned, as well as the reasons for their seizure. In addition, statements shall mention the offenses and measures to the imposed upon the offender, including the offence's opinion.

Statements shall be established in the presence of and read by the offender. In case the offender may not read, a third person will read the statement to the offender who will then sign or appose his thumb print on the statement together with customs officers.

Mention shall be made whether the offender refuse to sign or appose his thumb print. Statements shall be made in 2 copies. One copy to be keep in the files and another copy to be handed over to the offender.

In case no offender may be found, the established statement shall be placed before the customs office, post or in public places for twenty four hours at the latest to notify owners to claim their goods within twenty one days from the day the announcement is made. If such period of time is exceeded, the goods will be forfeited.

Article 64. Statements of customs procedures shall be effective until proof of the contrary. The court may consider a statement invalid when established inconsistently with the laws and regulations.

Customs statements, including transactions shall be exempted from stamps and court fees.

Article 65. Commodities and vehicles seized as evidence shall be preserved by customs officers. Responsibility for any damage or loss to such goods shall be taken by the preserving party according to the law.

Putrefied and rapidly degradable goods shall be sold by customs officers according to the regulations as provided in Article 17 of this Law.

The proceed from sale shall be preserved by customs officers until the lawsuit is terminated.

In case of non prohibited goods, customs authorities shall authorize the owners to take possession of seized goods and vehicles on a temporary basis pending the procedure's termination, but a guarantee of the commodities' and vehicle' value shall be deposited or such guarantee may be made by a reliable person.

Article 66. In case of fines, confiscation of goods or sale of confiscated goods after the lawsuit, civil servants or citizens having contributed to such activity shall congratulated by the Government or be given bonuses which will be governed by separate regulations outlined by the Government.

Chapter 2. Transaction

Article 67. Customs authorities are entitled to solve customs lawsuits at the offender's agreement to transact.

Article 68. In case the offender agrees to pay duties and fines as provided in the customs statement, customs officers shall establish a statement of transaction which will clearly provide the offender's transaction.

Duties and fines shall be immediately payable. In case immediate payment is not feasible, payment shall be made within fifteen days at the latest from the day the statement of transaction is made. After payment, non-prohibited goods and transport vehicles and materials used for concealment shall be returned to their owners.

Chapter 3 Procedures

Article 69. Customs authorities shall be entitled to induce procedures against offenders in the following cases:

1. No transaction for the payment of the payment of duties and fines;
2. Failure to comply with the statement of transaction;
3. Unknown identity of seized goods' and vehicles' owners;

4. Severe offense belonging to general criminal offenses.

Article 70. To induce procedures, customs authorities shall present a file to the authoritative people's prosecutor for the pursuance of procedures. Such file shall be presented in the form of an application, providing a summary of the offence, accusations, violated articles and purpose of the procedure to which the statement and other necessary documents shall be attached.

Article 71. During the performance of their duties, any call for assistance from customs officers shall be answered by the various agencies and armed forces.

Article 72. The prescription of a customs lawsuit shall comply with the Criminal Law.

Article 73. Customs authorities shall be entitled to withdraw their lawsuit before the court's final decision.

Article 74. Any claim against the customs authorities regarding suspicious paid duties and fined and review of customs documents may be made within one year from the goods' seizure or from the registration of the lawsuit the payment of duties and fines.

Article 75. The execution of a customs lawsuit's decision shall be coordinated between the court executor and customs officers.

Article 76. Procedures against customs infractions shall not only be liable to customs procedures, but also to other procedures depending on the nature of the case.

Article 77. Customs authorities shall refuse to hand over the seized evidence to prosecuted persons, if the decision is not yet definitive, except it such person has placed assets as collateral according to the regulations.

Chapter 4 Responsibilities and Joint Responsibility

Article 78. Persons possessing illicit goods or vehicles shall be considered as responsible for such goods or vehicles.

Article 79. Drivers of land, water or air transport vehicles may have customs and criminal liabilities only if transgressions to the Customs Law occur from their own acts.

Article 80. Customs declarers shall be responsible for irregularities in the declaration of goods to the customs authorities.

Article 81. In the performance of customs declaration business, customs declaration servicing party may have disciplinary, civil, servicing or criminal liabilities depending on the nature of such party's offenses.

Article 82. Those having entered agreements with the customs authorities shall strictly comply to such agreements.

Article 83. Collusion in customs infractions shall be subject to the conditions pertaining to collusion in criminal offence.

Article 84. Customs authorities shall be responsible for customs officers' acts during the performance of assigned duties as provided in Article 10 of the Contract Law.

In case of improper seizure of goods, their owners shall be entitled to claim compensations according to the laws and regulations from the day as seize until restitution.

Article 85. Owners of goods shall have civil liabilities on behalf of workers performing activities on their orders regarding customs declarations, duty payments and other fees according to the laws and regulations, duty payments and other fees according to the laws and regulations, including seized goods.

Article 86. Guarantors shall be responsible for the payment of customs duties and other fees according to the laws and regulations for which the guaranteed person is liable.

Article 87. Penalized persons for collusion in customs offenses shall be responsible according to the state of offence and shall be jointly responsible for the payment of customs duties and other fees according to the laws and regulations and for the seized goods.

PART X SANCTIONS AGAINST CUSTOMS OFFENSES
Chapter 1 Classification of Customs Offenses

Article 88. Customs offenses are classified in two categories : three degrees of minor offenses and two degrees of major offences.

Article 89. Minor offenses at the first degree include:

- Delayed detailed customs declaration;
- Inaccurate and incomplete declaration without impact on customs duties and on prohibition measures;
- Concealment, hindrance and refusal to present the necessary documents to customs officers' duties;
- Other offenses not classified under other categories.

Any persons guilty of minor offenses at the first degree shall be fined no less than ten thousand kips and no more than one hundred thousand kips.

Article 90. Minor offenses at the second degree include:

- Declaration of goods or containers in excess or less than the actual number;
- Declaration of goods or containers in excess or less than the actual number;
- Goods less or in excess to the actual quantity and failure to declare;

-    Other infractions not classified under other categories;

Any persons guilty of minor offences at the second degree shall be considered as responsible for customs evasion in view of reducing or avoiding payment of customs duty and shall pay customs duties and other fees in totality according to the law and regulations, together with fines equaling the evaded duties. At the second offence the fines shall be equal to two fold the payable customs duties.

Seized non-prohibited goods and materials used for concealment and vehicles used in the offence shall be restituted to their owners after payment of customs duties and fines in totality.

Article 91. Minor offences at the third degree includes:
-    Third minor offences at the second degree;
-    Import or export of non-prohibited goods into or out from the Lao People's Democratic Republic without detailed customs declarations;
-    Inaccurate data declaration influencing customs duties;
-    Voluntary false declaration of the mane of the freight forwarder at the point of departure and name of the actual freight receiver at the point of destination;
-    Inaccurate declaration for the purpose of receiving customs duty exemption;
-    Concealment of non-prohibited goods to elsewhere which does not enjoy privilege for the consumption of such goods.
-    Presentation of several units or containers grouped as one unit or container to customs officers;
-    Concealment of goods through the sue of vehicles or materials for customs evasion

Persons guilty of customs offenses at the third degree shall pay duties if such duty has not yet been paid and other fees in totality according to the laws and regulations, together with fines equaling who fold the evaded duties. At the second offence, the fine shall be equal to three fold.

Seized non-prohibited commodities and materials used for concealment and vehicles used in the offence shall be restituted to their owners after full payment of duties and fines.

In case of repeated offenses over two times, the offender shall be subjected to court procedures.

Article 92. A Major offence at the first degree includes the export or import, removal, procession of prohibited commodities without proper authorization.

Any person committing major offences at the first degree shall be subject to a lawsuit and fined two folds the goods' value while the illicit goods shall be confiscated in totality, including materials and vehicles used in the offence.

Article 93. A Major offence at the second degree includes the smuggled export or import, circulation or possession of prohibited goods jointly by a collective organization.

Any person guilty of major offences at the second degree will be subject to a lawsuit and fined three fold the goods' value, while the illicit goods shall be confiscated in totality, including materials and vehicles used in the offence.

Article 94. As customs officers discover illicit goods belonging to general criminals case, such as: weapons, opium, heroin or other narcotics, or if customs officers are offended, threatened or subjected to physical injuries, the customs authorities shall induce an initial lawsuit, then hand over the court file, the defendant and the evidence to the investigation police and establish a file for presentation to the prosecutor.

CHAPTER 2 CERTAIN ADDITIONAL PENALTIES FOR CUSTOMS OFFENSES

Article 95. In addition to the main offenses as mentioned in Article 89 to 94 above, goods shall be seized in the following cases:

- Substituted goods or goods to be substituted under the duty suspension regime;
- Substitution or withdrawal of goods during international transportation;
- Import or export of goods without passing through the border customs office;
- Replacement, withdrawal of goods placed under the customs' supervision.

Article 96. If the decides on venalities on the charge of transgression to the customs suspension regime, the offender shall not be authorized to temporarily import or export the goods, nor to send goods across the border, nor to store the goods in the warehouse.

Persons allowing offenders to use their names for the purpose of evading the above penalties shall be liable to receive equal penalty.

Article 97. If goods which should be confiscated are seized or not, but if there is sufficient evidence, the customs authorities may request the court to decide their confiscated in case.

Article 98. In case of offences belonging to several categories, either minor or major, additional penalty shall be decided in favor of the Government depending on the nature of the offence.

PART XI ORGANIZATION AND ACTICITIES OF THE CUSTOMS AUTHORITIES

Chapter 1 Organization

Article 99. The customs authorities is an organization under the management of the Ministry of Finance with the following organizational structure:

- Department of Customs and divisions;
- Customs offices in provinces, the municipality and special zones;
- Border customs;
- Customs control posts;
- Mobile customs control units.

The organizational chart, work methods, insignias and uniforms of customs, identity card shall be governed by specific regulations outlined by the Government.

Chapter 2 Scope of Activities of the Customs Authorities.

Article 100. Regular activities of the customs authorities are conducted within the customs radius. In certain necessary cases, as provided in Article 102 of this Law, customs officers may operate outside the customs radius.

CHAPTER 3 CRITERIA, RIGHTS AND DUTIES OF CUSTOMS OFFICERS

Article 101. All customs officers shall be qualified, have a clean personal history, be honest, organization conscious, disciplined, skilled and customs and laws and be in good health.

Article 102. In view of discovering smuggled goods, customs officers shall have the following rights:

- Physical search, search of goods, vehicles, identity cards or travel permits of individuals whether during the daytime or at nighttime within and outside the customs radius in case of suspicion;
- Order drivers of vehicles to stop for search in case of suspicion;
- Board crafts for search, monitoring and observe handing of goods. Navigators or owners of crafts shall cooperate with customs officers for searches on board;
- Enter the post office, including in the search room to inspect parcels under suspicion in the presence of post officers in accordance with the laws and regulation of the Lao People's Democratic Republic and international post federation agreement;
- Search building for smuggled goods in case such goods have been monitored without loosing them from sight, and such search as mentioned above shall strictly comply to the Law on criminal procedures;
- Wear and use weapons, devices and vehicles as provided in specific regulations;
- Request and receive cooperation and assistance from public organizations, the society, the population and receive legal protection;
- Executive other assigned rights and duties.

Article 103. In the performance of their duties, customs officers shall be entitled to demand and review documents related to customs at the following places and from the following person :

- Transport companies and representative companies and at other relevant premises;
- Customs declaration servicing persons and owners of import-export goods.

During inspection, customs officers shall have the right to retain necessary documents temporarily for facilitated work.

Article 104. In the performance of their duties, customs officers shall:

- Strictly implement instructions, customs regulations and law and other laws;
- Preserve documents and professional official confidentiality;
- Provide recommendations to persons, business persons and staff of various organizations on the implementation of the Customs Law;
- Outline measures to restrict and repress smuggling activities;
- Wear uniforms, insignias, present assignment cards, and adequate and correct attitude.

In certain necessary cases, customs officers may perform their duties undercover, but shall present their assignment cards to the searched persons.

Article 105. During the performance of their duties, customs officers abusing their rights and using their rights and duties for illegitimate personal interest or acting in a manner to disciplinary measures or penalties according to the laws and regulations.

PART XII FINAL PROVISIONS

Article 106. This Customs Law replaces the Decree No. 47/CCM, dated 26/6/1989, of the Council of Ministers on the State Tax Regime alone.

Article 107. The Government of the Lao People's Democratic Republic shall issue detailed provisions on the implementation of this Law.

Article 108. This Law is effective ninety days after its promulgation by the President of the Lao People's Democratic Republic.

LAW ON THE PROMOTION OF FOREIGN INVESTMENT

CHAPTER I GENERAL PROVISIONS

Article 1: Objectives

The Law on the Promotion of Foreign Investment determines principles, regulations and measures regarding the promotion, protection and management of foreign investment in the Lao PDR aiming at enhancing relationships, economic cooperation with foreign countries, and utilisation of financial resources and knowledge to enhance production capacity for purpose of industrialisation and progressive modernisation as well as to contribute to gradually improving the people's living conditions, and to strengthen and to develop the country.

ARTICLE 2: DEFINITIONS

Foreign investment means the importation of capital which includes assets, technology and expertise into the Lao PDR by foreign investors for business purposes.

Foreign investor means a foreign individual or juristic entity investing in the Lao PDR.

For additional analytical, business and investment opportunities information,
please contact Global Investment & Business Center, USA
at (703) 370-8082. Fax: (703) 370-8083. E-mail: ibpusa3@gmail.com
Global Business and Investment Info Databank - www.ibpus.com

Domestic investor means Lao individuals or juristic entities, or aliens or stateless persons residing in the Lao PDR who are shareholders or take part in joint ventures with foreign parties.

Asset means currency, materials and intellectual property.

Foreign enterprise means a 100% foreign owned enterprise, a joint venture and an enterprise established under a business cooperation contract incorporated in the Lao PDR.

Article 3: Promotion of Foreign Investment

Foreign investors may invest in all business sectors in the Lao PDR, except in business activities which are detrimental to national security or cause a negative impact on the environment in the present or long term, or are detrimental to health or national traditions.

The State promotes foreign investors investing in business sectors and areas of investment as provided in Article 16 and 17 of this Law by establishing policies on customs, taxes, regulations, measures and provision of information, services and other facilities to foreign investors.

Article 4: Protection of Foreign Investment

Assets and investment of foreign investors in the Lao PDR shall be fully protected by laws and regulations of the Lao PDR without seizure, confiscation or nationalisation, except if necessary for public purpose, in which case the foreign investors shall be compensated in accordance with laws and regulations.

CHAPTER II FORMS OF FOREIGN INVESTMENT

ARTICLE 5: FORMS OF FOREIGN INVESTMENT

Foreign investors may invest in the Lao PDR in the following forms:

1. Business Cooperation by contract;
2. Joint Venture between foreign and domestic investors;
3. 100% foreign owned enterprise

Article 6: Business Cooperation by Contract

A Business Cooperation by contract is business between domestic and foreign juristic entities without establishing a new juristic entity in the Lao PDR.

The objectives, forms, business term, rights and obligations, liabilities and benefits of each party shall be determined by contract.

Article 7: Joint Ventures

A Joint Venture is an enterprise established and registered under the laws of the Lao PDR, operated and jointly owned by foreign and domestic investors. The organisation, management, operation and the relationship between the shareholders of the Joint Venture are set out in an agreement made by both parties and in the Articles of Association of such Joint Venture.

Foreign investors investing in a Joint Venture shall contribute at least thirty percent (30%) of the Joint Venture's registered capital. Capital contributed in foreign currency shall be converted into Kip based on the exchange rate of the Bank of the Lao PDR on the day of the capital contribution.

Article 8: 100% Foreign Owned Enterprise A one hundred percent (100%) foreign owned enterprise is an enterprise in which the investment in the Lao PDR is made by a foreign investor only. Such enterprise may be incorporated as a new juristic entity or as a branch of a foreign enterprise.

Article 9: Registered Capital

The registered capital of a foreign enterprise shall not be less than thirty percent (30%) of its total capital. During the business operation of a foreign enterprise, the assets of the enterprise shall not be less than its registered capital.

Article 10: Representative Offices

A foreign juristic entity incorporated under the law of other countries may establish a representative office in the Lao PDR to collect information, study the feasibility of investment and coordinate for the purpose of applying for investment.

Representative offices or agents which operate for commercial purposes do not come under this Law.

Article 11: Investment Term

The investment term of a foreign enterprise depends on the nature, size and conditions of the business activities or project but will not exceed fifty (50) years and may be extended with the approval of the Government. However, the investment term of a foreign enterprise shall be for a maximum of seventy five (75) years.

CHAPTER III RIGHTS, BENEFITS AND OBLIGATIONS OF FOREIGN INVESTORS

ARTICLE 12: RIGHTS AND BENEFITS OF FOREIGN INVESTORS

Foreign investors shall have the following rights and benefits:

1. To receive support from the Government in establishing and operating their business in accordance with the laws and regulations;
2. To obtain protection of rights and legitimate interests related to business operations;

3. To own assets;
4. To receive benefits from the lease of or a concession over land such as the right to use, sell or use assets associated with the leased land or concession as security to any persons or financial institutions or for the purpose of joint venture, to sublease the right to use land, to transfer the land lease or concession agreement in accordance with the lease term, to use the land lease agreement or concession in Joint Ventures or as security with other persons. The details of the rights, benefits and obligations of foreign investors related to the land lease or concession shall be in compliance with the Land Law and other relevant laws;
5. To use foreign labourers, if necessary, but shall not exceed 10% (ten percent) of the enterprise's labour;
6. Foreign investors and their families, foreign professionals and employees of a foreign enterprise will be provided with facilities such as multiple entry visas and long term residence in the Lao PDR with the agreement of the Government; and will have the right to request Lao nationality in accordance with the Nationality Law;
7. To receive protection of their intellectual property which has been registered by the relevant authorities in the Lao PDR;
8. To transfer/repatriate profits, capital and other income after full payment of duties, taxes and other fees in accordance with regulations and laws, to their home countries or a third country through a commercial bank located in the Lao PDR;
9. To open a Kip account and a foreign currency account with commercial banks located in the Lao PDR;
10. To request an equitable decision from or to file a complaint to the relevant authorities when their business operations have been affected;
11. To obtain other rights and benefits as provided in the Laws.

Article 13: Obligations of the Foreign Investors

The obligations of foreign investors are:

1. To operate business activities in accordance with their licence, procedures set out in their feasibility study, any contract and laws and regulations;
2. To maintain accounts in accordance with the Enterprise Accounting Law of the Lao PDR. If necessary, an internationally recognised accounting system may be used with approval of the Ministry of Finance. To submit a report on business performance and an annual financial report to the Committee for Promotion and Management of Investment and other relevant authorities;
3. To fully pay duties, taxes and other financial obligations related to the business operations in a timely manner;
4. To facilitate the organisation and activities of the mass organisations in their enterprises;
5. To give priority in recruiting to Lao workers; to train and upgrade professional skills and transfer technology to Lao workers;
6. To address social security matters, health care and safety of employees in their enterprises;
7. To protect the environment, and ensure that business activities do not cause an adverse impact on the public, the national security or social order;

8. To maintain a reserve in accordance with laws and regulations;
9. To maintain insurance and social security policies in accordance with laws and regulations related to insurance and social security;
10. If an enterprise is relocated, the enterprise shall inform the relevant authorities and shall maintain its location in normal working condition;
11. To report on the performance of business operations to the Committee for Promotion and Management of Investment and other relevant authorities;
12. To perform other obligations as set out in the laws and regulations.

Article 14: Personal Income Tax of Foreign Employees

Foreign Employees working in a foreign investment enterprise shall pay personal income tax at the rate of ten percent (10%) of their total income to the Lao Government, except employees of a country with which the Lao Government has signed a Double Taxation Agreement.

CHAPTER IV INCENTIVES FOR FOREIGN INVESTMENT

ARTICLE 15: INCENTIVES FOR FOREIGN INVESTMENT

The State will consider granting incentives for foreign investment in accordance with the sectors and zones of investment promotion as provided in Article 16 and 17 of this Law.

Article 16: Promoted Activities

The Government determines promoted activities as follows:

1. Production for export;
2. Agricultural and forestry activities, agro-forestry and handicraft processing activities;
3. Activities relating to industrial processing, industrial activities using modern technology, scientific study and analysis activities and development, activities in relation to protection of environment and biodiversity;
4. Human resources development, skills development and protection of people's health;
5. Construction of infrastructure;
6. Production of raw materials and equipment to be supplied to key industrial activities;
7. Development of tourism and transit services.

Article 17: Promoted Zones

The Government specifies 3 promoted zones based on geographical location and socio-economic conditions. The zones are as follows:

Zone 1: Mountainous, plain and plateau zones with no economic infrastructure to facilitate investments. Zone 2: Mountainous, plain and plateau zones with a certain level of economic infrastructure suitable to accommodate investments to some extent. Zone 3: Mountainous, plain and plateau zones with good infrastructure to support investments.

The details of the promoted zones will be determined by the Government.

Article 18: Incentives Related to Duties and Taxes

Foreign enterprises investing in activities within the promoted sectors and zones determined in Article 16 and 17 of this Law will be entitled to the following duty and tax incentives:

Investments in Zone 1 will be entitled to a profit tax exemption for 7 years and thereafter will be subject to profit tax at the rate of ten percent (10%).

Investments in Zone 2 will be entitled to a profit tax exemption for 5 years, and thereafter will be subject to a reduced profit tax rate of half of fifteen percent (15%) for 3 years and thereafter a profit tax rate of fifteen percent (15%).

Investments in Zone 3 will be entitled to a profit tax exemption for 2 years and thereafter will be subject to a reduced profit tax rate of half of twenty percent for 2 years and thereafter a profit tax rate of twenty percent (20%).

Profit tax exemption starts from the date of the foreign enterprise's commencement of business operations. For some tree plantation activities, profit tax exemption commences from the date the enterprise starts making a profit.

Once the profit tax exemption period is over, the foreign investment enterprise shall pay profit tax in accordance with the laws and regulations.

In addition to the incentives mentioned above, the foreign investment enterprises shall be entitled to the following incentives:

1. During the tax exemption period and during the tax reduction period, the enterprise is entitled to an exemption of minimum tax;
2. The profit used for the expansion of licensed business activities will be exempted from profit tax during the accounting year;
3. Exemption of import duties and taxes on equipment, spare parts, vehicles directly used for production, raw materials which do not exist domestically or exist but are insufficient, semi finished products imported for manufacturing or for processing for the purpose of export; and
4. Exemption of export duty on export products.

Raw materials and semi finished products imported for manufacturing or assembly for import substitution will be exempted from import duties and taxes or will be subject to reduced rates of import duties and taxes.

Special economic zones, industrial zones, border trade areas and other specific economic zones shall follow the laws and regulations of such specific areas.

CHAPTER V APPLICATION FOR A FOREIGN INVESTMENT LICENSE

ARTICLE 19: APPLICATION FOR FOREIGN INVESTMENT

Application for foreign investment in the Lao PDR shall go through the one stop service of the Committee for Promotion and Management of Investment ("CPMI").

Foreign investors wishing to invest in the Lao PDR shall submit an application to CPMI at the central or provincial levels with attachments such as copies of passport and resume of the foreign investor; feasibility study or business plan; background information on the investor in the case of a juristic entity; and a Joint Venture Agreement in the case of a Joint Venture.

Article 20: Examination of a Foreign Investment Application

Upon receipt of a complete application in accordance with Article 19 of this Law, the CPMI shall coordinate with relevant sectors and local authorities when necessary to examine and to respond in writing to the foreign investor pursuant to the following timeframes:

- Projects which fall in the list of promoted activities - fifteen working days;
- Projects which fall in the list of open activities with conditions - twenty five working days;
- Projects which involve the grant of a concession - forty five working days.

Foreign investors who are qualified under this Law will obtain a foreign investment licence, an enterprise registration certificate and a tax registration certificate at the same time from the CPMI at the place where the foreign investors are licensed; thereafter they will be considered as enterprises established in conformity with the laws of the Lao PDR.

Within 90 days from the date of receipt of an investment licence, the foreign enterprise shall commence investment activities in accordance with the steps in the feasibility study provided in the foreign investment licence application and in conformity with laws and regulations of the Lao PDR. If such timeframe is not followed, the foreign investment licence may be withdrawn.

CHAPTER VI MANAGEMENT OF FOREIGN INVESTMENT

ARTICLE 21: MANAGEMENT AUTHORITIES RELATED TO FOREIGN INVESTMENT

Management authorities related to foreign investment are:

1. The Committee for Promotion and Management of Investment at central and provincial levels;
2. Relevant sectors and sections.

Article 22: Rights and Duties of CPMI at the Central Level

The Committee for Promotion and Management of Investment at the central level is established by the Prime Minister, located at the Committee for Planning and Investment and has the following rights and duties:

1. To develop strategies, incentives to promote and attract foreign investments and propose them to the Government for approval;
2. To issue decisions, orders, instructions and notifications regarding the protection and promotion of foreign investments;
3. To prepare a plan and a list of investment projects that are available for foreign investments;
4. To disseminate policies, laws and regulations; provide information and facilitate foreign investors;
5. To consider issuing or withdrawing a foreign investment licence within its scope of rights and duties, particularly within projects involving the grant of a concession,
6. To supervise and coordinate with the sectors and local authorities in implementing the Law on the Promotion of Foreign Investment;
7. To monitor, inspect, assess and report to the Government on the business operation of foreign investment enterprises;
8. To be a focal point in supporting, promoting and solving problems occurring in relation to the business operation of foreign investment enterprises;
9. To organise the annual meeting of CPMI and consultative meetings with foreign investors; and
10. To exercise and perform other rights and duties as prescribed in the laws and regulations.

Article 23: Rights and Duties of CPMI at Provincial Levels

The Committee for Promotion and Management of Foreign Investment at provincial levels is established by the Chairman of the CPMI at the central level. The CPMI at the provincial level acts as a support to the provincial Governors, the capital city Governor, the Special Zone Head and the CPMI at the central level in promoting and managing foreign investment. The CPMI at the provincial level located at the provincial Planning and Investment Divisions and has the following rights and duties:

1. To implement strategic plans and policies to promote and attract foreign investments at their local levels;
2. To disseminate policies, laws and regulations, provide information and facilitate foreign investors;
3. To consider issuing or withdrawing foreign investment licences within their scope of rights and duties;
4. To coordinate with various relevant sectors in implementing the incentive policies within the approved projects and in implementing the decisions, orders, instructions and notifications of the higher level authorities;
5. To monitor, inspect, assess and report to the provincial governors, the capital city governor or the Special Zone Head and CPMI at the central level regarding foreign investment;
6. To act as a focal point in solving problems related to foreign investment;

7. To organise the CPMI annual meetings at provincial levels and consultative meetings with foreign investors;
8. To exercise and perform other rights and duties as prescribed in the laws and regulations.

Article 24: Rights and Duties of other relevant Sectors and Sections

The relevant ministries, organisations equivalent to ministries and other relevant sectors shall assist in the promotion and management of foreign investments in accordance with their rights and duties as follows:

1. To coordinate with the CPMI at the central level in drafting laws, regulations, policies and plans in relation to foreign investment;
2. To prepare a plan and list of foreign investment projects to attract foreign investment to their sectors, to disseminate information to attract and promote investment;
3. To participate in the process of consideration and approval of investment projects;
4. To supervise the sectors both at central and local levels in implementing incentive policies and in revising procedures regarding implementation of investment projects;
5. To inspect and assess business operations of foreign investment enterprises and partners' business cooperation contracts within their scope of rights and duties and then report to the higher authorities;
6. To exercise and perform other rights and duties as prescribed in the laws and regulations.

The administrative authorities and sectors at the local level described above shall coordinate with the CPMI at the local level within the scope of rights and duties described in this Article.

CHAPTER VII DISPUTE RESOLUTION

Article 25: General Principles

If a dispute arises in relation to business operation, the parties shall mediate, arbitrate or file a petition to the court.

Article 26: Mediation of Disputes

Disputes related to business operation which cannot be mediated by the parties amicably shall be submitted for mediation to the CPMI that has issued the licence.

If the CPMI is not able to mediate such dispute, such dispute shall be submitted to the Economic Dispute Resolution Committee for arbitration.

Article 27: Filing of a case

The parties to a dispute related to business operation which can not be mediated may bring the case to the Committee for Economic Dispute Resolution or the People's Court for consideration in accordance with court procedures.

Chapter VIII Policies toward Those Who Have Performed Well and Measures Against Violators

ARTICLE 28: POLICIES TOWARD THOSE WHO HAVE PERFORMED WELL

Individuals or organisations who have had outstanding achievements in implementing this Law and in contributing to national socio-economic development will receive awards as deemed reasonable.

Article 29: Measures against Investors who violate the Law

Individuals or juristic entities who violate this Law shall be subject to penalties based on the seriousness of the violation in the form of warnings, suspension, withdrawal of their foreign investment licence or being sued in a court of law.

Article 30: Measures against other Violators

Individuals who violate investment laws and regulations by abusing their power or position to hinder or obstruct the promotion and approval of investment, falsify documents, mislead investors, receive bribes or commit any acts causing damage to the State or investors shall compensate for such damages and shall be subject to disciplinary and other measures in accordance with the laws of the Lao PDR.

CHAPTER VIII FINAL PROVISIONS

Article 31: Implementation

The Government of the Lao People's Democratic Republic shall implement this Law.

Article 32: Effectiveness

This Law will become effective sixty days from the date of the issue of a Promulgating Decree of the President of Lao People's Democratic Republic. Thereafter, the Law on the Promotion and Management of Foreign Investment No. 01/94/NA, dated 14 March 1994 shall cease to have effect, without prejudice to the rights and privileges granted to, and the obligations imposed upon, foreign investments under the Law No. 01/94/NA. Foreign investors who have been licensed under the Law No. 01/94/NA and wish to obtain incentives provided by this amended Law on Promotion of Foreign Investment shall submit an official written request within 120 days from the date this law become effective to the Committee for Planning and Investment for consideration.

The Chairman of the National Assembly

CUSTOMS REGULATIONS

A customs law was adopted by the National Assembly in late 1994, rationalising and consolidating the tariff system. Tariff reductions are under negotiation in the ASEAN Free Trade Area (AFTA) context and will be further reviewed in the light of Laos' request to accede to the World Trade Organisation (WTO).

Laos uses two types of customs valuations:

> I.) Valuation based on the transaction value of the imported item, which is usually based on the shipping invoice.

> II.) Valuation based on a certificate from the Lao embassy or a reputable organization having expertise on price and fair market value, such as the Chamber of Commerce of the country of origin.

If the importers cannot provide such documents, the customs valuation will be based on domestic price (the so-called general price), minus 15 percent. The importer must employ a certified customs specialist or certified customs clearance corporation to complete the report.

Lao law does not require an origin determination for imported goods, but relies upon the rules of origin from other countries.

TARIFFS AND IMPORT TAXES

The Lao import tax system aims at promoting the import of materials and equipment for investment and production, while protecting domestic production and limiting luxury imports. Foreign investors are required to pay a 1% import duty on imports of machinery for production, equipment, and spare parts. Raw materials and intermediate goods needed for export production are exempt from import taxes. Raw materials and intermediate goods imported for import-substituting industries can be accorded special treatment based on an incentive agreement.

There are six rates of import tariffs: five percent for promoted goods such as heavy equipment and machine tools; ten percent for some medicines and some materials used in light industry such as fabrics and some chemicals; twenty percent for some food products, such as frozen fish; thirty percent for certain kinds of fruit and vegetables; and forty percent for automobiles. Besides the import tariff, the government also imposes excise tax on a wide range of products, with the steepest assessed on autos (from 72% to 104%, depending on engine size); motorcycles, beer and cigarettes (50%); and alcohol (60%).

In addition to the excise tax, importers may also face a turnover tax of 5-10% on most goods. Goods are usually assessed at the higher 10% rate; most goods considered essential to domestic production (such as agricultural equipment, power tools, and construction equipment; fabric and cotton thread) are assessed at 5%. Tax-exempt goods include rice; fertilizer and animal feed; fire trucks and wheelchairs. The Lao government is expected to introduce a value-added tax, which will replace the turnover tax, by 2002.

IMPORT/EXPORT LICENSE REQUIREMENTS

Import License: Application for an import license must be made to the provincial trade authority where the importing enterprise is located. An import license is valid for three months, during which time payment for imports and import duties should be made. The Lao government limits the right to import autos to certain import-export companies.

Import/export documentation: for general goods, importers are required to have the following documentation for each shipment:

- Contract with a foreign supplier or purchase order;
- Import license (7 copies);
- Letter of credit or payment guarantee paper from a foreign exchange bank;
- Transport documents;
- Bill of lading;
- Customs clearance (import) report.

Importers of raw materials for re-export are required to have the same documents as other importers, except for the contract and import license for each shipment. Instead, they are required to provide an annual import plan to the provincial or municipal Industry and Handicraft Department where the factory is located.

Since the import of automobiles is restricted by a government-issued quota, automobile importers must show, in addition to the documents mentioned above, quota approval from the government, a technical specification approval from the Ministry of Communications and Transport, and an import license from the Ministry of Commerce and Tourism.

Exporters should have the following documentation when applying for an export declaration:

- application for export declaration;
- export permission from provincial trading authority;
- invoice;
- packing list;
- certificate of country of origin and generalized system of preferences certificate of origin if applicable;
- phytosanitary certificate for food exports; and
- industrial products certification for industrial products.

TEMPORARY GOODS ENTRY REQUIREMENTS

Products imported for the purposes of processing and assembly into finished products or for exhibition and subsequent re-export are exempt from duty. Trans-shipment of goods through Laos requires all the documents normally needed for both importing and exporting. In addition, the export-import company shipping goods through Laos must submit an annual trans-shipment plan to the related ministry (e.g., Agriculture and Forestry for wood products) and obtain further permission from the ministry for each trans-shipment. Goods travelling through Laos are not subject to import or export taxes.

SPECIAL IMPORT/EXPORT REQUIREMENTS AND CERTIFICATIONS

To import or export pharmaceuticals, food and chemical products, the importers must obtain a license from the Food and Drug Control Import Division of the Food and Drug Department of the Ministry of Public Health. For more information please contact Food and Drug Control Division of Ministry of Health at the following numbers: Tel: (856) 21 214-013 or 014; fax (856) 21 214015. Pre-shipment inspection is required for exported goods of any kind.

Prohibited Imports

Lao law prohibits the imports of weapons by private citizens; illegal drugs; toxic chemicals; hazardous materials; pornography; and agricultural produce which is grown domestically in sufficient quantities (i.e., eggplant, tomatoes, bananas, chilies, lemons, etc.).

Export Controls

The GOL uses quotas to control exports of timber and lumber. While export inspections are only required by law for a few items, in practice almost all shipments are inspected before export.

Lao law prohibits the export of weapons; antiques; Buddha images; illegal drugs; logs; 15 ft x 80 ft size and thicker sawed wood (regardless of length); raw rattan and basic processed rattan; and wildlife.

Standards

Laos has no specific law on standards for imported or exported goods. All imported goods are based on the standard certification of the country of export.

Free Trade Zones

Laos has no free trade zone, but the Ministry of Commerce has indicated its willingness to establish free trade zones in many areas of the country as an investment incentive on a case-by-case basis. Plans are currently underway for a free trade zone in Savannakhet province on the Vietnamese border in southeastern Laos.

Membership in Free Trade Arrangements

Laos became a member of ASEAN in 1997 and has committed to bringing all of its tariffs in line with its AFTA commitments by 2008. The following countries have granted MFN status to Laos: China; Myanmar; Thailand; European Union; and Russia. Laos has signed trade agreements with 15 countries, including Bulgaria; Czech Republic; India; Slovak Republic; Hungary; Germany; Cambodia; Mongolia; and Poland.

LAW ON VALUE-ADDED TAX

PART I GENERAL PROVISIONS

Article 1. Objective

The Law on Value-Added Tax defines principles, regulations, methods and measures relating to the value-added tax for the collection of obligations from consumers to the State budget, aiming at promoting production and business operations, and widening the circulation of goods 1 and services in conformity with the national plan for socio-economic development and integration with the regional and international communities.

Article 2. Value-Added Tax

The value-added tax is an indirect tax that is collected on the proportion of value added to goods and services occurring in all processes, ranging from production, distribution, service supply to consumption; and is [also] collected on the value of goods and services imported into the Lao PDR.

Article 3. Explanations of Terms

The meanings of the terms that are used in this law are as follows:

1. **Value-added-tax-liable targets** refers to goods and services used in manufacturing, business, consumption, distribution or supply in the Lao PDR;

2. **Value-added-tax-payable targets** refers to organisations, legal entities and individuals that do business and collect [value-added tax] from end consumers. They shall pay value-added tax to the State budget;

3. **Distribution of goods** refers to the assignment or transfer of rights to the usage of goods to other person(s) in return for remuneration in cash or other benefits 2 ;

4. **Services** refers to economic activities that supply labour, materials, equipment, or vehicles to other person(s) in return for remuneration, such as in the areas of transport, telecommunication, construction, repair, contracts for market management, land development for further sale of usage rights, the hotel business, tourism, food and beverage [business], entertainment, consultancy, brokerage, agency and other activities;

5. **Importation** refers to bringing goods or services into the Lao PDR, and includes import-related services;

6. **Exportation** refers to sending goods or services to other countries from the Lao PDR, and includes export-related services;

7. **Business undertaking or sector** refers to a business operation engaged in manufacturing [and/or] services in such different sectors as agriculture, forestry, handicraft, industry-commerce, mining, transport, banking, and others 3 ;

8. **Broker or agent** refers to an individual or legal entity that is authorised by other individuals or legal entities to make [an] agreement, conduct a negotiation and/or sign a business contract;

9. **Permanent business establishment** refers to an establishment where a taxpayer operates his business on a regular basis. Establishments considered to be permanent include administrative offices, branch offices, factories, mining-extraction sites, construction fields or sites, and any site where undertakings take place;

10. **Value-added tax input (value-added tax credit)** refers to the amount of value-added tax already paid by a taxpayer at the time of the purchase of goods or services for his value-added-tax-liable business operation;

11. **Value-added tax output** refers to the tax amount calculated on the sale value of output goods and services liable to value-added tax;

12. **Value-added tax payable** refers to the amount of value-added tax output minus the value-added tax input, or the tax amount calculated on the added portion of the sale value of goods and services liable to value-added tax;

13. **Tax period** refers to a monthly accounting period;

14. **Non-residents** refers to those who have no permanent residence to reside, make a living, and to do business in the Lao PDR.

1 The Lao language has two words for "goods". In this law both Lao words are virtually always used together. The translators believe that the single English word "goods" covers both these Lao words. Readers may wish to refer to footnote 3 to the translation of the Tax Law for a fuller discussion of the literal language.

2 The term "distribution" is intentionally defined and used in this law to refer to all kinds of sale (whether on a large scale or not).

3 The term "and others" is a literal translation and is not subject to further specificity.

4 The literal translation is "extended or normal". The translators are aware that the 1999 Enterprise Accounting Law (which was in force when this law was enacted) does not refer to these different accounting systems. The references here may be to the amended Enterprise Accounting Law which (as of July 2007) has just been passed. For

consistency, the translators have used the same translations as employed in Article 35 (1) of the Tax Law and by the Tax Authority.

5 If there is no market for the particular goods or services, this provision directs the calculator to determine the price of a private transaction in similar goods or services.

6 This is a literal translation of the Lao text. The translators are aware that value-added tax is typically excluded from, rather than included in, the calculation.

7 There is a connotation of re-issue.

8 These are translations of two Lao words that mean ticket. The first word refers to tickets made of ordinary soft paper and the second to tickets made of a thicker paper like the ones used for cards.

9 The descriptor "that are liable to and exempt from value-added tax" is a literal translation. The implication is that some of the output is liable to value-added tax and some is not.

10 There is a connotation that the other forms must be stipulated by laws.

11 In the Lao language, the same word is used to represent all of the following related (but slightly different) concepts: "control", "inspection", "supervision", "audit" and "monitoring". The translators have chosen "audit" for external audits of business operators and (consistent with most other laws), "inspection" for the inspection by the government of its own internal operations (as in Part V, Chapter 2).

12 For more detailed information on petitions, readers may wish to refer to the Law on the Handling of Petitions.

13 The term "policies" is often used as an indirect way of referring to "incentives' or "privileges" and the term "measures" is often used as an indirect way of referring to "sanctions".

14 Here, "re-education" does not mean the same as "re-education without deprivation of liberty" referred to in the Penal Law.

Article 4. State Policy on Value-Added Tax

The State determines the policy on value-added tax along with the policies on other taxes to handle double taxation and gradually decrease tax leakage, in stages from lower to higher levels, aiming to promote manufacturing, services, export, and domestic and foreign investment, and to strengthen the State budget to contribute to the constant growth of socio-economic development.

Article 5. Value-Added Tax Obligations of Individuals and Organisations

The value-added tax is an obligation of end consumers who consume goods and services. Business operators calculate and add value-added tax to the sale price of goods and services and pay it to the State budget.

Individuals, organisations and legal entities that consume or import goods and services have the obligation to pay value-added tax to the State completely and comprehensively in accordance with the laws and regulations.

Article 6. Scope of Application of the Law on Value-Added Tax

The Law on Value-Added Tax is applicable to individuals, organisations and legal entities, both domestic and foreign, that are operating businesses, manufacturing, and services on the territory of the Lao PDR as stipulated in this law.

Article 7. International Relations and Cooperation

The government opens up and promotes international relations and cooperation in the area of value-added tax for the sake of its development through the exchange of technical lessons, human resource development, exchange of information, and facilitation in different areas in line with international agreements or treaties which the Lao PDR has signed or acceded to.

PART II REGULATIONS ON VALUE-ADDED TAX

Chapter 1

Value-Added-Tax-Liable and Value-Added-Tax-Payable Targets

Article 8. Value-Added-Tax-Liable Targets

Goods and services used in manufacturing, business and consumption in the Lao PDR, including for self-consumption, non-business activities and free supply to others and one's own workers, are targets liable to value-added tax, except for the cases stipulated in Article 10 of this law.

Article 9. Value-Added-Tax-Payable Targets

Value-added-tax-payable targets are the following organisations, legal entities and individuals:

1. Business operators, which refers to operators engaged in manufacturing goods and [providing] services, whose annual turnover is higher or equal to the value-added tax threshold subject to the value-added tax system as stipulated in paragraph 1 of Article 13, or who have an annual business turnover lower than the threshold but who volunteer to enter the value-added tax regime in accordance with Article 15 of this law;

2. Importers of goods and services, who are liable to value-added tax regardless of whether the importation is for business operations or self-consumption, or on a continuous or occasional basis;

3. Those who are non-resident and not registered in the tax regime of the Lao PDR are all subject to value-added tax in accordance with Article 29 of this law for all acts of service supply to their customers in the Lao PDR, by using the method of determining business turnover to calculate the value-added tax levied on transactions made through permanent establishments in the Lao PDR.

Article 10. Value-Added Tax Exemptions

The goods and services listed below are all exempted from value-added tax:

1. Non-processed agricultural produce and handicraft products produced and sold by farmers, civil servants and members of cooperatives themselves;

2. Crop seeds and animals for breeding, pesticides, vaccines, [and] organic and chemical fertilizers;

3. Activities of sapling nurseries, afforestation, and plantation of industrial, fruit and medicinal trees;

4. Importation of materials, equipment, and chemicals that cannot be made domestically for scientific research and analysis by State administrative or technical agencies;

5. Importation of gold bars to secure the printing of bank notes, the minting of coins and the distribution of bank notes and coins[;] and importation of bank notes or coins;

6. Importation of, or activities relating to, tax or postage stamps for official use;

7. Importation of aircraft and equipment for air transport[;] and [importation] of goods, fuel and other oils for the service of international air transport;

8. Importation of goods for sale to diplomats, embassies, and international organisations in the Lao PDR in accordance with the authorisation of the Ministry of Foreign Affairs;

9. Personal effects of Lao diplomats, civil servants and students brought into the country following the completion of their overseas missions, training, or study, which have lasted for at least three months. The personal effects must be materials of a non-commercial nature. Cars and other vehicles will not receive exemption;

10. Production and sale of authorised textbooks, teaching manuals, newspapers, political magazines, and non-business television and radio programmes that disseminate political policies;

11. Educational operations such as childcare centres, kindergartens, primary and secondary schools, colleges, universities, vocational schools, and vocational training centres;

12. Operations relating to banking services, financial institutions, and the insurance of health, life, domestic animals and tree plantations;

13. Medical services, such as: examination, treatment, diagnosis, traditional medicines, organs for transplantation, and aids for patients and the disabled;

14. Vehicles for specific purposes, such as: fire engines, ambulances, vehicles equipped with repair facilities, outside television and radio broadcast vehicles, and others, for State administration, national defence and public security;

15. Goods and services supplied to grant aid projects, defined in agreements, treaties and contracts that the government has signed with the governments of foreign countries.

Chapter 2

System and Conditions for Implementation of Value-Added Tax

Article 11. Components of the Value-Added Tax System

The value-added tax system is a system within the general tax system. It replaces only the turnover tax.

The value-added tax system consists of principles and regulations on the registration, calculation, deduction, refund, filing, and payment of value-added tax.

Article 12. Conditions for Inclusion in the Value-Added Tax System

Inclusion in the value-added tax system shall depend on meeting conditions relating to:

• The annual business turnover of business operators;
• Use of a standard accounting system and invoices.

Article 13. Annual Business Turnover of Business Operators

As stipulated in paragraph 1 of Article 9 of this law, business operators who have a minimum annual business turnover of 400,000,000 Kip are subject to value-added tax registration with the tax authority, and are targets [required] to file value-added tax returns from the day they are registered in the value-added tax system.

If the prices of goods and services fluctuate by at least 20% or if there is a need, the government will adjust the level of the annual business turnover as stipulated above and in Article 15 of this law to conform to the local realities, and will report it to the next session of the National Assembly for approval.

Article 14. Maintenance of Standard Accounting System and Use of Invoices

Business operators registered in the value-added tax system have the obligation to maintain an advanced or ordinary 4 accounting system in line with the Enterprise Accounting Law. The standard of their accounting will be certified by relevant State organisations, or legally established accounting consultancy firms. They shall also use the invoice forms promulgated by the State in accordance with regulations.

Article 15. Voluntary Value-Added Tax Registration

A business operator who has an annual business turnover of less than 400,000,000 Kip, and who maintains correct accounts, and uses invoices and other certified documents, can voluntarily apply to the tax authority for registration in the value-added tax system and become a target to pay value-added tax starting from the month after it is authorised to be in the value-added tax system.

Chapter 3

Value-Added Tax Calculation

Article 16. Method of Value-Added Tax Calculation

Value-added tax can be calculated by multiplying the value of goods and services liable to value-added tax by the value-added tax rate.

Article 17. Basis of Value-Added Tax Calculation

The basis of value-added tax calculation is the value of goods and services liable to value-added tax, and the calculation can be made according to the following cases:

1. For imported goods, the calculation is based on the value declared at import plus customs duties, excise tax (if any), and the value of import-related services;
2. For goods and services on which excise tax is collected during the domestic production process [or] upon importation for domestic sale, the calculation is based on the sale price with excise tax (if any) but excluding value-added tax;
3. For goods and services used in domestic barter trade or for domestic consumption, including for self-consumption, consumption by others and employees and free supply, the calculation is based on the market sale price of goods and services excluding value-added tax, or on an equivalent price at the place of the transaction 5 ;
4. For the lease of assets of a business operator, the basis is the rental received for each period as stipulated in the contract;
5. For contracts for labour services, the calculation is based on the service fees including 6 value-added tax received under the contract; and for job placement services, it is based on the service fees received excluding value-added tax;
6. For goods and services sold on credit, the calculation is based on the total value, excluding value-added tax, that would be determined for the immediate sale of the goods or services, and not including interest;
7. For goods and services of specific nature, such as: tourism, telecommunication, internet services, lottery operation, operations of brokers and agents, and other undertakings for which it is difficult to establish the basis for value-added tax calculation, the government is responsible for defining detailed regulations to establish the basis of value-added tax calculation.

In calculating the basis of value-added tax for goods and services stipulated in this article, if there is additional income, the income will be added to the value-added tax calculation of business operators.

In the event that business operators earn business turnover in foreign currencies, it shall be converted into Kip to determine the basis of value-added tax calculation, based on the exchange rate of the Bank of the Lao PDR at the time of the transaction.

For additional analytical, business and investment opportunities information,
please contact Global Investment & Business Center, USA
at (703) 370-8082. Fax: (703) 370-8083. E-mail: ibpusa3@gmail.com
Global Business and Investment Info Databank - www.ibpus.com

Article 18. Adjustments to Value-Added Tax Basis

Adjustment to the value-added tax basis is possible in the following cases:

1. When the customer returns goods or [gets a refund of] the cost of services in whole or in part;
2. When there is a subsequent cancellation of sale or services;
3. When there is a discount on the price of goods or services.

The adjustment of value-added tax basis in the above-mentioned cases will be made when sellers issue 7 invoices that include value-added tax and report the value-added tax amount in their value-added tax returns.

Article 19. Rates of Value-Added Tax

The rates of value-added tax are set as follows:

1. A 10% rate is applied to imported [goods and services] and domestically produced and consumed goods and services liable to value-added tax;
2. A zero (0%) rate is applied to goods and services for export.

Article 20. Calculation of Value-Added Tax Payable

The amount of value-added tax payable is equal to the amount of value-added tax collected at the time of sale (output) minus the amount of value-added tax paid at the time of purchase (input) as credit that is deductible as stipulated in Article 22 of this law.

The amount of value-added tax collected at the time of sale (output) is equal to the actual sale price of goods or services multiplied by the value-added tax rate, which is indicated in the invoice issued at the time of sale of goods and services.

The amount of value-added tax at the time of purchase (input) as credit that is deductible is equal to the gross amount of paid value-added tax specified in invoices that indicate the amount of value-added tax at the time of purchase of goods and services, or in the receipts of value-added tax payment at the time of importation of goods and services.

As for transactions that are accompanied by other kinds of invoices (tickets, cards... 8) with fixed prices and with no separate indication of value-added tax (value-added tax is already included), the value-added tax output or input will be calculated by finding the value-added-tax-free price and multiplying it by the value-added tax rate.

Article 21. Timing of Value-Added Tax Calculation and Collection

The timing of value-added tax calculation and collection is set in the following cases:

1. For imported goods, the value-added tax will be calculated and collected at the same time as customs duties;

2. For the sale of imports or domestic goods and services, regardless of whether payment is made, the calculation and collection will be made according to the following cases:

a. In the case where the seller has issued an invoice and transferred the ownership of the goods, value-added tax will be calculated and collected at the time of the issuance of the invoice and the transfer of ownership;

b. In the case where the seller has delivered goods or supplied services to the buyer but invoices are not issued, value-added tax will be calculated and collected at the time of the delivery of goods or supply of services or at the time the goods are transported;

c. In the case where the buyer has made an advance payment to the seller in accordance with the contract but the seller has not yet issued an invoice, value-added tax will be calculated and collected at the time when the seller receives the payment;

d. In the case where one item is paid for in several instalments, value-added tax will be calculated and collected at the time of actual delivery of such goods and services to the buyer according to the total amount due;

3. For goods and services for self-consumption or free supply to others, and for the supply of goods or services to one's own employees, value-added tax will be calculated and collected at the time when the consumption or the supply takes place.

Chapter 4

Value-Added Tax Deduction and Refund

Article 22. Value-Added Tax Deduction

For business operators in the value-added tax system, the deductible value-added tax input is the amount of paid value-added tax according to an invoice issued at the time of purchase of goods and services, or indicated in a receipt of value-added tax payment at the port of entry, as in the following cases:

1. The amount of value-added tax input of goods and services used in manufacturing, business, and services that are liable to value-added tax is all deductible;

2. The amount of value-added tax input of goods and services used in manufacturing, business, and services that are liable to and exempted from value-added tax 9 is deductible only for the proportion of the goods and services used in such business operations that are liable to value-added tax;

3. The amount of value-added tax input of fixed assets used in manufacturing, business, and services that are liable to and exempted from value-added tax is all deductible;

4. The amount of value-added tax input of goods and services for export, including value-added-tax-exempt goods and services for export, will be deductible only if they meet the following conditions and are certified as follows:

a. The goods and services are exported with the certification of the Customs Authority;

b. [They] have contracts of sale; and

c. Payment [for such goods and services must be made] through banks, or in other forms, such as: exchange of goods and services, and settlement by other special forms as stipulated by the laws. 10
The deduction of value-added tax input for goods and services for export are prescribed in specific regulations;
5. For business operators in the value-added tax system whose amount of deductible value-added tax input exceeds the value-added tax output reported in the month, the balance can be carried forward for deduction in the following month but no longer than six months, except for the cases of value-added tax refunds stipulated in Article 24 of this law.

A request to deduct input value-added tax shall be made at the same time as value-added tax is calculated by submitting a written application to the tax authority within the month in which the value-added tax input is incurred, but no later than six months [after such incurrence].

Article 23. Non-deductible Value-Added Tax Inputs

The following are the cases of value-added tax inputs that are not deductible from value-added tax output:

1. Goods and services that are exempted from value-added tax as stipulated in Article 10 of this law;
2. Incorrect and incomplete receipts of the payment of value-added tax input at the time of purchase or importation of goods and services;
3. Goods and services that are not used in the operator's main business operations liable to value-added tax, such as: food, accommodation, tourism, entertainment, receptions, relief aid or in-kind donations, and the supply of goods and services free of charge to itself or to its own employees;
4. Fuel and lubricants that are used in business, manufacturing, and services that are liable to and exempted from value-added tax;
5. Costs of telephone, water supply, and electricity services, that are not used in the main business operations of the business operator;
6. Lease charges of materials, equipment, vehicles, or other assets;
7. Sale of vehicles, including their accessories and spare parts, that is not the main operation of the business.

Article 24. Value-Added Tax Refund

Value-added tax refund is possible in the following cases:

1. Value-added tax input of goods and services for export, including goods and services for export that are exempted in Article 10 of this law, will be refunded each month with the exception of the products of natural wood and minerals which are reserved by the government;
2. Value-added tax that has not been completely deducted or that has been overpaid by business operators as at the date of legal merger, separation, or bankruptcy in accordance with the laws;

3. The value-added tax amount subject to refund according to this law and in international agreements;
4. For business operators whose business income in an accounting period derives from domestic operations and export operations, if the value-added tax input is not completely deducted within the month, only the export proportion will be refunded.

Business operators shall make a written application to the competent tax authority to receive value-added tax refunds.

The scope of rights, timing, documents and financing sources for the establishment of funds for value-added tax refunds are prescribed in specific regulations.

PART III VALUE-ADDED TAX LICENSES

Chapter 1

General Principles on Value-Added Tax Licenses

Article 25. General Principles

The general principles on value-added tax licenses [cover] the following:

• Value-added tax registration;
• Value-added tax cancellation.

Article 26. Value-Added Tax Registration

Value-added tax registration refers to the systematic and continual recording of the main information on taxpayers into the registers of the tax authority.

The application for value-added tax registration shall be conducted through the submission of an application in the promulgated form used in the competent tax authority.

After receiving the application form for value-added tax registration, tax officers shall consider and issue a value-added tax registration license and tax identification number to the taxpayer within 15 official working days.

Those who are registered in the value-added tax system shall use their tax identification number for certification in their business and official activities as stipulated by the laws and regulations.

In the event of merger, separation, or change in business operations, business operators shall notify the competent tax authority within 30 official working days from the date of the merger, separation, or change in business operations.

Steps and detailed procedures for value-added tax registration will be defined in specific regulations.

Article 27. Value-Added Tax Registration for Business Operators

Business operators who have been running the businesses specified in paragraph 1 of Article 13 and in Article 15 of this law shall apply for registration in the value-added tax system with the competent tax authority.

New business operators are required to submit their annual business turnover plan as stipulated in paragraph 1 of Article 13 and in Article 15 of this law, and shall file an application form for registration with the competent tax authority. They will then be included in the value-added tax system and [be assigned] tax identification numbers within 30 official working days.

The value-added tax registration specified in this article will take effect after the value-added tax registration license is received.

Article 28. Cancellation of Value-Added Tax License

A business operator who wishes to give up his business operations shall apply for the cancellation of his value-added tax license at the competent tax authority with which the business is registered. The tax authority shall consider the application and issue a certificate for the cancellation within 30 official working days after the application is received. Business operators shall continue paying value-added tax until they receive the certificates of cancellation.

Chapter 2

Specific Principles on Value-Added Tax License

Article 29. Non-residents and Non-registered Operators in the Lao PDR

Business operators registered in the value-added tax system that receive services from operators who are non-residents or who are not registered in the value-added tax system in the Lao PDR, as stipulated in paragraph 3 of Article 9 of this law, shall withhold value-added tax when they pay service charges to such suppliers. The payment of the withheld value-added tax will be made at the same time as the normal tax filing in accordance with the accounting periods specified in Article 32 of this law.

If business operators that are not registered in the value-added tax system receive services from suppliers who are non-residents or who are not registered in the value-added tax system in the Lao PDR, they shall withhold value-added tax and pay it to the State within 30 days after the payment to the suppliers.

Article 30. Brokers and Agents

The supply of goods or services by an individual acting as a broker or agent for another person who is the owner of a business operation in the value-added tax system is considered an operation liable to value-added tax as stipulated in this law.

Article 31. Operators Outside the Value-Added Tax System

Business operators that are not registered in the value-added tax system in accordance with this law will be subject to turnover tax on the sale of goods and services in accordance with the Tax Law.

PART IV IMPLEMENTATION

Chapter 1

Value-Added Tax Filing and Payment

Article 32. Filing of Value-Added Tax Returns

The filing of value-added tax returns for payment shall proceed as follows:

> • Business operators shall file value-added tax returns on a monthly basis to the competent tax authority no later than the 15th of the following month;
> • Even if there is no value-added tax input and output [within a tax period], business operators are still obligated to submit value-added tax returns with complete and correct information to the tax authority, in accordance with the regulations;
> • Business operators that are registered in the value-added tax system shall file value-added tax returns from the day the registration takes effect;
> • Importers of goods and services shall file value-added tax returns and pay value-added tax for every importation at the same time as the declaration of customs duties.

Details of how to file tax returns and of tax return forms are specified in specific regulations.

Article 33. Value-Added Tax Payment

Business operators subject to value-added tax shall proceed as follows:

> • For the sale of goods or services, value-added tax shall be paid on a monthly basis by the 15th of the following month;
> • In the case of importation, value-added tax shall be paid fully at the time of the payment of customs duties;
> • If the amount of value-added tax input in an accounting period exceeds the amount of value-added tax output, the balance will be carried forward for deduction in the following tax period;
> • The value-added tax amount shall be paid in Kip to the State budget.

Chapter 2

Maintenance of Accounts and Invoices

Article 34. Maintenance of Accounts

Maintenance of accounts is the process of recording all business activities. In the process, the main data in invoices issued by business operators will be recorded into the accounting books in a systematic and continual manner in accordance with the laws and regulations.

Business operators registered in the value-added tax system shall maintain accurate and complete accounts for the monitoring, recording and maintenance of the files of invoices, receipts and accounting books relating to value-added tax.

All used accounting documents shall be kept for a period of 10 years and must be available at any time for inspection by auditors.

Article 35. Invoices

An invoice is a document certifying a sale of goods and services, a value-added tax payment at the time of purchase, a value-added tax collection at the time of sale, or a deduction or request (claim) for refund.

All sales of goods and services shall be accompanied by invoices as stipulated in the laws and regulations, as follows:

1. For every sale of goods and services, business operators in the value-added tax system have the obligation to issue invoices that include the value-added tax payable and to fill in correct and complete information as required by the invoice form. The information includes the sale price excluding value-added tax, fees received (if any), value-added tax amount, and the sale price including value-added tax. In the event that operators do not enter the value-added tax amount in the invoice at the time of sale, tax officers will take the sale price indicated in the invoice to be the value-added tax basis;
2. Business operators not registered in the value-added tax system are also obligated to issue invoices, but are not entitled to put the value-added tax amount in the invoices for their customers;
3. In the event that sellers do not issue invoices, buyers shall demand for them from sellers;
4. Stamps, tickets, and cards printed with fixed prices on them are considered to be receipts of payment in which value-added tax is included.

Article 36. Goods in Stock and Tax Deduction

Until the Law on Value-Added Tax takes effect, business operators that have goods in stock and that will be registered into the value-added tax system shall conduct a stocktaking to identify the accurate quantity, types, and value of goods in stock, and the amount of turnover tax paid at the time of purchase in order to report and declare to the competent tax authority.

The amount of turnover tax paid at the time of purchase of the goods mentioned above will be deductible from the value-added tax amount payable in the month as specified in Article 22 of this law after it enters into force.

Article 37. Audit 11

The audit of business operators subject to value-added tax is to ensure the correct, complete and timely performance of their obligations.

Audits can be carried out at places as follows:

  • Desk audit at the tax offices;
  • Field audit at the taxpayer's office;
  • Inspection at relevant sites, such as: [sites of] stocks or movement of goods within the country.

Audits can be conducted on a regular basis, with advance notice, and as emergency audits.

Auditors shall abide by the laws and regulations while the person under audit shall cooperate. After every audit, auditors shall make an audit memorandum in the presence of the audited business operator, read out all the phrases to him, and sign the memorandum.

Chapter 3

Settlement of Petitions 12 about Value-Added Tax

Article 38. Petitions by Business Operators

Value-added tax-payable business operators are entitled to file petitions about the value-added tax practices that they view as incompatible with the laws and regulations. The petition shall be lodged directly with the competent tax authority within 30 days from the date of the assessment notice, from the date any other notice issued by the tax authority is received, or from the time they witness the event or action viewed to be incompatible.

Pending settlement, the business operators shall put a sum of money accounting for 50% of the value-added tax assessment as security with the fund for value-added tax refund on a temporary basis.

If the business operators lodge a petition after the above-mentioned time limit, the tax authority will not consider such petition.

Article 39. Consideration and Settlement of Petitions

1. When a tax authority receives a petition about value-added tax enforcement from a business operator, it shall be considered and settled within 10 official working days from the date it is received. If it is complicated, the settlement can be prolonged but should take no more than 30 official working days;

2. Business operators will observe the decision of the settlement made by such tax authority. In the event of disagreement, they are entitled to petition within 10 official working days to the immediate higher authority of such tax authority for final decision;

3. For issues outside its mandate, such tax authority must transfer the files of the case or report the case to its immediate higher level for consideration and settlement;

4. The tax authority that receives the petition is entitled to require the petitioner to provide relevant documents and information. If nothing is provided, the tax authority is also entitled to refuse to settle the petition;

5. If the immediate higher authority of the competent tax authority decides that any acts of value-added tax enforcement, for example, calculation and penalties, are incorrect, the higher level tax authority shall make a decision, particularly returning the mistakenly collected taxes to the relevant business operators within 15 official working days from the date a decision on the settlement is made.

In the event that the business operators are not satisfied with the settlement by the final level of the tax authority, they are entitled to bring an action in accordance with the Law on the Handling of Petitions.

PART V MANAGEMENT AND INSPECTION OF VALUE-ADDED TAX

Chapter 1

Value-Added Tax Management

Article 40. Organisation for Value-Added Tax Management

The value-added tax management organisation is a centralised, uniform organisation along a vertical line of command from the central to local levels for the nationwide management and collection of value-added tax.

The value-added tax management organisation consists of:

- The Ministry of Finance;
- The tax authorities at each level:
- The Tax Department;
- The tax division in each province and city;
- The tax office in each district and municipality.

Article 41. Rights and Duties of the Ministry of Finance

In the management of value-added tax, the Ministry of Finance has the following main rights and duties:

1. To study and develop strategic plans, policy plans, laws and regulations on value-added tax for submission to the government for consideration;
2. To publicise and disseminate the Law on Value-Added Tax and other legislation according to its role;
3. To guide, monitor and inspect the implementation of the laws and other legislation on value-added tax;
4. To guide technical operations, to manage and train officers, to appoint, transfer and remove officers, to grant incentives to or take disciplinary actions against officers in charge of value-added tax, and to provide budget, vehicles, technical materials and equipment to the value-added tax machinery;
5. To coordinate with State organisations and other organisations relating to value-added tax;
6. To liaise and cooperate with foreign countries, regional and international communities in value-added tax activities;
7. To be responsible to the government for the management and inspection of the implementation of value-added tax nationwide;
8. To summarise and report on the implementation of value-added tax activities to the government.

Article 42. Rights and Duties of the Tax Department

The Tax Department serves as the secretariat to the Ministry of Finance in exercising rights and performing duties of the Ministry as specified in Article 41 of this law. It also has rights and duties in implementation, management, collection and decision-making relating to the refund of value-added tax.

Article 43. Rights and Duties of Provincial and City Tax Divisions Relating to Value-Added Tax Management

In the management of value-added tax, the tax division at each province or city has the following main rights and duties:

1. To study and make comments on draft strategic plans, policy plans, laws and regulations relating to value-added tax;
2. To make annual plans for revenue collection of value-added tax in the province or city;
3. To be responsible to the Ministry of Finance for the management and inspection of the implementation of value-added tax collection to ensure completeness and conformity with the laws and regulations;
4. To guide, manage, monitor and inspect the performance of district and municipal tax offices, and value-added tax officers under their control;
5. To publicise and disseminate within its jurisdiction the policies, laws, regulations and other legislation relating to value-added tax;
6. To make proposals for rewarding persons with outstanding achievements and imposing disciplinary actions against violators of the laws and regulations to the [relevant] provincial governor or city mayor for further submission to the Minister of Finance for consideration;

7. To make proposals regarding the appointment, transfer or removal of value-added tax officers under its control to the [relevant] provincial governor or city mayor, for further submission to the Minister of Finance for consideration;

8. To summarise and report on the implementation of value-added tax activities to the Ministry of Finance.

Article 44. Rights and Duties of District and Municipal Tax Offices Relating to Value-Added Tax Management

In the management of value-added tax, the tax office at each district or municipality has the following main rights and duties:

1. To study and make comments on draft strategic plans, policy plans, laws and regulations relating to value-added tax;

2. To publicise and disseminate within its jurisdiction the policies, laws, regulations and other legislation relating to value-added tax;

3. To be responsible for the implementation, management and collection of value-added tax within its district or municipality;

4. To guide, manage, monitor and inspect the performance of value-added tax officers under its control;

5. To summarise and report on the implementation of value-added tax activities to the [relevant] provincial or city tax division.

Chapter 2

Inspection of Value-Added Tax Activities

Article 45. Inspection Organisation

The inspection organisation includes the internal and external inspection agencies.

1. The internal inspection agencies include:
• The Ministry of Finance;
• The tax authority at each level;
2. The external inspection agencies include:
• Control committees;
• The State Audit Agency.

Local administrations, the Lao Front for National Construction, mass organisations, social organisations, the mass media and concerned parties are responsible for inspecting the implementation of the value-added tax according to their tasks and roles.

Article 46. Rights and Duties of Internal Inspection Agencies

The internal inspection agencies have rights and duties of regular systematic inspection on the implementation of laws, exercise of rights and performance of duties of value-added tax officers at each level, for example concerning calculation, collection, deduction and refund of value-added tax.

Article 47. Rights and Duties of External Inspection Agencies

The external inspection agencies have rights and duties of inspection on the performance of value-added tax officers, including inspection of value-added tax implementation by relevant organisations, to make the work relating to value-added tax efficient, transparent and fair.

Article 48. Types of Inspection

There are three types of inspection, as follows:

- Regular inspection;
- Inspection with advance notice;
- Emergency inspection.

Regular inspection refers to an inspection performed regularly according to plans at pre-determined times.

Inspection by advance notice refers to an inspection which is not included in the plan, which is performed when deemed necessary and for which advance notice is given.

Emergency inspection refers to a sudden inspection performed without advance notice to the person to be inspected.

PART VI POLICIES TOWARDS PERSONS WITH HIGH ACHIEVEMENT AND MEASURES AGAINST VIOLATORS 13

Chapter 1

Policies Towards Persons with High Achievement

Article 49. Policies Towards Persons with High Achievement

Individuals and organisations contributing to the efficient implementation of this law will receive rewards and other policies according to regulations.

Article 50. Policies for Taxpayers

Taxpayers who perform their obligations correctly, fully and on time will receive rewards and appropriate facilitation in their business operations in accordance with laws and regulations.

Chapter 2

Measures Against Violators

Article 51. Measures Against Violators

For additional analytical, business and investment opportunities information,
please contact Global Investment & Business Center, USA
at (703) 370-8082. Fax: (703) 370-8083. E-mail: ibpusa3@gmail.com
Global Business and Investment Info Databank - www.ibpus.com

Violators of this Law on Value-Added Tax will be subject to re-education, fines, disciplinary action, civil compensation, and criminal punishment depending on the severity of the case.

Article 52. Measures against Business Operators and Other Persons

Value-added-tax-payable business operators who violate the regulations on value-added tax registration, filing, and payment will face the following measures from case to case:

1. If a business operator whose annual turnover exceeds the level stipulated in paragraph 1 of Article 13 of this law does not apply for value-added tax registration as specified in Article 26 of this law, he will undergo re-education; if he does not comply with the re-education 14 measures, he will be fined in an amount equal to fifty percent of the value-added tax registration fee;
2. Business operators who do not use the tax identification number issued by the tax authority in their papers will be fined 200,000 Kip per instance;
3. Business operators who miss the deadline for filing or payment of value-added tax as specified in this law will be fined in an amount equal to five percent of the amount of value-added tax payable for each month of delay. In any case, the penalty shall not exceed the amount of value-added tax payable;
4. In cases of non-filing or underreporting of value-added tax, the tax authority shall demand action. If nothing happens, the following measures will be applied:
• In the first instance, the total amount of value-added tax payable shall be paid in full, and a fine of thirty percent of the total amount of value-added tax payable shall be imposed;
• In the second instance, the total amount of value-added tax payable shall be paid in full, and a fine of sixty percent of the total amount of value-added tax payable shall be imposed;
• If no filing is made or value-added tax is underreported after the second demand notice expires, business closure and temporary withdrawal of business and tax licenses for one month will be imposed. After the one-month period, measures in paragraph 5 below shall be applied;
5. In cases of non-payment of [value-added] tax and penalties after receiving the second demand notice, the following measures will be applied:
• [The offender] shall be fined five percent of the value-added tax payable for the issuance of the first demand notice, then ten percent of the value-added tax payable for the issuance of the second demand notice, and fifteen percent for the third one. The term of the demand notice for the payment of the tax shall be 10 days, each time;
• The business unit will be ordered to suspend its operations and its business and tax licenses shall be withdrawn temporarily for one month if the payment is not made after the deadline of the third demand notice. After the one-month period of suspension, if value-added tax is not paid, the business unit will be ordered to permanently terminate business and a claim shall be filed and presented to the court;
• Some of the business operator's money in bank accounts, the National Treasury and financial institutions (credit) will be garnished to pay value-added tax and fines;

The banks, the National Treasury and financial institutions (credit) have the obligation to garnish money in the deposit accounts of the business operator that does not pay the tax and fines to pay value-added tax and fines to the State budget in accordance with the decision of the tax authority or other competent agencies.

In the event that there is no money or insufficient money in the deposit accounts with the banks, the National Treasury, and financial institutions (credit) for the amount payable, the [relevant] tax authority shall establish a committee to seize or confiscate the assets of the business operator to secure the full recovery of the value-added tax and fines;

6. In cases of value-added tax fraud, failure to keep accounts, sale of goods or supply of services without issuing invoices, forgery of invoices or other accounting documents, hindering auditors in the performance of their duties, failure to provide accounting documents, or failure to respond to requests from the tax authority for the supply of evidence, explanation, information in due time, the following measures will be applied:
• In the first instance, the full amount of value-added tax payable shall be paid, [the offender] shall be fined fifty percent of the value-added tax assessed and shall [also] be fined according to the enterprise accounting regulations;
• In the second instance of violation, the full amount of value-added tax payable shall be paid[; the offender] shall be fined one hundred percent of the value-added tax assessed, shall be fined according to the enterprise accounting regulations, and shall be ordered to terminate the business operations[;] and an announcement shall be made in the mass media;
• If the above-mentioned measures are not observed, [the offender] will be subject to legal proceedings;
7. In cases of collusion in the improper deduction of value-added tax, the following measures will be applied:
• Return of the full amount of value-added tax to the budget;
• [The offender] shall be fined one hundred percent of the deducted value-added tax amount and in addition shall be subject to legal proceedings;

8. In cases where business operators or other persons hinder the performance of the tax authority or commit any other criminal offence, they will be prosecuted in accordance with the laws and regulations.

Article 53. Measures against Value-Added Tax Officers

Any officer in charge of value-added tax who commits any act that constitutes an offence will be subject to the following measures:

1. If the offence causes no severe impact to the laws and regulations, or the revenue and dignity of the tax authorities, re-education and warning will be applied;
2. In a case of irresponsibility or negligence causing damage to the interests of the State or taxpayers, compensation will be made for the damage, [and the

person shall also be subject to] prosecution according to the severity of the offence;

3. In a case of abuse of power, position, or duty, collusion, concealment of offences or other actions in violation of the laws, [the person shall be subject to] prosecution according to the severity of the offence;

4. In a case of abuse of power, position or duty, abuse of authority, any practice that violates the law, or embezzlement of value-added tax and fines, the offender shall pay back to the State the full amount embezzled and the taxes that are the subject matter of the abuse, shall be fined and shall be subject to prosecution.

PART VII FINAL PROVISIONS

Article 54. Implementation

The government of the Lao People's Democratic Republic is to implement this law.

Article 55. Effectiveness

This law shall enter into force after eighteen months following the date of the promulgating decree issued by the President of the Lao People's Democratic Republic.

This law replaces the amended Tax Law No. 04/NA, dated 19 May 2005, regarding turnover tax only, for business operators in the value-added tax system.

Vientiane, 26 December 2006

President of the National Assembly

[Seal and Signature]

Thongsing THAMMAVONG

For additional analytical, business and investment opportunities information, please contact Global Investment & Business Center, USA at (703) 370-8082. Fax: (703) 370-8083. E-mail: ibpusa3@gmail.com Global Business and Investment Info Databank - www.ibpus.com

PRACTICAL AND REGULATIONS FOR CONDUCTING BUSINESS

INVESTMENT CLIMATE

After eleven years of socialist policies, the Government of Laos (GOL) implemented the New Economic Mechanism (NEM) in 1986 to expedite the country's transition to a market economy. From the late 1980's to the mid-1990's trade was liberalized; price controls lifted; many state-owned industries privatized or commercialized; commercial banks established; and a comparatively open foreign investment law written. During the same period, the exchange rate stabilized and inflation remained relatively manageable.

After mid-1996 the rate of reform slowed considerably and Laos' economic performance, aggravated by the 1997 Asian financial crisis, suffered. Between June 1997 and June 1999, the local currency (kip) lost 87 percent of its value and inflation soared to 128.4 percent in 1999. GDP growth, which had fallen to four percent in 1998, rose again to over 5 percent in 1999. Tighter monetary policy has helped stabilize the rate since FY 2000, with monthly inflation averaging around 1 percent. The inflation rate remained between 10 and 15 percent between 2002 and 2005. Anticipated GDP growth of about 6.5 and 7 percent in 2004 and 2005 will depend largely on expected increases in agricultural output, (48 percent of GDP in 2004 and 2005), and upon extractive industries exploiting Lao timber and minerals. While income from hydropower will boost exports in FY 2005, greater growth in manufactured exports remains hampered by high transportation costs.

GDP growth stood at roughly 5.8 percent from 2000-2003, increased to 6.5 percent in 2004, and is expected to be around 7 percent in 2005. GDP growth will depend largely on agricultural output, which accounted for 48% of GDP in 2003, 47.2% in 2004, and 47.3 in 2005. Although agriculture's share of GDP is lower than in previous years, it still accounts for the largest share of GDP.

Laos' comparatively liberal investment law is significantly undermined by inconsistency in implementation. The decline in foreign direct investment after 1996, while partly due to the regional economic crisis, was rooted in other factors as well, such as bureaucratic impediments to the application process; a lack of transparency in the regulatory framework; and an uncertain domestic economic environment. Implementation of the Bilateral Trade Agreement (BTA) with the US, as well as Laos' efforts to become a member of the World Trade Organization may eventually help promote greater transparency and consistency in the legal and regulatory frameworks, but progress is slow.

OPENNESS TO FOREIGN INVESTMENT

The economic reforms adopted in 1988 and Decree No. 73/PO, dated October 22, 2004, purport to promote foreign direct investment as a means of boosting development and economic growth. Under the 2004 Law on the Promotion of Foreign Investment, foreign investors may invest in all business sectors and zones of investment in the Lao People's

Democratic Republic, except in business activities which are detrimental to national security, have a negative impact on the environment, or are regarded as detrimental to health or national traditions. In practice, however, some sectors are effectively closed to outside investors. The overall investment climate is poor, and rates very low in international indices of transparency and ease of doing business.

The investment term of a foreign investment enterprise depends on the nature, size, and conditions of the business project but normally cannot exceed fifty years. Under special circumstances, foreign investment enterprises may be extended with the approval of the government. However, foreign enterprises that receive extension approval from the government may not exceed a total investment term of seventy-five years.

Any foreign investor seeking to establish operations in Laos must submit project proposals to the Department for Promotion and Management of Domestic and Foreign Investment (DDFI), Committee for Planning and Investment (CPI). The proposal is then screened by the relevant line ministries and adjudicated by the Prime Minister's Office. Further to Prime Minister Decree No 301, dated on October 12, 2005, proposals for projects worth US $20 million or more require the approval of the Prime Minister. The President and Vice president of the Department of Domestic and Foreign Investment can sign approvals that involve investments of less than $10 million USD. FDI equal or less than $3 million USD can be approved at the provincial level by all provinces, and in large provinces the ceiling for provincial level approval is $5 million.

The screening process at the Department for Promotion and Management of Domestic and Foreign Investment (DDFI) in the Committee for Planning and Investment (CPI) takes into account the financial and technical feasibility of the project, input from relevant line ministries, and whether the proposed project conflicts with government policy. Upon receipt of an application, the CPMI must coordinate with relevant sectors and local authorities to consider and respond in writing to the foreign investor. Responses to projects, depending on project type, are supposed to be forthcoming within 15 – 45 working days.

Foreign investors shall obtain a foreign investment license, an enterprise registration certificate, and a tax registration certificate from the CPMI office nearest the place where the foreign investors are licensed. Thereafter they shall be considered as enterprises established in conformity with the laws of the Lao People's Democratic Republic. Within 90 days from the date of receipt of an investment license the foreign investment enterprise must commence business activities. If the investors fail to do so, the foreign investment license shall be terminated.

Besides the investment license, foreign investors are required to obtain other permits. These include a business registration which must be annually renewed from the Ministry of Commerce, a tax registration from the tax department in the Ministry of Finance, a business logo registration from the Ministry of Public Security, permits from each line ministry related to the investment (i.e., Ministry of Industries for manufacturing; Ministry of Communications for transportation, etc.), appropriate permits from local authorities, and an import-export license, if needed.

In mid-1999 the Lao government began imposing import restrictions on trading companies, whether foreign or domestic, in an effort to reduce the trade deficit. The Lao government requires them to file a joint annual import plan for approval by the Ministry of Commerce. Government documents articulating the restrictions and explaining the policy are difficult to obtain. Goods that are always prohibited for import and export range from explosives and weapons, to literature that presents a negative view of the Lao government, to certain forestry products and wildlife.

As of June 1, 2000 the Lao government began requiring pre-shipment inspection of all goods with an order value of US $2,500 and above. Because the garment manufacturing industry relies on imported inputs, some garment manufacturers expressed concerns about the additional delays and costs imposed on them by this requirement. Lao Bivac International, a joint venture between the Lao government and Bivac International of France, was the sole company given authority by the Lao government to perform the required inspections, but closed due to a lack of business. Many companies therefore rely on their own quality controllers to perform inspections.

Agriculture production, as well as the majority of manufacturing production is private. State-enterprises currently account for only one percent of total employment. Roughly 97 percent of manufacturing units are small (fewer than 10 employees). Among the medium and large units, 35 percent are privately owned by Lao citizens and 55 percent are joint ventures with foreigners. The rest are owned by the government (including provincial governments). Foreign companies interested in acquiring SOE's should apply through the Department for Promotion and Management of Domestic and Foreign Investment (DDFI) in CPI. Medium and large-sized SOE's can be obtained through a joint venture with the Lao government.

CONVERSION AND TRANSFER POLICIES

To facilitate business foreign investors generally open commercial bank accounts in both local and foreign convertible currency at domestic and foreign banks in Laos. Bank accounts must be maintained in accordance with the Enterprise Accounting Law. The law places no limitations on foreign investors transferring after-tax profits, income from technology transfer, initial capital, interest, wages and salaries, or other remittances to the company's home country or third countries so long as they request approval from the Lao government. These transactions are conducted at the official exchange rate on the day of execution, upon presentation of appropriate documentation. Supply of FOREX is sometimes limited in Laos, which imposes a de facto limit on repatriation of capital. Also, foreign enterprises must report on their performance annually and submit annual financial statements to the CPMI.

EXPROPRIATION AND COMPENSATION

Foreign assets and investments in Laos are protected by laws and regulations against seizure, confiscation, or nationalization except when this is deemed necessary for a public purpose, in which case foreign investors are to be compensated. Foreign investors in a joint venture must contribute at least thirty percent (30%) of the venture's registered capital. Capital contributed in foreign currency must be converted into kip based on the exchange rate of the Bank of the Lao People's Democratic Republic on the

For additional analytical, business and investment opportunities information,
please contact Global Investment & Business Center, USA
at (703) 370-8082. Fax: (703) 370-8083. E-mail: ibpusa3@gmail.com
Global Business and Investment Info Databank - www.ibpus.com

day of the capital contribution. Wholly foreign-owned companies may either be a new company or a branch office of an existing foreign company. During the business operation of a foreign investment enterprise, the assets of the enterprise must not be less than its registered capital.

DISPUTE SETTLEMENT

According to the Foreign Investment Law, investors involved in investment disputes must seek arbitration before taking legal action. If arbitration does not result in an amicable settlement, litigants may submit their claims to the economic arbitration authority of Laos, or that of the investor's country, or an international organization agreed on by both parties. The law does not reflect reality, as there are no adequate independent arbitration venues in Laos. Foreign investors are therefore generally advised to seek arbitration outside the country, since Laos' nascent domestic arbitration authority lacks enforcement powers. Laos is not a member of the International Center for the Settlement of Investment Disputes. It became a party to the New York Convention of 1958 on the Recognition and Enforcement of Foreign Arbitral Awards on September 15, 1998, but has never had to enforce a foreign arbitral award. Laos is a member of the United Nation's Convention on International Trade Law.

Laos' legal system is evolving, but remains incomplete in many regards. Laws sometimes contradict each other and often lack implementing regulations. For example, tax exemptions and low import duties guaranteed to foreign investors under the foreign investment law are not reflected in customs or tax law. Supported by the Japan International Cooperation Agency (JICA), Singapore, and the United Nations Development Program (UNDP), some laws have been officially translated into English. These include the business, tax, bankruptcy, customs, and secured transaction laws. Implementing regulations for the Foreign Investment Law, which are crucial to enforcement, were approved on October 10, 2005. The reliability of unofficial translations varies considerably, creating an environment of uncertainty and ambiguity among foreign investors.

Projects funded by the Australian government and the UN Development Program to assist Lao accession to the World Trade Organization (WTO) include components aimed at bringing Lao commercial law into conformity with WTO standards. A commercial court was established during 2003, and began to hear cases in 2005.

Laos has no anti-trust statutes. The bankruptcy law permits either the business or creditor the right to petition the court for a bankruptcy judgment, and allows the business the right to request mediation. There is no record of foreign-owned enterprises, whether as debtors or as creditors, petitioning the courts for a bankruptcy judgment.

PERFORMANCE REQUIREMENTS AND INCENTIVES

Laos does not impose performance requirements per se. Foreign investors are encouraged to give priority to Lao citizens in recruiting and hiring. Foreign personnel can be hired, though may not exceed ten percent (10%) of the enterprise's total labor force. Before bringing in foreign labor, the enterprise must apply for work permits from the Ministry of Labor and Social Welfare. A foreign personnel list must also be submitted to the Investment Service Center of the Department for Promotion and Management of Domestic and Foreign Investment (DDFI).

Incentives for Foreign Investment: Laos grants incentives for foreign investment depending on the sectors and zones of investment promotion. The government defines promoted activities under Article 16 as follows: 1) production for export; 2) activities relating to agriculture or forestry, and agricultural, forestry and handicraft processing activities; 3) activities relating to industrial processing, industrial activities using modern techniques and technology, research and development, and activities relating to the protection of the environment and biodiversity; 4) human resource development, skills development and public health; 5) construction of infrastructure; 6) production of raw materials and equipment to be supplied to key industrial activities; and, 7) development of the tourism industry and transit services.

Under Article 17, the government has determined three promoted zones for foreign investment based on geographical location and socio-economic conditions. The zones are as follows:

Zone 1:   Mountainous, plain and plateau zones with no economic infrastructure to facilitate investments.

Zone 2:   Mountainous, plain and plateau zones with a moderate level of economic infrastructure suitable to accommodate investments.

Zone 3:   Mountainous, plain and plateau zones with good infrastructure to support investments.

Under Article 18 of the Foreign Investment Law, foreign enterprises investing in activities within the promoted sectors and zones determined in Article 16 and 17 of the law on the Promotion of Investment shall be entitled to the following duty and tax incentives:

--Investments in Zone 1 shall be entitled to a profit tax exemption for 7 years, and thereafter shall be subject to profit tax at the rate of 10 percent.

--Investments in Zone 2 shall be entitled to a profit tax exemption for 5 years, and thereafter shall be subject to a reduced profit tax rate of half of fifteen percent for 3 years, and thereafter a profit tax rate of 15 percent.

--Investments in Zone 3 shall be entitled to a profit tax exemption for 2 years and thereafter shall be subject to a reduced profit tax rate of half of twenty percent for 2 years, and thereafter a profit tax rate of 20 percent.

The profit tax exemption starts from the date the foreign investment enterprise begins operations. For tree planting activities, profit tax exemption commences when the enterprise begins earning a profit. Once the profit tax exemption period is concluded, the foreign investment enterprise must pay profit tax. In addition to the aforementioned incentives, foreign investment enterprises shall be entitled to the following incentives:

For additional analytical, business and investment opportunities information,
please contact Global Investment & Business Center, USA
at (703) 370-8082. Fax: (703) 370-8083. E-mail: ibpusa3@gmail.com
Global Business and Investment Info Databank - www.ibpus.com

--During the tax exemption period and during the tax reduction period the enterprise is entitled to an exemption of minimum tax;

--The profit used for the expansion of licensed business activities shall be exempted from profit tax during the accounting year;

--Exemption from import duties and taxes on equipment, spare parts and vehicles directly used for production, on raw materials which do not exist domestically or which exist but are insufficient, and on semi-finished products imported for processing or assembly for the purpose of export;

--Exemption from export duty on export products; and,

--Raw materials and semi-finished products imported for processing or assembly for import substitution shall be exempted from import duties and taxes, or shall be subject to reduced rates of import duties and taxes.

Foreigners employed in Laos, including foreign investors, must pay an income tax of 10 percent of their total income to the Lao Government, unless they are citizens of a country with which the Lao Government has signed a double taxation agreement. The tax system includes taxes on profits, natural resources, agriculture, land, income, imports and exports, as well as excise and turnover taxes.

Foreign investors are not required to pay import duty on equipment, spare parts and other materials used in the operation of their enterprises. Raw materials and intermediate goods imported for the purpose of processing and re-export are exempt from import duties. Raw materials and intermediate goods imported for the purpose of import substitution are also eligible for import duty reductions on a case-by-case basis. On an individual basis, foreign investors are also eligible for profit tax and import duty reductions or exemptions, if the investment is significantly large or determined to have a significant benefit to Laos' socio-economic development.

Annual renewal of the business license (see section A.1. above) is contingent upon certification that all taxes have been paid. Given the lack of clarity in the tax law (see section A.4. above), foreign investors complain that taxes are often assessed in an inconsistent and capricious manner. Lao officials acknowledge ambiguities in the law. The tax code was streamlined and simplified in April 2005, but investors still report significant difficulties in obtaining tax certifications in a timely manner.

The Foreign Investment Law stipulates that foreign investors and their families, including foreign professionals and foreign employees of an enterprise, shall be facilitated by issue of multiple entry visas and, if approved by the government, long term residence in the Lao PDR. They shall also, in theory, have the right to apply for Lao nationality in accordance with the Law on Nationality.

RIGHT TO PRIVATE OWNERSHIP AND ESTABLISHMENT

The government recognizes the right of private enterprise ownership, and foreigners may transfer shares of a foreign-invested company without prior government approval.

However, the business law requires that all shareholders be listed in the articles of association, and changes in the articles of association of a foreign-invested company must be approved by DDFI-CPI. Thus, transferring shares in a foreign-invested company registered in Laos does require the indirect approval of the government (DDFI-CPI).

PROTECTION OF PROPERTY RIGHTS

Foreign investors are not permitted to own land. The government grants long-term leases, and allows the ownership of leases and the right to transfer and improve leasehold interests. Government approval is not required to transfer property interests, but the transfer must be registered and a registration fee paid. This includes mortgage leases.

Secured interests in property are inadequately covered by the Secured Transactions Law of 1994. Because the law offers no instructions for the creditor to enforce security rights (the creditor, for example, can only request repayment from the debtor), the law favors the debtor. Moreover, since the Ministry of Finance's registry system is not computerized, and cannot cross-reference records, it is difficult to determine if a piece of property is encumbered. Enforcement of a mortgage is further complicated by the legal protection given mortgagees against forfeiture of their sole place of residence.

Laos issued a trademark decree in January 1995. The Science, Technology, and Environment Agency (STEA), part of the Prime Minister's Office, controls the issuance of trademarks on a first-come, first-register basis. Applicants do not have to demonstrate prior use. There are currently over 12,200 trademarks registered in Laos.

Laos became a member of the ASEAN Common Filing System on patents in 2000 but lacks adequate personnel qualified to serve as patent examiners. A draft decree on patents was sent to the Prime Minister in February 2000 for approval and in 2002 the Prime Minister's Office issued patent regulations. However, the National Assembly is still in the process of researching the Intellectual Property Law and has not yet acted. Since Thailand and Laos have a bilateral Intellectual Property Rights (IPR) agreement, in principle a patent issued in Thailand would also be recognized in Laos.

Currently, no system exists to issue copyrights in Laos. Laos became a member of the World Intellectual Property Organization (WIPO) Convention on January, 1995 and the Paris Convention on the Protection of Industrial Property on October, 1998; it has not yet joined the Bern Convention on Copyrights. Although WIPO assisted Laos in drafting an intellectual property law in 1996, legislative action on the draft, however, remains pending and it appears that the draft law is dead.

TRANSPARENCY OF THE REGULATORY SYSTEM

The principal laws, regulations, decrees and guidelines governing international trade and investment, as well as the protection of intellectual property, are available to the public, although not all have been officially translated into English. Laws and their schedules for implementation are customarily published in the Lao daily newspapers, and relevant line ministries are beginning to put laws and regulations on websites.

For additional analytical, business and investment opportunities information,
please contact Global Investment & Business Center, USA
at (703) 370-8082. Fax: (703) 370-8083. E-mail: ibpusa3@gmail.com
Global Business and Investment Info Databank - www.ibpus.com

While Laos' body of commercial law is slowly developing, inconsistencies in the interpretation and application of existing laws is one of the greatest impediments to investment. A lack of transparency in a centralized decision-making process, as well as the difficulty encountered in obtaining information, augment the perception of the regulatory framework as arbitrary and inscrutable. While the government ostensibly streamlined the process by giving DDFI sole responsibility for foreign investment applications, the red-tape requirements associated with establishing a foreign investment have increased.

EFFICIENT CAPITAL MARKETS AND PORTFOLIO INVESTMENT

Laos does not have a developed capital market. Three-month treasury bills are occasionally offered for sale when there is a need to absorb excess liquidity in the economy. The country is just beginning to use checks and other financial instruments as methods of payment. The largest denomination of currency is 50,000 kip (about US $5). Credit is not available on the local market for large capital investments, although letters of credit for export can sometimes be obtained locally.

The banking system is under the supervision of the Bank of the Lao PDR and includes three state-owned commercial banks - Banque Pour le Commerce Exterieur Lao (BCEL), Lao Development Bank (LDB) and Agriculture Promotion Bank (APB); two joint-venture banks - Joint Development Bank and Lao-Viet Bank; five Thai banks - Bangkok Bank, Sam Commercial Bank, Krungthai Bank, Thai Military Bank, and Ayudhya Bank; one Malaysian bank - Public Bank; one Private Bank - Vientiane Commercial Bank; and one representative office - Standard Chartered Bank. Foreign banks are permitted to establish branches only in Vientiane. Total assets of commercial banks are estimated at 10-31 percent of GDP, with a single bank (BCEL) accounting for 45 percent of all bank assets and 57 percent of all foreign currency deposits. BCEL has correspondence arrangements with the following banks (US dollars):

- JP Morgan Chase Bank, New York
- Citibank, New York - Wachovia Bank, New York
- American express bank, Ltd., New York - HSBC Bank, New York
- Standard Chartered Bank, New York
- Barclays Bank Plc., London - Credit Suisse First Boston, Zurich - Bank of Tokyo-Mitsubishi, Ltd, Tokyo
- Natexis Banque Populaires, Singapore
- Standard chartered bank, Singapore - Bank for foreign trade of Vietnam, Hanoi - Thai Military
Bank Public Co. Ltd., Bangkok - Bank Thai Public Co. Ltd. Bangkok - Calyon, Bangkok

The poor condition of the financial sector is a significant barrier to business. Central bank supervision of the sector is lax, state-owned commercial banks (SCBs) border on being bankrupt, there is little enforcement of prudential guidelines and poor credit standards, and considerable directed crony lending. Although the SCBs were recapitalized as recently as 2003, results of a 2005 audit indicate that the institutions are insolvent, with non-performing loans accounting for 35 percent of their debt portfolio. The Asian Development Bank has provided both program loans and technical assistance to

For additional analytical, business and investment opportunities information, please contact Global Investment & Business Center, USA
at (703) 370-8082. Fax: (703) 370-8083. E-mail: ibpusa3@gmail.com
Global Business and Investment Info Databank - www.ibpus.com

Laos' financial sector, as have the World Bank and the IMF. These programs have not succeeded in eliciting significant reforms.

POLITICAL VIOLENCE

Although Laos is generally a peaceful and politically stable country, the remnants of an insurgency occasionally carry out small scale attacks on government personnel and civilians. Foreign persons are not deliberately targeted. Visitors are advised to use caution in public areas and when traveling in remote districts. The Lao PDR is a single-party Communist state controlled by the Lao People's Revolutionary Party (LPRP). At its Party Congress held every five years, the LPRP's Politburo sets government policies, including guidelines for all print and broadcast media. Dissent is rare and quickly quashed.

CORRUPTION

Corruption in Laos is rising. The Prime Minister's Office issued an anti-corruption decree in November 1999, but has not succeeded in slowing the growth of corruption. Although the 1999 decree specifically notes the responsibility of the state-owned mass media in publicizing corruption cases, there has been no reporting on this issue. Laos is not a signatory to the OECD Convention on Combating Bribery. The Counter-Corruption Committee in the Prime Minister's Office is the Lao government agency responsible for combating corruption. Both giving and accepting bribes are criminal acts punishable by fine and/or imprisonment. Besides bribes to low-level officials for the purpose of expediting time-sensitive applications, such as business licenses, importation of perishable items, customs, etc., and anecdotal evidence of more pervasive corruption is growing.

BILATERAL INVESTMENT AGREEMENTS

Laos has bilateral investment agreements with the following countries:

Country	Date Signed	Date Entered Into Force	Duration
France	12/12/89	3/8/91	10
Thailand	8/22/90	12/7/90	10
Malaysia	12/8/92	-	10
China	1/31/93	6/01/93	10
Mongolia	3/3/94	12/29/94	10
Indonesia	10/18/94	10/14/95	10
Australia	4/6/94	4/8/95	15
United Kingdom	6/1/95	6/1/95	10
Vietnam	1/14/96	6/23/96	10
USA (initialed)	3/8/96	3/26/96	20
Rep of Korea	5/15/96	6/14/96	15
Germany	8/9/96	3/24/99	10
Sweden	8/29/96	1/1/97	20
Switzerland	12/4/96	12/4/96	10
Russia	12/6/96	-	15
Singapore	3/24/97	3/25/98	10
Cuba	4/28/97	6/10/98	10
DPRK	8/20/97	8/22/99	10

Denmark 9/28/98 5/9/99 10
India 11/09/00 - 15
Myanmar 5/5/03 - -
Holland 16/5/03 - -
Pakistan 23/4/04 - -
On February 1, 2005 a Bilateral Investment Agreement (BTA) came into force between the U.S. and the Government of Laos. Laos and the United States do not have a bilateral taxation treaty.

OPIC AND OTHER INVESTMENT INSURANCE PROGRAMS

The United States and Laos signed an Overseas Private Investment Cooperation (OPIC) agreement in March 1996. In 1998 Laos signed an agreement with the Multilateral Investment Guarantee Agency (MIGA).

LABOR

Over 70 percent of Laos' work force of 2.6 million is engaged in subsistence agriculture. The Lao government estimated the total non-agricultural work force in 2005 to number 483,560 people, roughly 27,000 of who were employed in garment manufacturing. (Note: Active membership in the Lao Federation of Trade Unions, which totaled 98,000 in 2005, may offer a more accurate picture of the real size of the labor force). The total labor force is expected to increase by more than 30 percent over the next ten years.

The Labor Law passed in 1994 provides for the formation of trade unions; specifies working hours and compensation standards; allows for maternity leave and benefits; workers' compensation and retirement benefits; and establishes procedures for labor dispute resolution. The Lao government raised the official minimum wage to 200,000 kip per month (about $20 dollars) in 2005. Wages for unskilled labor at garment factories, including bonuses and lunch, now run about 290,000 kip or about US $30 monthly. Labor unions can be formed in private enterprises as long as they operate within the framework of the Lao Federation of Trade Unions (LFTU), which is controlled by the Lao People's Revolutionary Party. In mid-2005, there were 2,396 trade unions nationwide, and membership in the LFTU numbered 98,000. Strikes are not prohibited by law, but a government ban on subversive activities or destabilizing demonstrations makes them unlikely.

Laos has significant human resource deficiencies in virtually all sectors. English is not widely spoken. In 2005, about 27 percent of the population remained illiterate. The shortage of skilled labor is particularly acute in high-tech sectors. The country has a few technical colleges, one scientific research facility--the National Institute of Hygiene and Epidemiology--and almost no effective post-graduate degree programs. The Lao Government has dedicated very few resources to improve the country's education system and tends to rely heavily on international donors for support; there are a few state training programs and some foreign-funded programs. Potential investors should note the need to dedicate substantial resources, both human and capital, to train employees.

FOREIGN TRADE ZONES/FREE PORTS

The Foreign Investment Law allows for the establishment of free trade zones as an investment incentive. A zone in southern Savannakhet province, which borders both Vietnam and Thailand, is such a Special Economic Zone. Lao laws pertaining to trade are supposedly applied uniformly across the entire customs territory of Laos, including all sub-central authorities, special economic zones and border trade regions. In reality, however, customs practices vary widely at ports of entry in the provinces.

FOREIGN DIRECT INVESTMENT STATISTICS

From 2004-2005, the Lao government approved US $500 million in foreign investment projects. Hydropower schemes account for about 55 percent of that amount. The value of approvals for new investment licenses granted remained fairly constant in 2004 and 2005, while foreign direct investment fell by around 10 percent compared with 2003. Foreign direct investment figures, provided by the Bank of Lao PDR, follow:

Real FDI inflow through Bank of Lao PDR (in Million of US $)
2000 2001 2002 2003 2004 2005
33.9 23.9 4.5 19.5 16.9 NA
FDI approved (in Million of US $)
2000 2001 2002 2003 2004 2005
20.4 54 492 466 533 1,245
*These data are unavailable by sector or source.

Between 2000 and 2005, DDFI approved approximately US $2.7 billion in investment projects. These approvals do not reflect actual investment. For example, they include 15 projects listed by DDFI as U.S. investments (see below). In fact, US investment currently averages less than $1 million per annum. Only one new U.S. investment license was approved in 2005. Foreign investment now comes primarily from other Asian countries, particularly Thailand (traditionally Laos' largest trade and investment partner), China, and Vietnam. During 1994-95 Australia was briefly the largest investor, due to two large mining interests. During 2005 the value of Thai investment licenses approved grew by 36 percent, French investments accounted for 30 percent of the total approved (due to investment in the Nam Theun II hydropower project).

50. Foreign investment licensed in the Lao PDR by country of origin, from fiscal year 2000 to August 2005, in U.S. Dollars follows.

Rank	Country	Number of Projects	Capital
1	Thailand	102	606,537,630
2	Vietnam	56	469,818,157
3	France	34	415,654,500
4	Australia	17	340,977,528
5	China	131	278,468,609
6	Malaysia	23	83,338,237
7	Korea	64	60,370,450
8	Canada	6	46,960,000

9	Singapore	12	40,470,000
10	Switzerland	5	31,050,000
11	USA	15	15,254,560
12	Sweden	3	13,090,000
13	Norway	1	12,800,000
14	Japan	22	10,046,584
15	Taiwan	4	5,920,000
16	Russia	6	5,350,000
17	Cambodia	4	2,069,000
18	Germany	10	2,050,000
19	Island	2	1,100,000
20	England	8	1,009,700
21	Holland	1	1,000,000
22	India	2	330,000
23	Belgium	2	200,000
24	Myanmar	1	200,000
25	Srilanka	1	200,000
26	Cuba	1	185,000
27	Italy	1	100,000
28	Portugal	1	100,000
29	Spain	1	28,125

Total: 2,790,577,842
Lao Investment Share (In Joint Ventures) 325,301,999
Total (Combined Foreign and Lao Shares): 2,790,577,842
*Source: Department for Promotion and Management of Domestic and Foreign Investment (DDFI)

Foreign investment licensed in Lao PDR by sector, from 2000 through 2005, in US Dollars follows.

Rank	Sector	No. of Projects	Capital
Total		626	2,790,577,842
1	Electricity Generation	23	1,516,550,000
2	Mining	91	435,777,038
3	Industry & Handicraft	130	193,805,635
4	Trading	66	171,664,004
5	Agriculture	75	142,982,307
6	Services	110	125,604,816

7	Hotel & Restaurant	26	70,284,514
8	Telecom	3	39,940,000
9	Construction	20	29,086,874
10	Wood Industry	29	26,232,290
11	Banking	8	20,096,000
12	Garment	20	14,760,000
13	Consultancies	15	3,794,364

LEADING SECTORS FOR U.S. EXPORTS AND INVESTMENTS

OPPORTUNITIES FOR FOREIGN INVESTORS EXIST IN SEVERAL SECTORS DESPITE SUCH OBSTACLES AS THE LOW COST OF GOODS PRODUCED IN NEIGHBORING COUNTRIES, LIMITED SUPPLIES OF LOCAL CAPITAL, AND INFRASTRUCTURE DEFICIENCIES IN THE AREAS OF TRANSPORTATION, BANKING, BUSINESS MANAGEMENT AND LEGAL SYSTEMS.

TELECOMMUNICATIONS HAVE IMPROVED WITH ACCESS TO AN AUSTRALIAN COMMUNICATIONS SATELLITE, ALTHOUGH A LAO-THAI JOINT VENTURE COMMUNICATIONS SATELLITE PROJECT, UNDER DEVELOPMENT SINCE 1995, CONTINUES TO EXPERIENCE DELAYS. LAOS' SIGNIFICANT NATURAL RESOURCES, PROXIMITY TO LARGE EXTERNAL MARKETS, AND POTENTIALLY STRATEGIC POSITION FOR ENTREPOT TRADE ARE UNEXPLOITED ASSETS.

ENERGY

LAO PDR'S POTENTIAL FOR LARGE-SCALE GENERATION OF HYDROPOWER FROM MEKONG RIVER TRIBUTARIES IS WIDELY ACKNOWLEDGED. THESE RESOURCES CAN SUPPORT THE EXPORT OF LOW COST ELECTRICITY THROUGHOUT THE REGION. THAT SAID, THE ECONOMIC DOWNTURN IN THAILAND HAS MADE LAOS' LARGEST IMPORTER OF HYDRO-ELECTRICITY REVISE ITS FUTURE POWER NEEDS DOWNWARD, LEAVING SEVERAL LARGE-SCALE PROJECTS ON HOLD FOR THE TIME BEING. VIETNAM, WITH WHICH LAOS HAS SIGNED AN AGREEMENT TO SUPPLY 1500-2000 MW OF POWER BY 2010, IS ANOTHER POTENTIAL CUSTOMER IN THE FUTURE. POSSIBLE COMMERCIAL-SCALE RESERVES OF OIL AND GAS HAVE ALSO BEEN IDENTIFIED, ALTHOUGH A U.S. BASED COMPANY FINISHED EXPLORATORY DRILLING IN SOUTHERN LAOS IN 1997 WITHOUT A COMMERCIALLY VIABLE DISCOVERY.

WOOD-BASED INDUSTRIES: AN ESTIMATED 40% OF THE COUNTRY'S LAND AREA REMAINS FORESTED, WITH LARGE STANDS OF TROPICAL HARDWOODS INCLUDING TEAK, MAHOGANY AND ROSEWOOD. MARKET POTENTIAL IS APPARENT FOR DOMESTIC PROCESSING AND EXPORT OF ENVIRONMENTALLY SOUND FORESTRY PRODUCTS. IN AN EFFORT TO MAINTAIN CENTRAL CONTROL OVER THE COMMERCIAL LOGGING INDUSTRY, THE GOVERNMENT ALLOCATES LICENSES IN ACCORDANCE WITH A SYSTEM OF PROVINCIAL QUOTAS. LICENSES ARE REQUIRED FOR THE EXPORT OF WOOD PRODUCTS

AND VALUE ADDING IS ENCOURAGED. THE GOVERNMENT CURRENTLY DOES NOT ALLOW FOREIGN COMPANIES TO SET UP WOOD PROCESSING COMPANIES, BUT DOES ALLOW FOREIGN INVESTMENT IN THE EXPORT OF PROCESSED WOOD, INCLUDING PLYWOOD, PARQUET FLOORING, AND FURNITURE. THERE IS POTENTIAL FOR INVESTMENT IN FAST GROWING TIMBER SPECIES, AND THE INTERNATIONAL UNION FOR THE CONSERVATION OF NATURE (IUCN) AND OTHER MULTILATERAL AND BILATERAL AGENCIES ARE ALSO DEVELOPING COMMERCIAL OPPORTUNITIES OF NON-TIMBER BASED FOREST PRODUCTS.

ASSISTANCE CONTRACTING: THE SUPPLYING OF CONSULTING SERVICES, GOODS, AND EQUIPMENT FOR DEVELOPMENT PROJECTS FUNDED BY THE WORLD BANK, ASIAN DEVELOPMENT BANK (ADB), AND THE UN IS AN AREA WITH POTENTIAL FOR U.S. BUSINESS. TOTAL ASSISTANCE PLEDGES IN GRANTS AND LOANS BY THESE ORGANIZATIONS FOR THE PERIOD 1997-2000 AMOUNT TO USD 675.5 M: ADB $320M, WORLD BANK $180.5M, IMF $50M AND UN $125M. BID TENDERS ARE ADVERTISED IN "DEVELOPMENT BUSINESS" PUBLISHED BY THE UN AND "BUSINESS OPPORTUNITIES" BY ADB.

LIGHT MANUFACTURING: LOW-COST ENERGY AND LABOR RESOURCES SHOULD BE ATTRACTIVE TO PROSPECTIVE INVESTORS IN MANUFACTURING OF TEXTILES, GARMENTS AND HANDICRAFTS. GARMENT MANUFACTURING HAS BECOME ONE OF THE MOST PROMISING GROWTH INDUSTRIES IN LAOS, ESPECIALLY SINCE THE EUROPEAN UNION (EU) HAS REINSTATED GSP STATUS FOR LAOS FROM 1999 UNTIL DECEMBER 31, 2001. ALTHOUGH THE MANUFACTURING SECTOR GREW BY 10% IN 1998, AMOUNTING TO 21% OF GDP, INDUSTRIAL PRODUCTION IS STILL LOW AND GENERALLY INEFFICIENT, REFLECTING A LACK OF SIGNIFICANT RECENT INVESTMENT, OUTDATED PLANTS, DIFFICULTIES IN THE SUPPLY OF RAW MATERIALS, AND UNDERDEVELOPED ACCESS TO INTERNATIONAL MARKETS. MANUFACTURERS OF IMPORT-SUBSTITUTING CONSUMER GOODS HAVE NOT GENERALLY BEEN COMPETITIVE.

MINING/PETROLEUM: POTENTIALLY, THE MINING SECTOR IS ONE OF LAOS' MOST PROMISING LONG-TERM GROWTH AREAS. HOWEVER, SINCE COMPANIES FROM EUROPE AND THE U.S. HAVE THUS FAR EXPLORED POSSIBLE OIL AND MINERAL DEPOSIT SITES WITH VERY LIMITED RESULTS, THE FULL POTENTIAL FOR LAOS REMAINS AN UNKNOWN. SIZABLE LIGNITE AND COAL DEPOSITS ARE SET FOR IMMINENT DEVELOPMENT. ONE SMALL AMERICAN COMPANY, WHICH SEARCHED FOR COMMERCIALLY VIABLE AMOUNTS OF ALLUVIAL GOLD IN LUANG PRABANG PROVINCE WITHOUT SUCCESS, IS CURRENTLY MINING SOME ROCK GOLD. OTHER ONGOING MINING ACTIVITIES CONSIST OF EXTRACTION OF TIN AND GYPSUM USED MAINLY FOR DOMESTIC CONSTRUCTION AND SAPPHIRE MINING.

A MAJOR ATTRACTION TO INVESTORS HAD ONCE BEEN THE WILLINGNESS OF THE LAO GOVERNMENT, UNLIKE ITS NEIGHBORS, TO CONCLUDE "CRADLE TO GRAVE" AGREEMENTS WHICH CONFERRED EXCLUSIVE RIGHTS OVER EXPLORATION, MINING, PROCESSING AND EXPORTS IN CONCESSION AREAS.

For additional analytical, business and investment opportunities information,
please contact Global Investment & Business Center, USA
at (703) 370-8082. Fax: (703) 370-8083. E-mail: ibpusa3@gmail.com
Global Business and Investment Info Databank - www.ibpus.com

IN 1997, HOWEVER, A NEW MINING ACT PASSED BY THE NATIONAL ASSEMBLY GREATLY RESTRICTED INVESTORS' RIGHTS AND PROTECTIONS AND REDUCED BUSINESS INCENTIVES FOR LARGE SCALE EXPLORATION PROJECTS.

AGRIBUSINESS: THE AGRICULTURE SECTOR IS OF PARAMOUNT IMPORTANCE TO THE LAO ECONOMY, ACCOUNTING FOR ALMOST 52% OF GDP AND EMPLOYING 85% OF THE WORK FORCE IN 1997. ALTHOUGH RICE IS BY FAR THE LARGEST COMPONENT, UTILIZING 80% OF THE 752,000 HECTARES OF CULTIVATED LAND, PLATEAUS EXIST WITH SUITABLE SOIL AND CLIMATIC CONDITIONS FOR PLANTATION AGRICULTURE. PALM OIL, COFFEE, COTTON, GROUNDNUTS, SUGAR, FRUITS, VEGETABLES, TOBACCO AND FLOWERS ARE ALL VIABLE CROPS. AN AMERICAN BUSINESS IN BOKEO PROVINCE IS SUCCESSFULLY PRODUCING SOY BEANS FOR CATTLE FEED.

SMALL-SCALE TOURISM: INVESTMENT IS NEEDED FOR HOTEL AND GUESTHOUSE CONSTRUCTION AND MANAGEMENT, RESTAURANTS AND CATERING, IN-COUNTRY TRANSPORT (AIR, GROUND, AND WATER-BASED), TRAINING, AND RELATED SUPPORT SERVICES. SINCE 1990, OVER $600M IN INVESTMENT LICENSES FOR 34 PROJECTS IN THE TOURISM SECTOR HAVE BEEN APPROVED, AVERAGING A 50% PER YEAR GROWTH RATE OVER THAT PERIOD. FOREIGNERS ARE, HOWEVER, SPECIFICALLY PROHIBITED FROM OPENING TRAVEL AGENCIES OR TOUR GUIDE SERVICES. NATIONAL REVENUE FROM TOURISM REACHED ALMOST $80 MILLION IN 1998, BYPASSING GARMENTS FOR THE FIRST TIME. DURING 1999-2000, WHICH THE GOVERNMENT OF LAOS HAS DESIGNATED AS OFFICIAL TOURISM PROMOTION YEAR, THE NATIONAL TOURISM AUTHORITY EXPECTS TO INCREASE REVENUES UP TO $ 90 MILLION AND TO ATTRACT 700,000 FOREIGN TOURISTS.

SERVICES: GROWTH OF PRIVATE INVESTMENT AND COMMERCE WILL NECESSARILY GENERATE INCREASING DEMAND FOR BANKING, INSURANCE, ACCOUNTING, COMMUNICATIONS, AND CONSULTING SERVICES. IN 1998 THE SERVICES SECTOR GREW BY 4.8%, AND NOW CONSTITUTES MORE THAN 25% OF GDP.

LEADING TRADE PROSPECT

(IN USD MILLIONS)

1. COMPUTER SOFTWARE & HARDWARE AND ACCESSORIES

	1997	1998
TOTAL MARKET SIZE	0.928	4.17
TOTAL IMPORTS	0.92	4.17

2. CHEMICALS FOR PHARMACEUTICALS

	1997	1998
TOTAL MARKET SIZE	1.34	1.01
TOTAL IMPORTS	1.34	1.01

3. MEDICAL EQUIPMENT

	1997	1998
TOTAL MARKET SIZE	0.66	2.69
TOTAL IMPORTS	0.66	2.69

3. ELECTRONICS

	1997	1998
TOTAL MARKET SIZE	3.36	24.88
TOTAL IMPORTS	3.36	24.88

MARKETING U.S. PRODUCTS AND SERVICES

DISTRIBUTION AND SALES CHANNELS

IN GENERAL, IMPORT-EXPORT WHOLESALE COMPANIES IMPORT GOODS INTO LAOS, AND THEN SELL THE GOODS TO RETAILERS. GOODS MAY ENTER LAOS BY AIR, ROAD, OR LESS FREQUENTLY, BY RIVER. THERE IS NO RAILROAD. THE LACK OF A WELL-DEVELOPED ROAD SYSTEM AND BASIC INFRASTRUCTURE IN MANY AREAS MAKES DISTRIBUTION OUTSIDE OF THE MAIN URBAN AREAS IN VIENTIANE, LUANG PRABANG, SAVANNAKHET, AND PAKSE DIFFICULT, TIME-CONSUMING, AND COSTLY.

USE OF AGENTS AND DISTRIBUTORS; FINDING A PARTNER

MANY IMPORT-EXPORT COMPANIES EXIST IN VIENTIANE AND IN THE CITIES LOCATED AT OR NEAR BORDER CROSSINGS, SUCH AS PAKSE AND SAVANNAKHET. SOME IMPORT-EXPORT COMPANIES MAY BE ILL-EQUIPPED TO HANDLE LARGE-SCALE DISTRIBUTION. U.S. FIRMS LOOKING FOR A DISTRIBUTOR IN A PARTICULAR PROVINCE SHOULD CONTACT THE PROVINCIAL LAO NATIONAL CHAMBER OF COMMERCE (LNCC).

THE LNCC CAN ALSO HELP IDENTIFY BUSINESS PARTNERS. UNDER THE 1994 FOREIGN INVESTMENT LAW, A BUSINESS COOPERATION CONTRACT (SIMILAR TO A PARTNERSHIP) PROVIDES FOR THE DIVISION OF PROFITS AND LIABILITIES BETWEEN PARTNERS. IN THIS CASE, THE PARTNERS ASSUME FULL LIABILITY AS NO SEPARATE LEGAL ENTITY IS FORMED.
C) FRANCHISING

LAOS HAS NO SPECIAL LAW REGULATING FRANCHISES.

DIRECT MARKETING

BECAUSE OF LOW TELEPHONE DENSITY (ONLY ABOUT 1 PER EVERY 180 PEOPLE), POOR ROADS, AND HIGH ILLITERACY RATES (ABOUT 40 PERCENT), DIRECT MARKETING IS NOT GENERALLY EFFECTIVE IN LAOS.

JOINT VENTURES/LICENSING

THE FOREIGN INVESTMENT LAW RECOGNIZES JOINT VENTURES, BUT REQUIRES THE FOREIGN PARTNER TO CONTRIBUTE AT LEAST THIRTY PERCENT OF TOTAL EQUITY IN THE INVESTMENT. FOREIGN PARTNERS' EQUITY MAY BE FOREIGN CURRENCY, PLANT AND EQUIPMENT, CAPITAL GOODS, TECHNOLOGY, AND/OR SKILLS AND MANAGEMENT. LAO PARTNERS (INCLUDING THE LAO GOVERNMENT) MAY CONTRIBUTE MONEY, LAND, WATER RIGHTS, NATURAL RESOURCES, AND/OR CAPITAL GOODS. THE VALUE OF THE INPUTS AND ASSETS OF EACH SIDE ARE ASSESSED AT INTERNATIONAL MARKET RATES AND CONVERTED INTO LOCAL CURRENCY AT THE PREVAILING EXCHANGE RATE ON THE DATE OF EQUITY PAYMENT. THE INCORPORATION OF JOINT VENTURES MUST COMPLY WITH THE BUSINESS LAW OF THE LAO PDR.

ESTABLISHING AN OFFICE

TO APPLY FOR A FOREIGN INVESTMENT LICENSE, THE FOREIGN INVESTOR MUST PRESENT THE FOLLOWING DOCUMENTS TO THE FOREIGN INVESTMENT MANAGEMENT CABINET (FIMC), THE LAO GOVERNMENT AGENCY DESIGNATED BY THE PRIME MINISTER TO HANDLE ALL FOREIGN INVESTMENTS: A) STANDARD APPLICATION FOR A FOREIGN INVESTMENT LICENSE (SIGNED BY BOTH PARTIES IF A JOINT VENTURE); B) COMPANY BYLAWS AND FINANCIAL STATEMENT; C) FEASIBILITY STUDY;

ARTICLES OF ASSOCIATION.

JOINT VENTURE APPLICATIONS MUST ALSO INCLUDE AN AGREEMENT ON TECHNOLOGY TRANSFER AND A JOINT VENTURE AGREEMENT SIGNED BY BOTH SIDES. FIMC, THE MINISTRIES CONCERNED, AND THE PRIME MINISTER'S OFFICE WILL SCREEN THE PROPOSAL, AND ARE REQUIRED TO ISSUE OR DENY THE LICENSE WITHIN 60 DAYS.
(IN PRACTICE, HOWEVER, THE APPROVAL PROCESS GENERALLY TAKES ONE YEAR OR MORE.)

WITHIN 90 DAYS OF RECEIPT OF THE LICENSE, THE COMPANY MUST REGISTER WITH THE MINISTRY OF COMMERCE AND TOURISM IN ORDER TO OBTAIN A BUSINESS LICENSE; REGISTER WITH THE TAX DEPARTMENT AT THE MINISTRY OF FINANCE; AND RECEIVE AN INDUSTRIAL ESTABLISHMENT AUTHORIZATION FROM THE DEPARTMENT OF INDUSTRY, MINISTRY OF INDUSTRY AND HANDICRAFTS.

-TO ESTABLISH A REPRESENTATIVE OFFICE, THE FOREIGN COMPANY NEEDS TO PRESENT THE FIRST TWO DOCUMENTS MENTIONED ABOVE; A COMPANY

For additional analytical, business and investment opportunities information,
please contact Global Investment & Business Center, USA
at (703) 370-8082. Fax: (703) 370-8083. E-mail: ibpusa3@gmail.com
Global Business and Investment Info Databank - www.ibpus.com

PROFILE OR THE FOREIGN INVESTORS' BIO DATA; THE COMPANY'S FINANCIAL STATEMENT/ANNUAL REPORT; A LEASE AGREEMENT FOR OFFICE SPACE IN LAOS; VERIFICATION OF THE REPRESENTATIVE'S EMPLOYMENT WITH THE COMPANY; AND A COPY OF THE REPRESENTATIVE'S PASSPORT (IF A FOREIGNER).

SELLING FACTORS AND TECHNIQUES

U.S. PRODUCTS GENERALLY ENJOY A REPUTATION FOR TECHNOLOGICAL SOPHISTICATION AND HIGH QUALITY AMONG LAO. THE DOWN SIDE OF THAT REPUTATION, HOWEVER, IS THAT AMERICAN PRODUCTS ARE ALSO GENERALLY CONSIDERED TOO ADVANCED AND TOO COSTLY FOR LAOS' NEEDS. THE LAO MARKET CAN THUS BE DIFFICULT FOR U.S. PRODUCTS, WHICH ARE OFTEN MORE EXPENSIVE AND LESS KNOWN THAN IMPORTS FROM NEIGHBORING COUNTRIES, TO ENTER. TO COMPETE SUCCESSFULLY, SOME U.S. FIRMS HAVE COMBINED ROUTINE ADVERTISING WITH WORKSHOPS, TRAINING PROGRAMS, TRADE SHOWS, AND PRODUCT LAUNCHING EVENTS FOR MAJOR WHOLESALERS AND DISTRIBUTORS, AS WELL AS CUSTOMERS. THE THAI AND LAO LANGUAGES, WHILE SIMILAR, ARE NOT IDENTICAL, AND AMERICAN PRODUCTS THAT INCLUDE LAO-LANGUAGE PACKAGING AND/OR PROMOTIONAL MATERIALS ARE WELL REGARDED.

ADVERTISING AND TRADE PROMOTION.

ADVERTISING AND TRADE PROMOTION ARE IMPORTANT MARKETING TOOLS IN LAOS FOR U.S. PRODUCTS. SINCE NEARLY ALL LAO WHO OWN TELEVISIONS WATCH PROGRAMS (AND ADVERTISEMENTS) BROADCAST FROM THAILAND, A GOOD REPUTATION AND STRONG ADVERTISING CAMPAIGN IN THAILAND WILL LIKELY YIELD BENEFITS ACROSS THE BORDER AS WELL.

IN LAOS, MANY COMPANIES ADVERTISE IN TWO LAO LOCAL NEWSPAPERS: VIENTIANE MAI, WHICH IS A LAO LANGUAGE NEWSPAPER, AND VIENTIANE TIMES, AN ENGLISH LANGUAGE NEWSPAPER.

I) PRICING PRODUCT

GIVEN THE MODEST PER CAPITA INCOME (UNDER $300 IN 1998), PRICE SENSITIVITY IS ESPECIALLY IMPORTANT IN DETERMINING SUCCESSFUL PRODUCT SALES. LINGERING FALL-OUT FROM THE ASIAN FINANCIAL CRISIS, IN WHICH THE LAO LOCAL CURRENCY PLUMMETED SHARPLY AGAINST THE U.S. DOLLAR AND THAI BAHT, CONTINUES TO MAKE MANY IMPORTED GOODS PROHIBITIVELY EXPENSIVE. MARK-UP ON MOST CONSUMER GOODS RANGES FROM THREE TO FIVE PERCENT, WHILE THE MARK-UP ON ELECTRONIC EQUIPMENT GENERALLY RUNS FROM TEN TO FIFTEEN PERCENT.

J) SALES SERVICE/CUSTOMER SUPPORT

IN LIGHT OF THE GENERALLY LOW LEVEL OF TECHNOLOGICAL SOPHISTICATION, SALES SERVICE AND CUSTOMER SUPPORT ARE CRUCIAL TO

SELLING PRODUCTS LIKE MEDICAL EQUIPMENT, OFFICE AND TELECOMMUNICATIONS EQUIPMENT, AND COMPUTER SOFTWARE AND HARDWARE. SINCE LAOS HAS LIMITED ACCESS TO THE WORLD MARKET AND MEDIA, U.S. COMPANIES MAY WISH TO SUPPORT LOCAL AGENTS OR CLIENTS IN PROVIDING TRAINING OR SEMINARS TO EDUCATE NEW USERS ABOUT PRODUCTS AND TECHNOLOGY. THE LIMITED AVAILABILITY OF LOCAL SOURCES OF CAPITAL (SEE CHAPTER VIII) MAY MAKE OFFERING GENEROUS FINANCING TERMS (ESPECIALLY FOR FIRST-TIME CLIENTS) A CONSIDERATION.

K) SELLING TO THE GOVERNMENT

SINCE FOREIGN ASSISTANCE ACCOUNTED FOR MORE THAN 40% OF THE NATIONAL BUDGET IN 1997, GRANTS AND LOANS FROM FOREIGN GOVERNMENTS, AID AGENCIES, MULTILATERAL ORGANIZATIONS, AND INTERNATIONAL FINANCIAL INSTITUTIONS, ACCOUNT FOR A SIGNIFICANT PERCENTAGE OF GOVERNMENT PROCUREMENT. OPPORTUNITIES IN GOVERNMENT SALES EXIST IN A VARIETY OF FIELDS, INCLUDING INFRASTRUCTURE DEVELOPMENT; CONSTRUCTION; ENGINEERING SERVICES; POWER GENERATION AND TRANSMISSION, INFORMATION TECHNOLOGY (BOTH GOODS AND SERVICES); MEDICAL EQUIPMENT AND PHARMACEUTICALS; AND AGRICULTURAL TOOLS AND MACHINERY. HOWEVER, GIVEN THE MODEST MEANS OF THE LAO GOVERNMENT, CONTRACTS ARE OFTEN AWARDED TO THE LOWEST BIDDER, AND AMERICAN BIDS ARE FREQUENTLY NOT CONSIDERED COMPETITIVE. IN GENERAL, SUCCESSFUL BIDDERS ON GOVERNMENT CONTRACTS NEED A REPUTABLE LOCAL REPRESENTATIVE WITH EXTENSIVE CONTACTS AND LONG-STANDING FAMILIARITY WITH PROCUREMENT PRACTICES AT A PARTICULAR AGENCY.

L) PROTECTING YOUR PRODUCTS FROM IPR INFRINGEMENT

IN JANUARY 1995, THE PRIME MINISTER ISSUED A DECREE ON TRADEMARKS, WHICH PROVIDES FOR THE REGISTRATION OF TRADEMARKS. LAOS IS A MEMBER OF THE WORLD INTELLECTUAL PROPERTY ORGANIZATION (WIPO), WHICH HAS ASSISTED IN DRAFTING AN INDUSTRIAL PROPERTY LAW THAT ADDRESSES PATENTS, INDUSTRIAL DESIGN, LAY-OUT DESIGN, INTEGRATED CIRCUITS, SPECIALLY-BRED PLANT SPECIES, AND TRADE SECRETS. THIS LAW IS IN THE PROCESS OF DISCUSSION AMONG RELATED MINISTRIES BEFORE BEING SUBMITTED TO THE NATIONAL ASSEMBLY FOR CONSIDERATION. LAOS IS ALSO A MEMBER OF THE PARIS CONVENTION ON THE PROTECTION OF INDUSTRIAL PROPERTY; IT HAS NOT YET JOINED THE BERNE CONVENTION ON COPYRIGHTS. LAOS IS IN THE PROCESS OF DRAFTING A LAW ON COPYRIGHTS MODELED ON WIPO STANDARDS, IN HARMONY WITH TRIPS (TRADE RELATED ASPECT ON INTELLECTUAL PROPERTY RIGHTS). (NOTE: THE APPROVAL PROCESS FOR DRAFTED LEGISLATION IS A LENGTHY ONE. SINCE THIS DRAFT IS STILL IN ITS INITIAL STAGES, WE DO NOT EXPECT LEGISLATIVE ACTION ON THIS IN THE NEAR FUTURE.)

LAOS IS NOT ON THE U.S. TRADE REPRESENTATIVE'S PRIORITY WATCH, WATCH, OR SPECIAL MENTION LISTS FOR COUNTRIES FAILING TO PROVIDE ADEQUATE IPR PROTECTION. SINCE THAILAND AND LAOS HAVE A BILATERAL

IPR RIGHTS AGREEMENT, PROTECTION MAY BE GRANTED IF AN INVESTOR ALREADY HAS OBTAINED A PATENT IN THAILAND.

M) NEED FOR A LOCAL ATTORNEY

THE BODY OF COMMERCIAL LAW IN LAOS REMAINS COMPARATIVELY UNDERDEVELOPED AND CAN SOMETIMES APPEAR INCONSISTENT. SINCE FEW LAO LAWS HAVE BEEN TRANSLATED INTO ENGLISH (AND NONE HAVE BEEN OFFICIALLY TRANSLATED) AND THE LOCAL BUREAUCRACY CAN BE APPALLINGLY CUMBERSOME, MANY FOREIGN BUSINESSPEOPLE VIEW THE NEED FOR LOCAL LEGAL COUNSEL AS IMPERATIVE. THE EMBASSY PROVIDES THE NAMES OF THE FOLLOWING LAWYERS AS A SERVICE TO U.S. CITIZENS SEEKING LEGAL ADVICE. THE EMBASSY OFFERS NO RECOMMENDATIONS REGARDING THESE LAWYERS NOR DOES THE EMBASSY ACCEPT ANY RESPONSIBILITY FOR THEIR COMPETENCE.

MR. KHAMPHAY BOTHAPANITH
106 BAN WAT NAK, SISATTANAK DISTRICT
VIENTIANE
TEL: (856) 21 312397

MR. TODD DIRKSEN/MS. MARY FLIPSE
DIRKSEN FLIPSE DORAN & LE
MEKONG COMMERCIAL BUILDING NO. 1
LUANGPRABANG RD.
SITHANNEUA, VIENTIANE
E-MAIL: DFDLLAOS@LOXINFO.CO.H
TEL: (856) 21 216927-9; FAX: (856) 21 2216919

MR. PASITH PHOMMARAK
BAN SPHANTHONG , SISATTANAK DISTRICT
VIENTIANE
E-MAIL: DFDLLAOS@NOXINFO.CO.CH
TEL/FAX: (856) 21 216927-9; FAX: (856) 21 2216919

KPMG LAO LTD.
LUANGPRABANG RD.
BAN KHOUNTA THONG
P.O. BOX: 6978, VIENTIANE
TEL: (856) 21 222-042 or 219-491; FAX: (856) 21 219-490

MR. SABH PHOMMARATH
191, UNIT 17, NONGBOUATHONG TAI
VIENTIANE
TEL: (856) 21 222346

MR. BONG XAYAKOUMMANE
MINISTRY OF JUSTICE/PRESIDENT OF THE LAO BAR ASSOCIATION

THE LAO MINISTRY OF JUSTICE ALSO EMPLOYS A NUMBER OF LAWYERS WHO, UNDER SOME CIRCUMSTANCES, MAY TAKE PRIVATE CASES.

EXPORT DOCUMENTS AND PROCEDURES

PART I : DOCUMENTATION

- Cargo Control Document
- Invoice
- Declaration Form
- Certificate of Origin

You will be able to obtain release of your goods upon presentation of a fully completed declaration package consisting of the following:

1. 3 copies of the cargo control document
2. 2 copies of the invoice
3. 2 carrier advice notes
4. 2 copies of any permit issued by a relevant Ministry or Department
5. 2 certificates of origin showing origin of goods
6. 3 sets of the declaration form

CARGO CONTROL DOCUMENT

A cargo control document in the form of an airway bill for goods arriving by air or a manifest for goods arriving by highway or river will be sent to you together with an advice note issued by the carrier to inform you that a shipment has arrived and is awaiting customs clearance.

You will need the cargo control number from the airway bill or manifest to complete the appropriate field on the declaration form.

Three copies of the cargo control document and two copies of the advice note must accompany the declaration form.

INVOICE

For all shipments entering or leaving Lao PDR, a commercial invoice which indicates the buyer and seller of the goods, the price paid or price payable, and an adequate description of the goods including quantity of the goods contained in the shipment, should be produced to support the declaration. The invoice must be prepared by the exporter. Locally produced invoices are not acceptable. Click here to download an invoice sample

Declaration Form

Certificate of origin

PART II :CLASSIFICATION OF GOODS

- Harmonized System

General Information on the Harmonized Commodity Description and Coding (HS) Based Tariff

The H.S. based tariff is logically structured and divided into twenty-one sections. For the most part, commodities are arranged in these sections according to the decree of manufacture or processing.

Within the twenty-one sections there are 99 chapters. Chapter 77 is reserved for possible future expansion. The last chapter, 99 is set aside for special use by individual countries.

Chapters are arranged according to levels of processing, with primary commodities classified in the earlier chapters and technically more complex products treated later on.

Each chapter begins with a title page. Section and chapter legal notes precede certain chapters and sections. However, these notes only define the scope and limits of the chapter and sections they precede. Following the chapter notes, you will find the classification numbers of all products covered by the chapter.

STRUCTURE OF THE CLASSIFICATION NUMBER

Classification in the HS is a systematic process. To use this process, it is essential to understand the structure of the classification number.

With the entry of Lao PDR in ASEAN, the classification number consists of eight digits. This eight-digit number is sub-divided at various levels to provide greater details and definitions for a product than the previous level at the six digits.

Each level is identified as follows:

01.01 HEADING
01.01.20 1st SUB-HEADING
01.01.20.00 2sd Sub-Heading

International Lao and ASEAN
Requirement Requirement

The first six digits represent the international portion of the classification number and are the numbers that will be used by all countries acceding to the Harmonized System. The last two digits reflect the Lao and ASEAN requirements for tariff and statistical purposes.

The structure of the classification number, i.e., the breakdown of the number by heading, and sub-headings is the basis for classifying your product in the H.S. Once a product has been located in a heading, an appropriate eight-digit number of sub-headings within the selected heading must be determined.

PART III : VALUE FOR DUTY

- Transaction Value Method
- Other Methods of Valuing Imports
- Importer's Responsibility
- Importer's Rights

The Lao PDR system of valuing imported goods is known as the transaction value system. It is based on an internationally approved set of rules, under the General Agreement on Tariffs and Trade. The system is now used by most trading nations and provides for a fair and uniform means of valuing goods for customs duty.

The transaction value system stipulates that the transaction value method must be used whenever possible. This value method bases the customs value on the price paid by the importer to the exporter for the imported goods. If the transaction value method cannot be used, one of the other five methods must be used, in the sequence presented. These other methods are known as

- Transaction value of identical goods
- Transaction value of similar goods
- Deductive value
- Computed value
- Flexible value

TRANSACTION VALUE METHOD

1. The transaction value method will be used for valuation of most imported goods, except in situations where there is a relationship between the importer and exporter that may influence the value, or where the imported goods are rented or leased, or are sent on consignment, or where the exporter imposes certain conditions such as restricting the trading level or the area of resale, or barter trade.

2. When using the transaction value method, the following costs must be included in the customs value:
- Transportation costs to Lao PDR
- Insurance costs
- Packing, packaging and special handling costs
- Fees paid to the exporters for royalties, licenses, etc.
- Storage charges in the country of export that are paid by the importer
- All escalation costs charged after the goods are ordered
- All selling costs such as commissions, etc that are charged to the importer
- Assists are goods or services supplied by the importer to the exporter free or at a reduced cost that were used in the production of the goods.

3. Costs which may be deducted from the customs value are:
- Discounts for volume purchases, payment for the goods in advance or within an agreed period (such discount must be shown on the invoice and granted before importation)
- If goods were sold by the exporter on a duty and tax paid basis, deduct the amount paid for duties and taxes
- Amount paid to the exporter for work that will be performed in Lao PDR, such as construction, erection, assembly, maintenance or technical assistance related to the imported goods (such costs must be shown separately on the invoice or in a contract)

OTHER METHODS OF VALUING IMPORTS

The five other methods of valuation are more complex and the necessary information may not be readily available. The following is therefore only for the importer's information and, if it is necessary to apply these methods the importer may wish to consult with a customs officer to determine the value for duty.

IDENTICAL OR SIMILAR GOODS METHOD

Under these methods the value for duty is based on the customs value of other identical or similar goods which have been previously exported to Lao PDR, at or about the same time as the goods being imported. The customs value can be adjusted to allow for differences in the trade level of purchases and in the cost of transportation. It is unlikely that the importer will be able to use these methods, as it requires information on values declared to customs for imports of identical or similar goods. Values for duty under these methods is therefore usually calculated in conjunction with the assistance of a customs officer.

DEDUCTIVE VALUE METHOD

Under the deductive value method, the value for duty is based on the most common selling price of goods imported into Lao PDR. From this resale price is deducted an amount which represents the average profit and general expenses involved in selling the goods in the Lao PDR. Included in the general expenses involved in the expenses will be items such as Lao PDR duties and taxes, all transportation, warehousing, selling and distribution costs, also any packaging or further processing costs in Lao PDR, should also be deducted in calculating the value for duty.

The purpose behind this method is to determine what the cost of the goods would have been had they been purchased, in the same condition as when imported, from an unrelated exporter. This method would only be used in situations such as goods being imported on consignment or barter trade.

COMPUTED VALUE METHOD

The computed value method is the cost of production of the imported goods, plus an amount for normal profit and general expenses experienced by the exporter, when selling the same type of goods to importers in Lao PDR.

As most exporters are reluctant to release this information, the use of this valuation method will generally be limited to those importers who are related to the exporter and where the exporter is the manufacturer of the goods being appraised.

FLEXIBLE METHOD

If the other methods of valuation can not be used, the flexible method must be applied. This method does not provide specific rules, but stipulates that the rules of one of the other five methods is applied in a flexible manner and that the information used is available in the Lao PDR.

IMPORTER'S RESPONSIBILITY

The importer of commercial goods into Lao PDR is responsible for the self-assessment of the duty and tax liabilities on all goods imported. This means that the importer or his authorized agent must prepare all necessary documents for presentation to customs.

CUSTOMS' RESPONSIBILITY

Customs is responsible to ensure that all legislation governing the importation and exportation of goods into and out of the Lao PDR have been fully complied with. Customs is also responsible to insure that all applicable duties and taxes have been paid. Customs will also review customs declarations after release of the goods and may issue notices for payment of additional, duties and tax as a result of the review, or reassessment of value or redetermination of tariff.

IMPORTER'S RIGHTS

An importer has the right to request customs to reconsider any reassessment of value and any redetermination of tariff classification. Further, the importer has the right to appeal the customs reassessment notice to higher authorities.

PART IV : CODING INSTRUCTIONS

Annex
I List of Customs Offices and Codes
II List of Country and Currency Codes
III List of Regional Customs Offices and Addresses

THE DECLARATION FORM

The declaration form or single administrative document is used for all customs transactions; import, export or transit. It must be complete to be acceptable in customs.

Click here to view a sample form

THE DECLARATION FORM HAS THREE SEGMENTS.

1. In the first section(Boxes No.1-23) enter general information on importer, exporter and declarant as well as transport and transaction details.

2. In the second section (Boxes No.24-42) enter details on the item declared, including amount of duties and taxes payable or exempted.

3. Summary of Payment and Responsibility of Declaration Section.

It is presented in the form of (i.) a header sheet, which is used to declare importation, exportation or in transit information for each commodity item (ii.) continuation sheets to declare other commodity items and (iii.) section sheet for official use.
Note. Declaration forms are on sale at all Regional Customs offices.
Instructions to fill each box of the form.

BOX NO.1 DECLARATION REGIME

Inscribe one of the following codes to identify the type of transaction the declaration is for:

Regime Code Description
10 Exportation of domestic Goods
14 Exportation under a drawback regime
20 Temporary Exportation
35 Re-Exportation
40 Importation of goods for Home consumption.
4A Importation of goods for diplomatic use, returning residents, and humanitarian assistance; samples, educational materials and certain religious articles.
4B Goods ex-warehoused to duty free shops
4C Goods ex-warehoused for exportation out of Lao PDR
45 Home Consumption of Goods after temporary admission
47 Home Consumption of Goods entered under a warehousing regime
50 Temporary Importation
62 Re-Importation of Goods Exported temporarily
70 Warehousing of Goods
80 Transit

Office Codes.

Enter the code of the office where the declaration is presented. See Annex I for a list of all customs offices and their codes.

MANIFEST /AIRWAY BILL NUMBER.

Enter the cargo control number from the air waybill if the goods arrive or leave by air or from the manifest if goods arrive or leave by any other mode of transport.
Declaration Number and Date.

Customs will assign the declaration number and the date when the declaration is presented and registered with customs.

BOX NO.2 EXPORTER AND ADDRESS

If you enter goods for exportation, indicate your name and address as well as the taxpayer identification number (TIN) issued by the Tax Department. If you have not yet been issued a TIN please obtain a number from the nearest tax office and use it on all subsequent customs declarations. Also include your office telephone number. For diplomatic and personal exportations, leave the number field blank.

BOX NO.3 GROSS MASS KG.

Indicate the gross weight in kilograms of the entire consignment of goods as declared on the manifest or air waybill.

BOX NO.4 ITEMS

Indicate the total number of items as shown on the invoice.

BOX NO.5 TOTAL PACKAGES.

Indicate the total number of packages as declared on the manifest or airway bill. In case of bulk cargo, indicate BULK only.

BOX NO. 6 IMPORTER AND ADDRESS

If you enter goods for importation, indicate your name and address as well as the taxpayer identification number (TIN) issued by the Tax Department. If you have not been issued a TIN please obtain a number from the nearest tax office and use it on all subsequent customs declarations. Also include your office telephone number. For diplomatic and personal importations, leave the number field blank.

BOX NO.7 CONSIGNEE.

If you are importing goods on behalf of another person, or the other party holds title to the good at time of importation indicate the name and address of the consignee as well as the TIN issued by the Tax Department. Please contact the nearest tax office for a number and use on all subsequent declarations, or obtain the TIN number from the consignee if one has been issued to the consignee by the tax department. For diplomatic importations, leave the number field blank.

BOX NO.8 DECLARANT.

If you are a licensed agent authorized to transact business in customs, enter the TIN issued by the Tax Department. If you do not have a TIN, contact the nearest tax office.

BOX NO.9 COUNTRY OF CONSIGNMENT/DESTINATION.

For importation, indicate the country and the code from where the goods have been consigned.
For exportation, indicate the country and the code to where the goods are exported or re-exported.

See Annex II: List of Country and Currency Codes.

Box No.10 Type of License.

Indicate the type of trade or industry license held by you.

Box. No.11 Delivery Terms.

Indicate the terms of delivery of goods either CIF for importation, or FOB for exportation.

Box No.12 Total Invoice in Foreign Currency.

For importation, indicate the total amount of the invoice in foreign currency. See list of Country and Currency Codes in Annex II.

Box No.13 Total Invoice in Local Currency.

Enter here the total value of the invoice in Kip by converting the value declared in box No. 12 with the rate of exchange indicated in box No.16. If there is only one item, this value should correspond to the value declared in box no.38. If there are many items, the total value should correspond to the total of values declared in all the boxes no.38 on the Continuation sheets.

Box No.14 Total FOB (Exports)

Indicate the FOB value of the goods in foreign currency.
(if known)

Box No. 14 Total FOB (Imports)

Enter the FOB value in foreign currency. (if known)

Box No.15 Total FOB Ncy (Import/Export)

For import, leave blank.
For export, indicate the FOB value of the goods in Kip.

Box No.16 Rate of Exchange.

For additional analytical, business and investment opportunities information,
please contact Global Investment & Business Center, USA
at (703) 370-8082. Fax: (703) 370-8083. E-mail: ibpusa3@gmail.com
Global Business and Investment Info Databank - www.ibpus.com

Indicate the rate of exchange of the foreign currency to the Kip and the code of the foreign currency. (The exchange rate shall be that which is in force at time of importation, unless otherwise advised).

Box No.17 Mode of Transport.

Indicate the mode of transport, the voyage number. Also the country code of the nationality of the aircraft, truck or ship.
(if known)

The codes for mode of transport are:

SEA 1
RAIL 2
ROAD 3
AIR 4

Box No.18 Port of Loading/Unloading.

For imports indicate the name and the code of the foreign country where goods are loaded,
For exports, indicate the name and the code of the foreign country where goods are destined.

See Annex II for a list of Country Codes.

Box No.19 Place of Shipping/ Landing.

For imports, indicate the place in Lao PDR where goods have arrived. At export, or re-export, indicate the place in Lao PDR from where the goods are exported or re-exported.

Box No.20 Entry/Exit Office.

Indicate the code of the Lao customs office where the declaration is presented for clearance.

In a transit operation, indicate the code of the customs office where the transit operation commences. Also indicate the code of the exit customs office where the transit operations is to be terminated.

Box No.21 Identification Warehouse (Leave blank until bonded warehouses are established)

Indicate the code of the bonded warehouse where goods are to be warehoused or ex-warehoused.

Box No.22 Financial and Banking Data.

For additional analytical, business and investment opportunities information,
please contact Global Investment & Business Center, USA
at (703) 370-8082. Fax: (703) 370-8083. E-mail: ibpusa3@gmail.com
Global Business and Investment Info Databank - www.ibpus.com

Indicate the terms of payment of the transaction, as well as the name of the bank and the branch where payment for the commercial transaction is made.

Box No.23 Attached Documents.

Indicate the codes of attached documents, which support your declaration. (Documents must be originals or certified as true copies).

1234567891011 InvoiceManifestAirway billPacking ListCertificate of Origin (If required)Phytosanitary Certificate (If required)Import Permit from Ministry of Trade (If required)Import permit from Ministry of Agriculture (If required)Import Permit from Ministry of Heath (If required) Authorization from Department of Transport (If required)If claiming duty and tax exemptions, documents authorizing such exemptions must be presented with the declaration.

Box No.24 Marks, Numbers and Description of Goods

Indicate the marks and numbers of the packages as shown on the manifest or airway bill.

If goods arrive or leave by containers, indicate the container number as shown on the manifest.

The total number of packages should correspond to the total number of packages indicated in box No.5.

Give a detailed description of the goods. Avoid, as far as possible, trade names. Except in the case of vehicles and electronic devices, provide make and model.

Box No.25 No. of Items.

Indicate the number of items on the invoice.

Box No.26 Tariff Code

Indicate the classification code of the commodity imported. This classification code in based on the AHTN and must be eight digits.

Box No.27 Customs Procedure Codes.
(Leave blank at this time)

Box No.28 Country of Origin/Destination

For imports, indicate the code of the country of origin of the goods imported, if the country of origin of the goods is different from the country where the goods have been consigned.

Box No.29 Zone.
It the goods originate from ASEAN member countries and are supported by a certificate of origin enter ASEAN. For other countries enter GEN. At export enter XPT.

Box No.30 Valuation Code

Indicate the code of the valuation method used to determine the customs value for duty.

There are six valuation methods and coded as follows:

Valuation Method Code
Transaction Method 1
Identical Goods Method 2
Similar Goods Method 3
Deductive Method 4
Computed Method 5
Flexible Method 6

Note: The transaction valuation method must be used as the primary method for valuation if possible.

Box No.31 Gross Mass.

Enter the gross weight in kilograms for the item on the first page only. The total weight of all items on the continuation sheets in the declaration should be equal to the weight declared in box no.3 of the general segment.

Box No.32 Net Mass.

Enter the net weight of the goods in kilograms for each item declared. If a continuation sheet is used a net mass must be inscribed for each item.

Box No.33 FOB Foreign Currency.

Enter the FOB value of the item in foreign currency (if known).

Box No.34 FOB Local Currency, only if transport and insurance are not prepaid by exporter. If prepaid, enter the value that includes transportation and insurance.

Enter the FOB value of the item in Kips, only if transport and insurance are not prepaid by exporter. If prepaid, enter the value that includes transportation and insurance.

Box No. 35 Freight.

Enter the amount of freight paid or payable for the item in Kip. For a shipment of various items, the freight charges are apportioned according to freight paid or payable and by weight. If freight is prepaid by exporter and included in the value, mark the box "Prepaid".

Box No.36 Insurance.

Enter the amount of insurance in Kip for the item.

For a shipment of various items, the insurance paid or payable is to be apportioned.

If the insurance is prepaid by the exporter and included in the value, mark the box "prepaid"

Box No.37 Other Costs.
Enter other costs and expenses incurred for the import of goods and paid to the exporter for the imported goods.

Box No.38 Customs Value in Local Currency.

Enter the customs value for the item, which is the total of values of boxes 33, 34, 35 and 36.

Box No. 39 Supplementary Unit/Quantity.

Some of the most common international units of quantity are as follows:

Unit Code
Cubic Metre MTQ
Gigawatt-hour GWH
Hundred CEN
Kilogram KGM
Litre LTR
Metre MTR
Number NMB
Number of packs NMP
Square Metre MTK
Ten TEN
Ten Pairs TPR
Thousand MIL
Tonne TNE

Enter any of the code, which describes the unit quantity of goods imported/exported. If the units of imports or exports are not included in this list, consult a customs officer for more detailed lists.

Box No.40 Duty Payable.

Enter the amount of duties and taxes payable for the item declared per category of duty, tax and excise.

Enter also the taxable base for each category of duty, tax and excise. Duty rate is calculated on the Customs value. The tax is calculated on the customs value plus the

For additional analytical, business and investment opportunities information,
please contact Global Investment & Business Center, USA
at (703) 370-8082. Fax: (703) 370-8083. E-mail: ibpusa3@gmail.com
Global Business and Investment Info Databank - www.ibpus.com

duty payable. The excise tax is calculated on the customs value plus duty payable plus tax payable.

For other items of the declaration, on the continuation sheets enter the duty, tax and excise payable.

Box No.41 Permit Numbers.

Enter permit number and date of issue for the shipment, if required.

Box No.42 Previous Declaration.

If the declaration refers to a previous declaration, the registration number and date of the previous declaration is entered here.

Present a copy of the previous declaration with the declaration you have just prepared.

Responsibility of Declaration

You must enter your full name, indicate the capacity in which you are acting. And sign the declaration.

You must also indicate the mode of payment by which duty and taxes are to be paid.

After you have completed your declaration, you can now lodge it at the designated customs office where your goods are held.

After customs review and approval of the declaration, please make the payment of all applicable duties and taxes, and present a copy of the payment receipt to the customs office where the declaration was presented.

On receipt of the customs release note, present the release note to the warehouse keeper for delivery of the imported goods and sign for receipt of the goods or have the carrier sign for receipt.

FOREIGN INVESTMENT OPPORTUNITIES IN LAOS

FOREIGN INVESTMENT LICENSED IN LAOS

Rank	Countries	Number of Projects	Investment in US $ x 1000	Percentage
1.	Thailand	233	$2,278,289	44.78%
2.	USA	39	1,482,717	29.14

3.	R. Korea	17	394,785	7.76
4.	France	68	312,806	6.15
5.	Malaysia	11	188,731	3.71
6.	Australia	41	134,026	2.63
7.	Taiwan	31	64,764	1.27
8.	Norway	1	56000	1.10
9.	China	61	38,921	0.76
10.	UK.	13	28,685	0.56
11.	Hong Kong	23	28,266	0.56
12.	Canada	13	17,914	0.35
13.	Russian	12	17,564	0.35
14.	Singapore	16	12,217	024
15.	Japan	17	7,913	0.16
16.	Indonesia	2	5,140	0.10
17.	DPK Korea	1	3300	0.06
18.	Germany	7	3,019	0.06
19.	Vietnam	10	2,724	0.05
20.	Macao	2	2,560	0.05
21.	Sweden	7	2,203	0.04
22.	Italy	6	1,973	0.04
23.	Holland	3	770	0.02
24.	New Zealand	5	734	0.01
25.	India	2	645	0.01
26.	Belgium	2	500	0.01
27.	Denmark	6	406	0.01
28.	Switzerland	2	240	0.00
29.	Ukraine	1	200	0.00
30.	Austria	3	172	0.00

31.	Myanmar	3	65	0.00
	Laos' Shares		1,158,400	
	TOTAL:	658 projects	US$6,246,649,000	100%

SELECTED BUSINESS AND INVESTMENT OPPORTUNITIES

AGRO-FORESTRY SECTOR

Agriculture : The economic growth of the Lao PDR **Depends to a large extend,** upon the, performance of the Agricultural sector which contributed in 1993 for 56% of the GDP and employed about 0% of the labor force.

Coffee is by far the most promising **product for export.** In 1992, export of coffee accounted for around 80% of the export value in the agricultural sector and contributed for 7.4% of the total export value of the country. Export also includes several annual and perennial corps of limited quantities.

The Lao PDR has the **highest potential land/person** in the Greater Mekong Subregion large and unexploited fertile land and favorable climatic conditions, particularly in the **boloven basaltic plateau.** This could offer promising **opportunities** for low-intensive investment in the **agro-processing industry** for export based on annual and perennial crops.

The on-going improvement of main National Roads linking major provinces, together with the high rate of urbanization have created **favorable conditions** for investment in the **import-substitution** agro-processing industries.

Forestry : It has been estimated that the Lao PDR has **the highest ratio** of forest to total area in ASIA. Wood products including lumber are one of the main **export earning** of Lao PDR. In 1993, it accounted for **22% of the total export value.** In view of the long term sustainable development and the preservation of the environment, the Government has been implementing the policy of striking **a balance** between exploitation and conservation and shifting from exports of logs and lumbers towards the **promotion of wood** processing. Due to **shortage** of capital and the technical know-how in the country, the development of wood processing subsector also needs the investment and the introduction of new technology of the **foreign investors.**

ENERGY SECTOR

Electricity requirements in the region-. are increasing rapidly it has been predicted that 23,958 MW of new generation will be needed between now and year 2000. Lao PDR. is rich in energy resources: **Hydropower, coal, oil and gas. The uneven distribution** of the energy resources among the countries, particularly the hydropower resources : Countries with higher power demand have limited resources while those with limited requirements are well endowed with the hydropower resources.

For additional analytical, business and investment opportunities information,
please contact Global Investment & Business Center, USA
at (703) 370-8082. Fax: (703) 370-8083. E-mail: ibpusa3@gmail.com
Global Business and Investment Info Databank - www.ibpus.com

Lao PDR has a hydropower potential of about **15,000 MW** within its territory. Up to now, slightly over 1% of the total potential has been developed with 70 to 75% of the production exported to Thailand.

With the huge resources located close to the biggest power demand country in the subregion **(Thailand)** and the low domestic demand, the hydropower sector will continue to be **one of the main foreign exchange earning of Lao PDR.**

Without other financial sources than **The public investment funds and the external soft loan** the hydropower development would provably continue with the similar **slow rate** as experienced in the eighties. This would lead to a loss of opportunity for foreign exchange earning badly needed for development of other sectors.

On the basis of the above and in line with the new economic policy, the Government has begun, since the beginning of the nineties, **to seek participation of foreign investors** for projects beyond the financial capacity of the public and soft loan investment.

Within the short timeframe, experiences have proven that such policy is correct and several projects with the aggregate generation capacity about **10 times higher than the existing capacity** are being implemented in 1994 and expected to be completed by **the 2000** as shown 'm the attached figure.

The funds for these projects are from both the private sector **(BOT schemes)** for large schemes and soft loan for small/medium schemes. Agreements between the Government and the developers have been signed for most of the BOT schemes of the 1994-2000 peroid.

All the a above-mentioned BOT schemes have a provision for **equity sharing by the government** ranging from 25% to 60%.

Information given in following tables and figures are aimed to show the potential and the relative advantages of the hydropower resources in Lao PDR. It also indicates the, long-term forecast of power and electric energy demands of the countries in the Greater Mekong Subregion.

MINING SECTOR

Foreign investment is particularly sought in the Mining Sector because of its capital-intensive investment combined with scarce domestic financial resources and its high potential for export.

In 1991, the foreign investment in this sector was ranked second in terms of aggregate value (about 25% of the total).

Fiscal regulations such royalty rate, income taxes and incentives in the Mining Sector are widely recognized as **competitive** by international standard. This indicates the firm commitment and strong support of the Government to **pave the way** for foreign investment in the sector.

For additional analytical, business and investment opportunities information,
please contact Global Investment & Business Center, USA
at (703) 370-8082. Fax: (703) 370-8083. E-mail: ibpusa3@gmail.com
Global Business and Investment Info Databank - www.ibpus.com

The following location maps of various minerals and fossil fuels such as coal lignite, oil and natural gas show that the country possess huge mineral resources.

Market for fossil fuel in **Thailand** is tremendous as the country has to import about **60% of its requirements.** This would be an area of **high prospects** for foreign investors. Recently, an agreement was signed with private investors to implement a **lignite power plant** project in Hongsa (Northwest of Lao PDR) for exporting the electricity to Thailand.

In the **short-term,** other minerals having high prospects for export would be gemstones which require simple extraction equipment and could be easily transported.

Some **medium-and long-term** investment opportunities offered by the Ming Sector would be :

a). **The potash production** in the **Vientiane** province, the largest known deposits in the subregion with the estimated reserves exceeding by far those in Thailand;

b). The significant **iron ore** deposits in the province of **Xiengkhouang,** the occurrences of **base metals** (components needed for steel) and the planned hydropower development on the Nam Ngum river, both in the northeast of Vientiane and in Xiengkhoang Province, suggest the region could provide opportunities for both iron ore and steel export;

c). The **boloven** basaltic plateau in the southern Laos well endowed with both the competitive **hydropower** potential and **bauxite** might also offer opportunities for aluminum melting plants.

Having been fully aware that the absence of railways and inadequacy -of the road network are the major constraints for the development of the Mining Sector, the Government is now seeking all financial means to develop the transport sector including the **concession arrangement** with private investors Mining and transport development could be tied together in a **Single package** for concession arrangement.

ROADS

The Second and Third conferences in Subregion Economic Cooperation have identified the following priority projects in the road subsector :

a). Upgrading of the **Ho Chi Minh City- Phnom Penh- Bangkok road connection,** including possible extension to Vung Tau in Vietnam;

b). Construction of a **Thai- Lao PDR- Vietnam east-west Corridor;**

c). Development of a good quality road linking **Chiang Rai-Kunming via Myanmar;**

d). Development of a good quality road linking **Chiang Rai-Kunming via Lao PDR;** and

For additional analytical, business and investment opportunities information, please contact Global Investment & Business Center, USA at (703) 370-8082. Fax: (703) 370-8083. E-mail: ibpusa3@gmail.com Global Business and Investment Info Databank - www.ibpus.com

UPGRADING KUNMING -LAOSHIO ROAD SYSTEM.

RAILWAY, WATER AND TRANSPORT SUB-SECTOR

The Subregion Transport Sector Study by ADB considers 3 projects in railway subsector, 2 in the water transport subsector and 2 in the air transport subsector which are directly concerned Lao PDR.

a). **Projects in railway subsector** :

- Yunnan Province- Thailand Railway Project with two out of three optimal via Lao PDR.

- Extension Thailand Railway to Lao PDR (150 km) through the firstinternational Mekong bridge.

- Construction of new railway line from Lao PDR's Xiengkhouang Province to a Cualo port in Vietnarn mainly for export of iron ore.

b). **Water Transport Subsector** :

- Upper Mekong River Navigation Improvement Project.

- Southem Lao PDR- Cambodia River Navigation Improvement Project.

c). **Air Transport Subsector** :

- Project to upgrade the airport in Lao PDR

- Project to Establish New Subregional Air Routes involving Luang Prabang.

TOURISM AND HOTEL SECTOR

Within the Subregion, links and networks in the tourism sector **already exist :** Government-to-government and the commercial sector.

The commun interest among all six countries is to promote nature and culture types of tourism. The major problem is the **gaps** in most countries in the **basicinfrastructure** and **support services** necessary for maximizing tourism potential.

The subregional cooperation will primarily focus on :

1. **Promoting the Subregion as a tourism destination.**
2. **Establishing Subregional Tourism Forum.**
3. **Training the trainers in the basic craft skills of tourism.**
4. **Training the Resource Management in Conservation and Tourism.**
5. **mekong River Tourism Promoting Study.**

TRANSPORT

For additional analytical, business and investment opportunities information, please contact Global Investment & Business Center, USA at (703) 370-8082. Fax: (703) 370-8083. E-mail: ibpusa3@gmail.com Global Business and Investment Info Databank - www.ibpus.com

In most countries, transportation infrastructures are inadequate and are considered as a **major impediment** to trade , cooperation and the exploitation of rich mineral resources, particularly those located in the hinterlands.

Further major commitments are required before minimum standards can be satisfies and most of the shortcomings could only be addressed by **cooperation efforts**.

Through several meetings and consultations, the six countries have agrees that :

a). **Priority** should be on to the improvement and rehabilitation of existing facilities and Subregional projects on which there is already agreement among the countries directly concerned;

b). **The formulation of projects** should consider trade generation impacts, especially considering the economic transformation taking place in the Subregion;

c). Transport projects should be **implemented in sections or stretches** in order to facilitate project(s) implementation and provide immediate benefits;

d). Given financial constraints, **criteria** for project(s) selection will need to be established, including consideration of the subregional versus national character of the project and financial resources available.

TRADE AND SERVICES SECTOR

Most of the countries trade more often with countries outside the subregion than within.

However, trade and investment **within the subregion** are being **development steadily** owing to the growing openness and revitalization of the economies, and the favorable legal and regulatory framework for local and foreign investors.

The countries in the subregion have many **commun problems** (such as severe infrastructure shortage) and also commun goals (such as outward-oriented economy and promotion of the participation of private sector). All countries recognize that the attraction of foreign investor **depend to a great extend** on the trade and investment environment.

The cooperation aiming at improving the Trade and Investment Climate in the Subregion would enable investors to consider their own strategies in the **subregional context** which is more attractive than the national context. Projects and initiatives emerged from the Third Conference on the Economic Cooperation in the Greater Mekong Subregion includes :

(a) Two Projects aiming at Facilitating and Enhancing Trade Flows
(b) Three Projects aiming at Improving Investment Climates
(c) Two Projects on Building a Strong Science and Technology Base
(d) One Project aiming at Increasing the Role of Private Sector

STRATEGIC BUSINESS AND INVESTMENT OPPORTUNITIES

20 MILLION ENVIRONMENT & SOCIAL PROGRAM

1. The proposed USD20 million loan project for Lao's Environment and Social program project is expected to be approved by the Asian Development Bank's (ADB) Board on **December 6, 2001**. This cable is intended to:

-- Alert Embassies and AID missions to ADB-financed projects, and

-- Provide U.S. businesses with as much lead time as possible concerning procurement and consulting opportunities.

-- For more information on this project or ADB lending opportunities, firms should contact Ms. Chantale Wong, Alternate U.S. Executive Director, Asian Development Bank at phone no. (63-2) 632-6051, and fax no. (63-2) 632-4003 or Mr. Stewart Ballard, The U.S. Commercial Liaison Office for the ADB at telephone nos.: (63-2) 887-1345 to 46 and fax no. (63-2) 887-1164. For in-country inquiry, please contact Mr. Scott Rolston, Commercial Officer, American Embassy, Vientiane; Tel.: (856-21) 212-581; Fax: 212-584.

2. For post, USADB requests AmEmbassy and AID mission views on the Project before **December 06, 2001** based on currently available information.

A. PROJECT RATIONALE:
- Lao People's Democratic Republic (Lao PDR) is a small landlocked country, characterized by its mountainous terrain, low population density, limited skilled human resources, and a wealth of natural resources and environmental assets. As natural resources underpin economic development and poverty reduction prospects) the Government attaches priority to conserving the environment and ensuring the environmental and social sustainability of all development activities.

- Improving environmental management and social safeguards performance has been the subject of considerable policy dialogue and technical assistance. Enactment of the Environment Protection Law (EPL) in 1999 was a breakthrough. Together with environmental provisions in laws on electricity, roads, land, water resources, and forests, the EPL provides a framework for implementing safeguards. However, effective enforcement requires the adoption of enabling regulations, compliance mechanisms, and measures to enhance Government capacity and financial sustainability. Without this, the integration of environmental management and social safeguard issues across sectors will remain elusive.

- The Government aims to go beyond case-by-case remedial action on environment and social impacts towards a pro-active approach that integrates these concerns within national, sectoral, and area-based planning. The Government has sought Asian Development Bank (ADB) assistance to develop and implement a program aimed at shifting the country onto a more sustainable development trajectory, focusing initially on the energy and transport sectors. This will require five closely related sets of constraints to be addressed: (i) incomplete policy and regulatory framework; (ii) lack of implementation capacity at sectoral and provincial levels; (iii) inadequate compliance and enforcement mechanisms; (iv) absence of integrated area-based planning frameworks to guide investments in energy and transport; and (v) insufficient attention to sustainable finance for environment management.

B. PROJECT OBJECTIVES:
- The objective is to support the Government's policy reform agenda for improved environmental management and social safeguards in the energy and transport sectors. The scope covers five closely linked priority areas for policy action: (i) strengthening national policy and regulatory framework for environment management and social safeguards; (ii) enhancing policy implementation measures and capacity at sectoral and provincial levels; (iii) improving compliance and enforcement; (iv) promoting river basin management as a multi-sectoral and integrated planning framework for energy and transport development; and (v) establishing sustainable financing mechanisms, including an environment fund.

C. PROJECT DESCRIPTION:
- The Environment and Social Program (the Program) will assist the Lao PDR implement a targeted policy reform agenda for environmental management and social safeguards in the energy and transport sectors, focusing on hydropower and roads, with a proposed program loan of USD20.0 million.

D. EXECUTING AGENCY:
- The Science, Technology and Environment Agency (STEA) will be the Executing Agency for the Program, in close coordination with the Committee for Planning and Cooperation (CPC), Ministry of Finance (MOF), Ministry of Communication, Transport, Post and Construction (MCTPC), Ministry of Industry and Handicrafts (MIH), and Ministry of Agriculture and Forestry (MAF). STEA will have overall responsibility for ensuring effective implementation of the Program. MOF will monitor the use of loan proceeds and counterpart funds.

E. TOTAL PROJECT COST: USD20.0 million

F. PROGRAM PERIOD AND TRANCHING:
- The Program period will be 36 months (FY2002- FY2004). The proposed loan is to be disbursed in three tranches. The first tranche of USD5.0 million will be made available upon loan effectiveness, while the second tranche of USD10.0 million will be disbursed within 14 months after the first tranche, subject to the Government's compliance with the conditions set for the release of that tranche. A third tranche of USD5.0 million will be made available when the Government establishes a proposed environment fund during the 36 months of loan utilization.

G. PROCUREMENT:
- The proceeds of the loan will finance the full foreign exchange costs, excluding local duties and taxes, of imports procured in and from ADB's member countries, other than those specified in the list of ineligible items and those financed by other multilateral and bilateral official sources. Procurement of eligible items

under ADB's loan will be based on normal commercial practices for procurement by the private sector or standard Government procurement procedures acceptable to ADB for procurement by the public sector. In the case of goods commonly traded on international commodity markets, procurement will be done in accordance with procedures appropriate to the trade and acceptable to ADB.

H. COUNTERPART FUNDS:
- The Government will use counterpart funds generated by the loan to (i) finance additional public investment costs in transport and power projects to ensure strengthened social and environment safeguards; (ii) build institutional capacity to plan, design, and enforce environment and social safeguards; (iii) provide local counterpart resources for development projects aimed at river basin planning and management; (iv) address mitigation costs of existing infrastructure where social and environment costs were not adequately addressed; and (v) establish an environment fund.

I. CONSULTING SERVICES:
- No consulting services are required under the Program.

J. PROJECT BENEFITS:
- Program benefits include: (i) reducing the environmental and social costs of projects developed with inappropriate safeguards; (ii) increasing equity and resource use efficiency by internalizing social and environmental considerations in sector development; (iii) reducing the costs associated with "fixing" environmental and social problems resulting from inadequate regulatory framework and weak enforcement of safeguards; (iv) attracting increased commercial investment in infrastructure development; and (v) ensuring more sustainable and less risky project designs that better reflect local concerns, needs, and opportunities.

- The Program will also contribute to the country's poverty reduction goals. Improved environmental management will help maintain and enhance the livelihood base of the rural poor. Land use planning and watershed management will improve prospects for sustainable use of natural resources. Road transport developed, conceived within an area based planning framework, will directly benefit isolated communities through improved market linkages and access to services. Over the medium term, it is expected that revenues from hydropower projects will also allow the government to increase the share of public expenditure allocated to health, education and social development. Introduction of social safeguards in infrastructure development will ensure that vulnerable groups are not impoverished or marginalized by adverse impacts.

PREPARATORY TECH ASSISTANCE PROJECTS

This report alerts U.S. firms to US$3.6 million in new, potential national procurement of consulting services under the Asian Development Bank's (ADB) technical assistance (TA) grant programs. Opportunities are reported for Azerbaijan, India, Laos, Maldives, and Pakistan. In 2000, U.S. firms, including many small consulting firms, succeeded in winning USD 57 million ADB-funded national technical assistance contracts out of a total

For additional analytical, business and investment opportunities information,
please contact Global Investment & Business Center, USA
at (703) 370-8082. Fax: (703) 370-8083. E-mail: ibpusa3@gmail.com
Global Business and Investment Info Databank - www.ibpus.com

ADB-financed consulting budget of USD 348 million.

The ADB selects a consultant for a TA grant based on its prior Expression of Interest (EOI). An EOI can be transmitted on-line through the ADB's website (www.adb.org); afterward it will be acknowledged automatically. Firms may opt to send a hardcopy follow-up EOI addressed to Mr. S. Thuraisingham, Manager, Consulting Services Division, with a copy to the ADB Project Officer. The EOI should relate a firm's experience and expertise to the ADB project. It is important for a U.S. firm to emphasize its similar project experience in the country or in a similar geographic area rather than presenting a general profile of its consulting activities. A separate EOI should be submitted for each project. The project name indicated in the EOI should exactly match that listed in the ADB Business Opportunities publication to avoid confusion.

To be considered for employment, consultants must register on the ADB's DACON (Data on Consulting Firms) and DICON (Data on Individual Consultants) Systems, otherwise, their EOIs will not be accepted. DACON and DICON registration can now be done on-line at www.adb.org/consulting.

Firms may also send a notification copy of their EOIs to the U.S. mailing address for the U.S. Commercial Liaison Office for the ADB, Attention: Stewart Ballard, Senior Commercial Officer, PSC 500 Box 33, FPO AP 96515-1000, or to the same office at its international mailing address: 25th Floor Ayala Life-FGU Center, 6811 Ayala Avenue, Makati City, Metro Manila, Philippines 1226; Phone: (63-2) 887-1345; Fax: (63-2) 887-1164; E-mail: manila.adb.office.box@mail.doc.gov. This office works closely with the Office of the U.S. Executive Director to the ADB to increase American awareness of, and participation in, the ADB's activities.

The projects listed in this cable are now being actively processed by the ADB. For more information on these projects, the name of the ADB project officer is indicated in the project brief. The U.S Commercial Liaison Office is ready to provide assistance to U.S. firms upon request. (Please see paragraph 4.)

The following TA projects will be listed for the first time in the January 2002 issue of the Asian Development Bank's (ADB) Business Opportunities (ADBBO). (Note: The ADBBO is also available on the ADB's website <http://www.adb.org>.

NAME OF PROJECT: GMS: Northern Economic Corridor
Project No.: LAO34231-01
Executing Agency: Ministry of Communication, Transport, Post and Construction, Lanexang Avenue, Vientiane, Lao PDR
Fax: 856-21-414132
Tel. No.: 856-21-412741
TA Amount: US$600.0 Thousand
Sector/Subsector: Transport and Communications/Roads and Road Transport

Objectives and Scope: The Project will help to improve access and potential market linkages of a remote area of the Lao PDR to two large and growing economies in the region. Two main objectives of this TA are (i) to assist the Government to update all project parameters of the pre-feasibility study for the existing road in the Lao PDR from

Houei Sai to Boten, and (ii) to prepare a pre-investment study to determine feasibility of developing a viable economic corridor. The TA will adopt a holistic approach to plan integrated development of the region. It will undertake surveys and hold stakeholder consultations with potential business leaders and private investors to identify projects and investment opportunities. The pre-investment study will also identify policy, institutional and human resource constraints and suggest an action plan to develop this region into a vibrant economic corridor.

Consulting Services: The TA is expected to commence in January 2002 and completed by December 2002 and will have duration of 12 months.

The TA will involve a total of 66 person-months of consulting services, divided between international (about 18 person-months) and domestic (about 48 person-months) consultants. The TA will be implemented with a multidisciplinary team of international and domestic consultants, headed by an economist as team leader with the main output related to update the cost estimates and providing overall supervision of the TA. Other expertise and skills required for the TA include engineers, environmental, social and resettlement experts, transport economist, business economist, and financial analyst. Familiarity with transport and communication sectors and region's economies, especially of the private sector operations will be essential.

Recruitment of Consultants: No action has yet been taken to recruit consultants.
Environmental Analysis: Required
Project Processing Stage:
SRC Completed: 3 Dec 2001
Project Officer: Rita Nangia (632-6801)
Transport and Communications Division West
In-country Commercial Officer: Scott Rolston, Commercial Officer, U.S. Embassy, Vientiane; E-mail: RolstoSL@state.gov.

NAME OF PROJECT: Northern and Central Water Supply and Sanitation Sector
Project No.: LAO34197-01
Executing Agency: Ministry of Communication, Transport, Post and Construction, Lane Xang Avenue, Vientiane
TA Amount: USD700.0 Thousand

Sector/Subsector: Social Infrastructure/Water Supply and Sanitation
Objectives and Scope: The ensuing Project will address the Government's highest priorities in the water supply sector and will help in its long-term vision of providing safe and convenient water supplies and sanitation facilities to 80 percent of all urban communities as contained in the Government's Sector Investment Plan. The Project will identify the demand for expanded urban water supply and sanitation services in the selected small urban communities, develop selection criteria for the participation of urban communities, develop strategies to strengthen the regulatory framework and build institutional capacity, and prepare new investment project covering a number of small urban communities in the Northern and Central regions.

Consulting Services: Consulting services yet to be determined.
Recruitment of Consultants: Requirements for consulting services to be completed during Fact-finding Mission.

Environmental Analysis: Not Required

Project Processing Stage:
Beginning of Fact-finding Mission: Jan 2002.
Project Officer: Keiichi Tamaki (632-6843)
Water Supply, Urban Development and Housing Division West
In-country Commercial Officer: Scott Rolston, Commercial Officer, U.S. Embassy,
Vientiane; E-mail: RolstoSL@state.gov.

U.S.$37 MILLION VIENTIANE URBAN INFRASTRUCTURE & SRV PROJ

. The proposed USD 37 million loan project for Laos' Vientiane Urban Infrastructure and
Services project is expected to be approved by the Asian Development Bank's (ADB)
Board on August 23, 2001. This report is intended to:

-- Alert Embassies and AID missions to ADB-financed projects, and

-- Provide U.S. businesses with as much lead time as possible concerning procurement
and consulting opportunities.

-- For more information on this project or ADB lending opportunities, firms should contact
Ms. Cinnamon Dornsife, U.S. Executive Director, Asian Development Bank at phone no.
(63-2) 632-6051 and fax no. (63-2) 632-4003 or Mr. Stewart Ballard, The U.S.
Commercial Liaison Office for the ADB at telephone nos.: (63-2) 887-1345 to 46 and fax
no. (63-2) 887-1164. For in-country inquiry, please contact Ms. Patricia Mahoney,
American Embassy, Vientiane; Tel.: (856) 21-212581; Fax: 856) 21-212584; e-mail:
mahoneypa@vientiwpoa.us-state.gov.

2. For post, USADB requests AmEmbassy and AID mission views on the Project before
August 23, 2001 based on currently available information.

A. BACKGROUND
- Current deficiencies in urban infrastructure and services in Vientiane impede economic
growth and undermine the quality of life of the urban residents. especially the poor.
Despite the recent investments in primary road and drainage networks, the poor
condition of secondary and tertiary infrastructure constrains the full potential of and
benefits from recent improvements to primary infrastructure and services. The
inadequate infrastructure and services at community level has a particularly adverse
impact on the lives of the poor, the majority of whom live in low-lying land, flooded for
most of the year. Sustained growth and the quality of life of the residents are further
constrained by the present urban institutional framework and nascent urban
management that are still evolving in the process of ongoing reforms for
decentralization. While considerable progress has been made toward a decentralized
form of urban governance and development of Vientiane Urban Development
Administration Authority (VUDAA) as a new entity responsible for urban management in
Vientiane, the extent of further reforms yet needed to fully achieve decentralized urban
governance requires extensive and long-term support. There is a need at this stage to
shift the focus of efforts to secondary and tertiary infrastructure and services to ensure
that environmental improvements are felt by all, especially the poor. Equally important is

For additional analytical, business and investment opportunities information,
please contact Global Investment & Business Center, USA
at (703) 370-8082. Fax: (703) 370-8083. E-mail: ibpusa3@gmail.com
Global Business and Investment Info Databank - www.ibpus.com

the further progress in the decentralization process and development of VUDAA with adequate management systems and skills and financial resources.

B. PROJECT OBJECTIVES

- The Project aims to improve the quality of life of the urban residents and especially the poor and enhance urban productivity and economic growth in Vientiane urban area. To this end, the Project has two specific objectives. One is to support decentralization and urban governance reforms and the process toward an autonomous, well-functioning, and self-sufficient urban local government that is capable of planning, managing, and financing urban development and providing services in a sustainable manner. The second is to target investments in infrastructure and services to maximize the utility of existing infrastructure by completing the remaining gaps and focussing on secondary and tertiary level infrastructure and services. The Project represents AD6's second investment in the Vientiane urban area, and builds on lessons learned from the experience of the first intervention, Vientiane Integrated Urban Development Project.

The scope of the Project includes (i) Part A: citywide urban infrastructure and services, comprising critical missing links of primary and secondary roads and drainage, efficiency improvements in solid waste management, traffic management and safety , and institutional infrastructure and maintenance improvements; {ii) Part B: village area improvements (VAI), adopting a demand-led and participatory approach, seeking as a prerequisite the willingness of villages to participate in and contribute to a portion of the cost of the improvements, and combining community infrastructure and services with community-level capacity building and awareness raising in environmental health, participatory local planning and community-based infrastructure development and service delivery; and (iii) Part C: a comprehensive capacity building program to support the accomplishment of the urban policy and institutional reform agenda, and enhance planning, operation and maintenance, revenue mobilization and financial management capabilities of VUDAA.

C. PROJECT DESCRIPTION

- The Project is designed to improve the urban environment in Vientiane and reinforce the Government's reforms for effective and responsive urban management. It combines physical infrastructure and service improvements with interventions for decentralized urban governance and extensive capacity building of VUDAA. Physical investments consist of improvements to drainage, roads, traffic management and safety, solid waste management, and sanitation. The Project incorporates a social strategy to ensure active participation of the urban communities in the implementation of the Project and effective targeting of the poor and vulnerable. The Project area covers a hundred urban villages with a population of about 162,000 residents within Vientiane that falls under the jurisdiction of VUDAA.

D. EXECUTING AGENCY

- Vientiane Prefecture (the Provincial Government of
- Vientiane City)
- Contact: Mr. Thongmy Phomvisay, President
- Fax: 856-21-212104

E. TOTAL PROJECT COST: USD 37.0 MILLION

- Foreign Exchange : USD 20.0 million
- Local Currency: USD 17.0 million

F. MEANS OF FINANCING
- Bank Loan: USD 25.0 million
- Government and Community: USD 7.6 million
- AFD Cofinancing: USD 4.4 million

G. PROCUREMENT
- Procurement will be carried out by VUDAA. All procurement will follow the ADB's Guidelines for Procurement. International competitive bidding (ICB) procedures will be used for major civil works contracts estimated to cost over USD 1.0 million and for supply contracts estimated to cost over USD 500.000. For civil works, with a value up to USD 1.0 million, local competitive bidding (LCB) procedures will be used. The package of work per village under VAI component is relatively small ranging from USD 30,000 to USD 100,000. The works are labor-intensive and do not require sophisticated technologies. Therefore, for the works, estimated to cost less than USD 50,000 and where the capacity of the community to undertake the works is adequate, community participation in procurement will be applied.

H. CONSULTING SERVICES
- The selection and engagement of consultants under the loan will be in accordance with ADB's Guidelines on the Use of Consultants and other arrangements satisfactory to ADS for engaging domestic consultants. A team of consultants with a total input of 270 person-months (76 international and 194 domestic) is required to assist PIMU in overall Project implementation management, detailed engineering design, construction supervision, demand-led village area improvements, and development of legal and financial reforms for decentralized governance. Additionally, services of domestic consultants are required to assist in community preparation and awareness program and construction supervision. A further 191 person-months of consultancy inputs, including 173 person-months (65 international and 108 local) for capacity building and 18 person-months (5 international and 13 local) for traffic management and safety components will also be provided under a parallel financing arrangement funded by AFD.

I. PROJECT BENEFITS

- The Project will benefit about 162,000 Vientiane urban residents, 18 percent of whom belong to low-income groups. The overall population will benefit from the Project directly or indirectly through upgrading of roads, improved traffic and safety conditions, and enhanced urban management capacities within VUDAA, leading to sustainable delivery of urban services. The Project will directly improve the living conditions of 81,000 residents of Vientiane through improved community infrastructure and services under VAI, a partially coincident 60,000 people through drainage improvements, and 50,000 people through improved solid waste collection and disposal. The Project will promote good governance through supporting decentralized urban governance and empowerment of village communities in local planning, project implementation, and operation and maintenance of urban infrastructure and services.

3. For U.S. businesses and consultants: The shorlisted consultants will receive a request for proposals, selection of and contract negotiation with the firm submitting the best technical proposal will be completed, and preparation of bid specifications and contract documents will begin.

- Potential equipment suppliers and contractors should maintain regular contact with the executing agency and its consultants so that they may act quickly when tenders or prequalification notices are issued. Procurement notices and prequalification announcements are also released by the U.S. Commercial Liaison Office for the ADB and the Commerce Business Daily. These are also published on http://www.adb.org.

NEW ADB LOAN PROJECTS

. This report alerts U.S. firms to USD 101.2 million in new, potential national procurement of goods and services in Cambodia, Laos, and Nepal. These opportunities are an example of the many procurements financed by Asian Development Bank (ADB) loans to 33 ADB member developing countries. In 2000, U.S. contractors and equipment suppliers succeeded in winning USD 196 million in such national procurements as well as another USD 153 million in national consulting services financed by ADB loans.

This report notifies prospective U.S. exporters early on the current formal consideration of development projects by the ADB Board of Directors. Generally tender documents are issued 12-24 months later. Interested prospective U.S. contractors and equipment suppliers should contact the persons listed below to position themselves for future opportunities. U.S. consultants should contact the persons listed below and submit an Expression of Interest (EOI) to the national executing agency to market their firms' expertise and experience on similar past projects.

3. U.S. Consultants must also register with the ADB DACON (Data on Consulting Firms) system. DACON registration may now be completed on-line at <http://www.adb.org/consulting/dacon>. For loan projects, primary responsibility for hiring consultants rests with the executing agency in the borrowing country. A good way to facilitate contact with the executing agency is by working with the appropriate U.S. Commercial Service officer listed below.

4. Firms may also send a notification copy of their EOIs to U.S. Commercial Liaison Office for the ADB, Attention: Stewart Ballard, Senior Commercial Officer, PSC 500 Box 33, FPO AP 96515-1000, or to the same office at its international mailing address: 25th Floor Ayala Life-FGU Center, 6811 Ayala Avenue, Makati City, Metro Manila, Philippines 1226; Phone: (63-2) 887-1345; Fax: (63-2) 887-1164; E-mail: manila.adb.office.box @mail.doc.gov. This office works closely with the Office of the U.S. Executive Director to the ADB to increase American awareness of, and participation in, the ADB's activities.

5. The projects listed in this cable are now being actively processed by the ADB. For more information on these projects, the name of the ADB project officer is indicated in the project brief. The U.S Commercial Liaison Office is ready to provide assistance to U.S. firms upon request. (Please see paragraph 4.)

6. The following loan projects will be listed for the first time in the August 2001 issue of the Asian Development Bank's (ADB) Business Opportunities (ADBBO). (Note: The

ADBBO is also available on the ADB's website <http://www.adb.org>.

7. LOAN PROJECTS FOR CAMBODIA, LAOS, AND NEPAL

A. CAMBODIA
NAME OF PROJECT: Rural Development
Project No.: CAM34207-01
Executing Agency: Ministry of Rural Development
Contact: His Excellency Ngy Chanphal, Undersecretary
Fax: 855-23366-790
Loan Amount: USD 25.0 Million
Sector/Subsector: Agriculture and Natural Resources/ Irrigation and Rural
Development

Objectives and Scope: The project will target poor, rural populations in selected rural
areas where significant number of soldiers will be demobilized and will settle in host
communities. Activities in support of area development would include rural infrastructure
(rural roads, water supply, village-level social infrastructure), facilitating provision of
social services (rural finance, skill training, microenterprise development) through
existing provider programs, institutional strengthening and capacity building.

Procurement:
Goods: To be determined.
Services: To be determined.

Environmental Category: B

Project Processing Stage:
Fact-Finding in Field: 2 Jul 2001
Project Officer: Alain Goffeau (632-6955)
Agriculture and Rural Development Division West
In-country Commercial Officer: Bruce Levine, Economic and Commercial Officer,
American Embassy Phnom Penh

LAOS
NAME OF PROJECT: Second Education Quality Improvement Project
Project No.: LAO31345-01
Executing Agency: Ministry of Education
Department of Planning and Cooperation
Vientianne
Contact: Dr. Sikhamtath Mitaray, Director
Fax: 856-21-216006
Tel. No.: 856-21-217927

Loan Amount: USD 20.0 Million

Sector/Subsector: Social Infrastructure/Education
Objectives and Scope: The Project will: (i) improve the relevance, quality and efficiency
of primary and secondary education, by providing teacher training programs, and by

For additional analytical, business and investment opportunities information,
please contact Global Investment & Business Center, USA
at (703) 370-8082. Fax: (703) 370-8083. E-mail: ibpusa3@gmail.com
Global Business and Investment Info Databank - www.ibpus.com

introducing measures to improve the professional status and development of teachers; (ii) expand access to and improve retention in primary schools in the poor, underserved areas, by constructing new complete and/or multigrade schools, and renovating existing schools; and (iii) strengthen the institutional capacity to manage education at the MOE, PES, DEB, village/community, and school levels.

Procurement:
Goods: None.
Services: To be determined.
Environmental Category: C
Project Processing Stage:
Appraisal Completed: 15 Jun 2001
Project Officer: Yasushi Hirosato (632-6949)
Education, Health and Population Division West
In-country Commercial Officer: Patricia Mahoney, Commercial Officer, American Embassy Vientiane

USD 1.55 MILLION ADB BUSINESS OPPORTUNITIES

1. This report alerts U.S. firms to USD 1.55 million new, potential national procurement of consulting services under the Asian Development Bank's (ADB) technical assistance (TA) grant programs. Opportunities are reported for Cook Islands, Laos, and Nepal. In 2000, U.S. firms, including many small consulting firms, succeeded in winning USD 57 million ADB-funded national technical assistance contracts out of a total ADB-financed consulting budget of USD 348 million.

2. The ADB selects a consultant for a TA grant based on its prior Expression of Interest (EOI). An EOI can be transmitted on-line through the ADB's website (www.adb.org); afterward it will be acknowledged automatically. Firms may opt to send a hardcopy follow-up EOI addressed to Mr. S. Thuraisingham, Manager, Consulting Services Division, with a copy to the ADB Project Officer. The EOI should relate a firm's experience and expertise to the ADB project. It is important for a U.S. firm to emphasize its similar project experience in the country or in a similar geographic area rather than presenting a general profile of its consulting activities. A separate EOI should be submitted for each project. The project name indicated in the EOI should exactly match that listed in the ADB Business Opportunities publication to avoid confusion.

3. Although not required for employment, consultants should register on the ADB's DACON (Data on Consulting Firms) and DICON (Data on Individual Consultants)
Systems, otherwise, their EOIs will not be accepted. DACON and DICON registration can now be done on-line at www.adb.org/consulting.

4. Firms may also send a notification copy of their EOIs to the U.S. mailing address for the U.S. Commercial Liaison Office for the ADB, Attention: Stewart Ballard, Senior Commercial Officer, PSC 500 Box 33, FPO AP 96515-1000, or to the same office at its international mailing address: 25th Floor Ayala Life-FGU Center, 6811 Ayala Avenue, Makati City, Metro Manila, Philippines 1226; Phone:

(63-2) 887-1345; Fax: (63-2) 887-1164; E-mail: manila.adb.office.box @mail.doc.gov. This office works closely with the Office of the U.S. Executive Director to the ADB to increase American awareness of, and participation in, the ADB's activities.

5. The projects listed in this cable are now being actively processed by the ADB. For more information on these projects, the name of the ADB project officer is indicated in the project brief. The U.S Commercial Liaison Office is ready to provide assistance to U.S. firms upon request. (Please see paragraph 4.)

6. The following TA projects will be listed for the first time in the July 2001 issue of the Asian Development Bank's (ADB) Business Opportunities (ADBBO). (Note: The ADBBO is also available on the ADB's website http://www.adb.org.

7. PROJECT PREPARATION TECHNICAL ASSISTANCE
FOR COOK ISLANDS, LAOS, AND NEPAL

COOK ISLANDS
NAME OF PROJECT: Outer Islands Development
Project No.: COO29645-01
Executing Agency: Ministry of Finance and Economic
Management
TA Amount: USD 250.0 Thousand
Sector: Others
Objectives and Scope: To prepare a project to help accelerate outer islands development.
Procurement: About 10 person-months of international consultants and 10 person-months of domestic consultants.
Status of Consulting Services: No action has yet been taken to recruit consultants.
Environmental Analysis: Not Required
Project Processing Stage: Beginning of Fact-finding Mission: Sep 2001.
Project Officer: Michel D. Latendresse (632-6129)
Pacific Operations Division
In-country Commercial Officer: c/o AmConsul Auckland

LAOS
NAME OF PROJECT: Northern Community-Managed Irrigation Sector Project
Project No.: LAO34188-01
Executing Agency: Department of Irrigation
Vientiane, Lao PDR
Contact: Mr. Phuovieng Latdavong,
Permanent Secretary
TA Amount: USD 700.0 Thousand

Sector/Subsector: Agriculture and Natural Resources/ Irrigation and Rural Development
Objectives and Scope: The objective of the TA is to prepare a follow-on sector investment project which will address the poverty reduction, environmental protection and gender issues through the development of community-managed irrigation (CMI)

schemes in selected northern provinces. CMI development demonstrated the effectiveness to increase the yields of rice and other value crops and to reduce the shifting cultivation under the ongoing Project (ADB's Community-Managed Irrigation Sector Project: Loan No. 1488-LAO). The TA will comprise the following major activities: (i) review relevant water sector policies; (ii) review the lessons learnt from ongoing Projects; (iii) undertake institutional capacity analyses of organizations; (iv) determine the northern provinces to be included in the proposed project by taking into consideration the stakeholders' demand, Government's strategy, implementation capacity, etc.; (v) review and upgrade the completed appraisal studies on sample subprojects; (vi) conduct a social and environmental assessment of sample subprojects with particular emphasis on poverty reduction and environmental protection; (vii) analyze the cost effectiveness and financial sustainability; and (viii) develop a sector investment package and necessary supporting mechanism for sustainable and affordable CMI considering all above. The investment package may have sustainability of CMI schemes in the following components: (i) community mobilization and training; (ii) development of community-managed irrigation schemes; and (iii) institutional support for CMI development.

Procurement: The TA work will be carried out by a team of experts from an international consulting firm in association with domestic consultants.
Other details of consulting services to be required will be determined during the fact-finding mission. Procurement of one service vehicle will be proposed to facilitate the work of the consultants.
Status of Consulting Services: No action has been taken to recruit consultants.
Environmental Analysis: Required
Project Processing Stage:
Fact-Finding in Field: 11 Jun 2001
Project Officer: Toshio Kondo (632-6779)
Forestry and Natural Resources Division West
In-country Commercial Officer: Patricia Mahoney, Commercial Officer, AmEmbassy Vientiane

NEPAL
NAME OF PROJECT: Third Irrigation Sector
Project No.: NEP33209-01
Executing Agency: Department of Irrigation, Kathmandu
Jawalakjel, Lalitpur
Fax: 977-1-537169
E-mail: doi@jwlk.mos.com.np
TA Amount: USD 600.0 Thousand

Sector/Subsector: Agriculture and Natural Resources/ Irrigation and Rural Development
Objectives and Scope: Farmer-managed irrigation schemes are a major focus of the Government's irrigation strategy. This PPTA will prepare a sector project to cover about 300 small farmer-managed irrigation schemes covering about 40,000 ha for as many households.

Main components of the project will include water users' associations mobilization and training, construction and rehabilitation of irrigation schemes, provision of vehicles and equipment to the executing agency, staff training and capacity building for both the Department of Irrigation and Agriculture. The TA will develop specific intervention package including measures for improving sector policy, plan, and institutions through (i) water sector policy and institutions/review; (ii) assessment of ongoing Second Irrigation Sector Project; and (iii) feasibility study of sample subprojects.

Procurement: A total of about 45 person-months (pms) of consulting services' inputs : (i) 15 pms of international consultants including water resource institutional specialist (Team Leader); water resource engineer; resource economist; agronomist; environmental and social specialists; and (ii) 30 pms of water resource planner (Deputy Team Leader); water resource institutional specialist; agronomist; agricultural economist; environmental, social and poverty specialists.

Status of Consulting Services: No action has yet been taken to recruit consultants.

Environmental Analysis: Required
Project Processing Stage:
Beginning of Fact-finding Mission: Jul 2001.
Project Officer: Kenichi Yokoyama (632-6937)
Forestry and Natural Resources Division West
In-country Commercial Officer: John Dyson, Political/Economic Officer, AmEmbassy Kathmandu

PRIMARY HEALTH CARE EXPANSION PROJECT

The proposed loan grant application for Lao for the Primary Health Care Expansion Project is expected to come to the ADB Board in about five weeks. This cable is intended to:
Alert Embassies and AID missions to upcoming ADB-financed projects, and
Provide U.S. businesses with as much lead-time as possible concerning procurement and consulting opportunities. For more information on this project of ADB lending opportunities, firms should contact Ms. Cinnamon Dornsife, U.S. Executive Director, Asian Development Bank at phone no. (63 2) 632 6051 and fax no. (63 2) 632 4003 or Mr. Alex Severens, The U.S. Commercial Liaison Office to the ADB. For in-country inquiry, please contact Ms. Trish Mulhoney of AmEmbassy Vientiane at telephone nos.: (856 21) 212581, 212582, 212585 and fax no.: 212584.

2. For Post: USADB requests AmEmbassy and AID Mission views on the said Project on or before August 20 based on currently available information.

Background: With a per capita income of $283 and half of the population living in poverty, Lao PDR is one of the poorest countries in the Asia and Pacific Region. The rural poor, in particular women and children, ethnic minorities and other vulnerable groups living in the inaccessible northern hills suffer from extremely poor health. Life expectancy of only 51 years is the lowest in the region. Most sickness and deaths are from common communicable diseases such as malaria, acute respiratory infections, diarrhea and measles, most of which are preventable or easily curable. Maternal and infant mortality and fertility are among the highest in the region, yet maternal and child health and family planning services are not readily available. The existing network of health facilities has inadequate coverage and mainly provides a limited range of curative services of often sub-standard quality. Much as half of the rural population does not have access to preventive and promotive services and first referral care, in particular in the northern hills.

The Government, as a cornerstone of its social policy, accords high priority to the improvement of the health status of the population. Primary health care (PHC) has been identified as the most cost-effective approach to provide basic health services. The Government recently approved a PHC policy that aims to make a basic package of health care available to the entire population, and restructured Ministry of Health (MOH) in support of PHC. The Government has requested Asian Development Bank (ADB) to support expansion and improvement of PHC delivery, strengthen PHC planning and management, and develop an effective financial mechanisms. The Project is specially designed to improve the health status of women and children, ethnic minorities and the rural poor.

Project Objectives: The Project will contribute to the Government's goals of improving the health status and reduce poverty of the population of Lao PDR. The Project will improve PHC for the rural poor by (i) expanding and improving the quality of PHC in the northern region, and (ii) strengthening the institutional capacity of PHC.

The Project will target women and children, ethnic minorities and the rural poor by (i) increasing their physical, social and financial access to essential services, (ii) focusing on interventions and diseases that affect them disproportionally, and (ii)improving the quality of services for these groups. The Project will give priority to cost-effective interventions benefiting women and children including health promotion, reproductive health care, prevention and treatment of common infections and micronutrient deficiencies, and first referral services.

Component 1 will develop PHC in the northern provinces by (i) increasing access to PHC at health center and village levels; (ii) improving the quality of PHC including training of ethnic minority staff, (iii) strengthening maternal and child health and family planning services, and (iv) supporting village health care and promotion.

Component 2 will strengthen the institutional capacity for PHC nationwide by (i) strengthening PHC coordination; (ii) standardizing management systems; (iii) supporting staff development and training for PHC management; and (iv) testing innovating financing approaches.

Project Description: The Project will develop primary health care (PHC) in the eight northern provinces of Bokeo, Louang-Namtha, Phongsali, Houaphan, Louangphrabang, Xiangkhoang, Oudamxai, and Xaignabouri. It will improve access to and quality of essential preventive, promotive and curative health services at village, health center and district levels in 34 underdeveloped districts with a total population of 0.9 million, and improve referral services for 1.7 million people. It will also strengthen the institutional capacity of the MOH and all Provincial Health Offices to plan, manage, monitor and finance PHC.

Executing Agency:

Ministry of Health
PHC Extension Project
Contact: Dr. Prasongsidh Boupha, Project Director
Fax No.: (856 21) 223146
Tel.No.: (856 20) 518422

Total Project Cost: $25.0 million (Foreign Exchange: $8.4 million; Local Currency: $16.6 million)

Procurement: All ADB-financed procurement for the Project will be in accordance with ADB's Guidelines for Procurement. Related equipment and material will be combined into packages to simplify procurement. Supply contracts costing more than $500,000 equivalent or less will follow international shopping procedures, except for some equipment and supplies like hostel beds and furniture that are locally manufactured and unlikely to attract foreign suppliers. These will be procured through local competitive bidding in accordance with Government procedures acceptable to ADB. Packages of less than $100,000 may be procured on a direct purchase basis. Equipment and materials required at provincial level and costing less than $10,000 may be procured by the PIO according to Government procedures acceptable to ADB.

The Project includes construction of 41 health centers and seven hospitals and renovation or upgrading of six health centers and 17 hospitals. The health facilities are located in remote and scattered locations and are unlikely to attract international bidders. Civil works contracts will be awarded according to local competitive bidding procedures acceptable to ADB. However, if any package is estimated to cost $1.0 million or more, international competitive bidding procedures will be followed.

g.) All consultants financed under the loan will be selected and engaged in accordance with ADB Guidelines on the Use of Consultants and other procedures acceptable to ADB on the recruitment of domestic consultants. Six international and six domestic individual consultants and one domestic firms will be provided. The international consultants will include chief technical adviser (36 person-months), education and training specialist (6 person-months), management specialist (12 person-months), health sector financing specialist (6 person-months), procurement specialist (6 person-months), and architect (6 person-months). Domestic consultants will include education and training specialist (72 person-months), management specialist (72person-months), health sector financing specialist (72 person-months), accountant (72 person-months), procurement specialist (72 person-months), and architectural monitoring and evaluation specialist (72 person-months). A domestic firms will be contracted for five years for building design and construction supervision.

For US Businesses and Consultants: The loan is now at a point where, shortly after ADB Board approval, shortlisted consultants will receive a request for proposals, selection of and contract negotiation with the firm submitting the best technical proposal will be completed, and preparation of bid specifications and contract documents will begin.

Potential equipment supplies and contractors should maintain a regular contact with the executing agency and its consultant so that they may act quickly when tenders or prequalification notices are issued. Procurement notices and prequalification announcement are also released by the U.S. Commercial ADB Liaison Office and made available on the National Trade Data Bank (NTDB) and the Commerce Business Daily. These are also published on the Asian Development Bank's homepage, http//www.adb.org.

For additional analytical, business and investment opportunities information,
please contact Global Investment & Business Center, USA
at (703) 370-8082. Fax: (703) 370-8083. E-mail: ibpusa3@gmail.com
Global Business and Investment Info Databank - www.ibpus.com

IMPORTANT LAWS AND REGULATIONS AFFECTING BUSINESS AND TAXATION

LAW ON THE PROMOTION AND MANAGEMENT OF FOREIGN INVESTMENT IN LAO PDR2

SECTION ONE: GENERAL PROVISIONS

Article I : The Government of the Lao People's Democratic Republic encourages foreign persons, either individuals or legal entities, to invest capital in the Lao People's Democratic Republic (hereinafter "the Lao PDR") on the basis of mutual benefit and observance of the laws and regulations of the Lao PDR. Such persons hereinafter shall be referred to as "foreign investors ".

Article 2 : Foreign investors may invest in and operate enterprises in all fields of lawful economic activity such as agriculture and forestry, manufacturing, energy,, mineral extraction, handicrafts, communications and transport. construction, tourism trade, services and others.

Foreign investors may not invest in or operate enterprises which are detrimental to national security, the natural environment, public health or the national culture, or which violate the laws and regulations of the Lao PDR.

Article 3 : The property, and investments in the Lao PDR of foreign investors shall be fully- protected by the laws and regulations of the Lao PDR. Such property and the investment may not be requisitioned. confiscated or nationalized except for a public purpose and upon payment of prompt, adequate and effective compensation.

SECTION TWO: FORMS OF FOREIGN INVESTMENT

Article 4 : Foreign investors may invest in the Lao PDR in either of two forms:

(1) A Joint Venture with one or more domestic Lao investors-; or
(2) A Wholly Foreign-Owned Enterprise.

Article 5 : A Joint Venture is a foreign investment established and registered under the laws and regulations of the Lao PDR which is jointly owned and operated by one or more foreign investors and by one or more domestic Lao investors.

The organization, management and activities of the Joint Venture and the relationship between its parties shall be governed by the contract between its parties and the Joint Venture's Articles of Association, in accordance with the laws and regulations of the Lao PDR.

---

[2] National Assembly No. 01/94

Article 6 : Foreign investors Who invest in a Joint Venture must contribute a minimum portion of thirty percent (30%) of the total equity investment in that Venture. The contribution of the Venture's foreign party or parties shall be converted in accordance with the laws and regulations of the Lao PDR into Lao currency at the exchange rate then prevailing on the date of the equity payment(s), as quoted by the Bank of the Lao PDR.

Article 7 : A wholly Foreign-Owned Enterprise is a foreign investment registered under the laws and regulations of the Lao PDR by one or more foreign investors without the participation of domestic Lao investors. The Enterprise established in the LAO PDR may be either a new company or a branch or representative office of a foreign company.

Article 8 : A foreign investment which is a Lao branch or representative office of a foreign company shall have Articles of Association which shall be consistent with the laws and regulations of the Lao PDR and subject to the approval of the Foreign Investment Management Committee of the Lao PDR.

u The incorporation and registration of a foreign investment shall be in conformity with the Enterprise Decree of the Lao PDR.

SECTION THREE: BENEFITS, RIGHTS AND OBLIGATIONS OF FOREIGN INVESTORS

Article 10 : The Government of the Lao PDR shall protect foreign investments and the property of foreign investors in accordance with the laws and regulations of the Lao PDR. Foreign investors may lease land within the Lao PDR and transfer their leasehold interests; and they may own improvements on land and other moveable property and transfer those ownership interests.

Foreign investors shall be free to operate their enterprises within the limits of the laws and regulations of the Lao PDR. The Government shall not interfere in the business management of those enterprises.

Article 11 : Foreign investors shall give priority to Lao citizens in recruiting and hiring their employees. However, such enterprises have the right to employ skilled and expert foreign personnel when necessary and with the approval of the competent authority of the Government of the Lao PDR.

Foreign investors have an obligation to upgrade the skills of their Lao employees , through such techniques as training within the Lao PDR or abroad.

u The Government of the Lao PDR shall facilitate the entry into, travel within, stay within, and exit from Lao territory of foreign investors, their foreign personnel, and the immediate family members of those investors and those personnel. All such persons are subject to and must obey the laws and regulations of the Lao PDR while they are on Lao territory.

Foreign investors and their foreign personnel working within the Lao PDR shall pay to the Lao government personal income tax at a flat rate of ten percent (10 %) of their income earned in the Lao PDR.

Article 13 : Foreign investors shall open accounts both in Lao currency and in foreign convertible currency with a Lao bank or foreign bank established in the Lao PDR.

Article 14 : In the management of their enterprises, foreign investors shall utilize the national system of financial accounting of the Lao PDR. Their accounts shall be subject to periodic audit by the Government's financial authorities in conformity with the applicable Lao accounting regulations.

Article 15 : In conformity with the law and regulations governing the management of foreign exchange and precious metals, foreign investors may repatriate earnings and capital from their foreign investments to their own home countries or to third countries through a Lao bank or foreign bank established in the Lao PDR at the exchange rate prevailing on the date of repatriation. as quoted by the Bank of the Lao PDR.

Foreign personnel of foreign investments may also repatriate their earnings, after payment of Lao personal income taxes and all other taxes due.

Article 16 : Foreign investments subject to this law shall pay a Lao PDR'. annual profit tax at a uniform flat rate of twenty percent (20%), calculated in accordance with the provisions of the applicable laws and regulations of the Lao PDR.

Other Lao taxes, duties and fees shall be payable in accordance with the applicable laws and regulations of the Lao PDR.

For foreign investments involving natural resources exploitation and energy generation, sector-specific taxes and royalties shall be prescribed in project agreements entered into between the investors and the Lao Government.

Article 17 : Foreign investments shall pay a Lao PDR import duty on equipment, means of production, spare parts and other materials used in the operation of their investment projects or in their productive enterprises at a uniform flat rate of one percent (1%) of their imported value. Raw materials and intermediate components imported for the purpose of processing and then re-exported shall be exempt from such import duties. All exported finished products shall also be exempted from export duties.

Raw materials and intermediate components imported for the purpose of achieving import substitution shall be eligible for special duty reductions in accordance with the Government's applicable incentive policies.

Article 18 : In highly exceptional cases and by specific decision of the Government of the Lao PDR, foreign investors may be granted special privileges and benefits which may possibly include a reduction in or exemption from the profit-tax rate prescribed by Article 16 and/or a reduction in or exemption from the import-duty rate prescribed by Article 17, because of the large size of their investments and the significant positive impact which those investments are expected to have upon the socioeconomic development of the Lao PDR.

In the event of the establishment of one or more Free Zones or Investment Promotion Zones. the Government shall issue area-specific or general regulations or resolutions.

Article 19 : After payment of its annual profit tax, a foreign investor shall devote a portion of its profit each year to various reserve funds necessary for the operation and development of the enterprise in order to continuously improve the enterprise's efficiency, in accordance with the policy and the Articles of Association of the enterprise.

Article 20 : Foreign investments approved under this law shall at all times be operated in accordance with the laws and regulations of the Lao PDR . In particular, foreign investors shall take all measures necessary and appropriate to ensure that their investments' facilities, factories and activities protect the natural environment and the health and safety of the workers and the public at large, and that their investments contribute to the social insurance and welfare programs for their workers in conformity with the policy and the laws and regulations of the Lao PDR.

Article 21 : In the event of disputes between foreign parties within a foreign investment, or between foreign investors and Lao parties , the disputants should first seek to settle their differences through consultation or mediation.

In the event that they fail to resolve the matter , they shall then submit their dispute to the economic arbitration authority of the Lao PDR or to any other mechanism for dispute resolution of the Lao PDR, a foreign country or an appropriate international organization which the disputants can agree upon.

SECTION FOUR: THE ORGANIZATION OF FOREIGN INVESTMENT MANAGEMENT

Article 22 : The Government of the Lao PDR has established a State organization to promote and to manage foreign investment within the Lao PDR titled the Foreign Investment Management Committee (hereinafter called "the FIMC").

The FIMC is responsible for administration of this law and for the protection and promotion of foreign investment within the Lao PDR.

Article 23 : All foreign investments established within the Lao PDR shall be assisted, licensed and monitored through the "1-stop-service " of the FIMC, acting as the central focal point for all Government interactions with the investors, with the collaboration of the concerned ministries and the relevant provincial authorities.

Article 24 : A foreign investment shall be considered to be legally established within the Lao PDR only upon the investment's receipt of a written foreign investment license granted by the FIMC.

Article 25 : A foreign investor which seeks a license for a foreign investment shall submit to the FIMC an application and such supporting documentation as the FIMC may prescribe by regulation.

The FIMC may grant preliminary approval-in-principle for investment projects being specially promoted by the Government.

Article 26 : Upon receipt of a completed application and supporting documentation, the FIMC shall screen them, take a foreign-investment licensing. decision and notify the applicant of that decision within 60 days of the application's submission date.

Within this same overall 60-day period, concerned ministries and provincial authorities consulted by the FIMC for their views shall have a maximum of 20 days in which to reply.

Article 27 : Within 90 days of receiving its foreign investment license from the FIMC. a foreign investor shall register that license and commerce operation of its investment in conformity with the implementation schedule contained in the investment's feasibility study and with the terms and conditions of the license granted by FIMC, and in accordance with the laws and regulations of the Lao PDR.

Article 28 : The FIMC has responsibility to coordinate with other concerned ministries and provincial authorities in monitoring and enforcing the implementation of a foreign investment in conformity with the investment's feasibility study and with the terms and conditions of the investment license, and in accordance with the laws and regulations of the Lao PDR.

The concerned ministries and provincial authorities have the responsibility to perform their respective monitoring and enforcement obligations.

Article 29 : If a foreign investor violates the agreement and the terms and conditions of its foreign investment license or the laws and regulations of the Lao PDR, the investor shall be notified of the detected violation and shall be instructed to promptly desist. In the event the investor fails to desist or in case of a serious violation, the investor's foreign investment license may be suspended or revoked and the investor may additionally be subject to other sanctions under the applicable laws and regulations of the Lao PDR.

SECTION FIVE: FINAL PROVISIONS

Article 30 : This law shall come into force 60 days after its ratification.

Upon the entry into force of the present law, the foreign investment law of the Lao people's Democratic Republic No. 07/PSA dated 19 April 1988 shall cease to have effect, without prejudice to the rights and privileges granted to, and the obligations imposed upon, foreign investments under the law.No. 07/PSA.

Notwithstanding this provision, a foreign investor which received its license tender the prior law may elect to petition the FIMC in writing, within 120 days of the coming into force of this law, to become subject to the terms of this law. The FIMC may grant such petitions at its discretion. For a foreign investor whose petition is granted, the rights and benefits previously granted. and the obligations previously imposed under the law No. 07/PSA shall thereafter prospectively cease to have effect .

Article 31 : The Government of the Lao PDR shall, by decree, issue detailed regulations for the implementation of this law.

LAW ON THE PROMOTION AND MANAGEMENT OF FOREIGN INVESTMENT IN THE LAO PEOPLE'S DEMOCRATIC REPUBLIC

SECTION: GENERAL PROVISIONS

Article 1: The Government of the Lao people's Democratic Republic encourages foreign persons, either individuals or legal entities, to invest capital in the Lao People's Democratic Republic (hereinafter "the Lao PDR") on the basis of mutual benefit and observance of the laws and regulations of the Lao PDR. Such persons hereinafter shall be referred to as "foreign investors".

Article 2: Foreign investors may invest in and operate enterprises in all fields of lawful economic activity such as agriculture and forestry, manufacturing, energy, mineral extraction, handicrafts, communications and transport, construction, tourism, trade, services and others.

Foreign investors may not invest in or operate enterprises which are detrimental to national security, the natural environment, public health or the national culture, or which violate the laws and regulations of the Lao PDR.

Article 3: The property and investments in the Lao. PDR of Foreign investors shall be fully protected by the laws and regulations of the Lao PDR. Such property and investments may not be requisitioned, confiscated or nationalized except for a public purpose and upon payment of prompt, adequate and effective compensation.

SECTION TWO: FORMS OF FOREIGN INVESTMENT

Article 4: Foreign investors may invest in the Lao PDR in either of two forms:

1. A Joint Venture with one or more domestic Lao investors or (2) A Wholly Foreign-Owned Enterprise.
2. A Wholly Foreign-Owned Enterprise.

Article 5: A Joint Venture is a foreign investment established and registered under the laws and regulations of the Lao PDR which is jointly owned and operated by one or more foreign investors and by one or more domestic Lao investors.

The organization management and activities of the Joint Venture and the relationship between its parties shall be governed by the contract between its parties and the Joint Venture's Articles of Association, in accordance with the laws and regulations of the Lao PDR.

Article 6: Foreign investors who invest in a Joint Venture must contribute a minimum portion of thirty percent (30%) of the total equity investment in that Venture. The contribution of the Venture's foreign party or parties shall be converted in accordance with the laws and regulation of the Lao PDR into Lao currency at the exchange rate then prevailing on the date of the equity payment(s), as quoted by the Bank of the Lao PDR

Article 7: A wholly Foreign-Owned Enterprise is a foreign investment registered under the laws and regulations of the Lao PDR by one or more foreign investors without the participation of domestic Lao investors. The Enterprise established in the Lao PDR may be either a new company or a branch or representative of5ce of a foreign company.

Article 8: A foreign investment which is a Lao branch or representative office of a foreign company shall have Articles of Association which shall be consistent with the laws and regulations of the Lao PDR and subject to the approval of the Foreign investment Management Committee of the Lao PDR.

Article 9: The incorporation and registration of a foreign investment shall be in conformity with the Enterprise Decree of the Lao PDR.

SECTION THREE: BENEFITS, RIGHTS AND OBLIGATIONS OF FOREIGN INVESTORS

Article 10: The Government of the Lao PDR shall protect foreign investments and the property of foreign investors in accordance with the laws and regulations of the Lao PDR. Foreign investors may lease land within the Lao PDR and transfer their leasehold interests; and they may own improvements on land and other moveable property and transfer those ownership interests.

Foreign investors shall be free to operate their enterprises within the limits of the laws and regulations of the Lao PDR. The Government shall not interfere in the business management of those enterprises.

Article 11: Foreign investors shall give priority to Lao citizens in recruiting and hiring their employees. However, such enterprises have the right to employ skilled and expert foreign personnel when necessary and with the approval of the competent authority of the Government of the Lao PDR.

Foreign investors have an obligation to upgrade the skills of their Lao employees, through such techniques as training within the Lao PDR or abroad.

For additional analytical, business and investment opportunities information, please contact Global Investment & Business Center, USA at (703) 370-8082. Fax: (703) 370-8083. E-mail: ibpusa3@gmail.com Global Business and Investment Info Databank - www.ibpus.com

Article 12: The Government of the Lao PDR shall facilitate the entry into, travel within, stay within, and exit from Lao territory of foreign investors, their foreign personnel, and the immediate family members of those investors an those personnel. All such persons are subject to and must obey the laws and regulations of the Lao PDR while they are on Lao territory.

Foreign investors and their foreign personnel working within the Lao PDR shall pay to the Lao government personal income tax at a flat rate of ten percent (10%) of their income earned in the Lao PDR.

Article 13: Foreign investors shall open accounts both in Lao currency and in foreign convertible currency with a Lao bank or foreign bank established in the Lao PDR.

Article 14: In the management of their enterprises, foreign investors shall utilize the national system of financial accounting of the Lao PDR. Their accounts shall be subject to periodic audit by the Government's financial authorities in conformity with the applicable Lao accounting regulations.

Article 15: In conformity with the law and regulations governing the management of foreign exchange and precious metals, foreign investors may repatriate earnings and capital from their foreign investments to their own home countries or to third countries through a Lao bank or foreign bank established in the Lao PDR at the exchange rate prevailing on the date of repatriation, as quoted by the Bank of the Lao PDR.

Foreign personnel of foreign investments may also repatriate their earnings, after payment of Lao personal income taxes and all other taxes due.

Article 16: Foreign investments subject to this law shall pay a Lao PDR annual profit tax at e uniform flat rate of twenty percent (20%), calculated in accordance with the provisions of the applicable laws and regulations of the Lao PDR.

Other Lao taxes, duties and fees shall be payable in accordance with the applicable laws and regulations of the Lao PDR.

For foreign investments involving natural resources exploitation and energy generation, sector-specific taxes and royalties shall be prescribed in project agreements entered into between the investors and Lao Government.

Article 17: Foreign investments shall pay a Lao PDR import duty on equipment, means of production, spare parts and other materials used in the operation of their investment projects or in their productive enterprises as a uniform flat rate of one percent (1%) of their imported value. Raw materials and intermediate components imported for the purpose of processing and then re-exported shall be exempt from such import duties. All exported finished products shall also be exempted from export duties.

Raw materials and intermediate components imported for the purpose of achieving import substitution shall be eligible for special duty reductions in accordance with the Government's incentive policies.

Article 18: In highly exceptional cases and by specific decision of the Government of the Lao PDR, foreign investors may be granted special privileges and benefits which may possibly include a reduction in or exemption from the profit-tax rate prescribed by Article 16 and/or a reduction in or exemption from the import-duty rate prescribed by Article 17, because of the large size of their investments and the significant positive impact which those investments are expected to have upon the socio-economic development of the Lao PDR.

In the event of the establishment of one or more Free Zones or Investment Promotion Zones, the Government shall issue area-specific or general regulations or resolutions.

Article 19: After payment of its annual profit tax, a foreign investor shall devote a portion of its profit each year to various reserve funds necessary for the operation and development of the enterprise in order to continuously improve the enterprise's efficiency, in accordance with the policy and the Articles of Association of the enterprise.

Article 20: Foreign investments approved under this law shall at all times be operated in accordance with the laws and regulations of the Lao PDR. In particular, foreign investors shall take all measures necessary and appropriate to ensure that their investments facilities, factories and activities protect the natural environment and the health and safety of the workers and the public at large, and that their investments contribute to the social insurance and welfare programs for their workers in conformity with the policy and the laws and regulations of the Lao PDR.

Article 21: In the event of disputes between foreign parties within a foreign investment, or between foreign investors and Lao parties, the disputants should first seek to settle their differences through consultation or mediation.

In the event that they fail to resolve the matter, they shall then submit their dispute to the economic arbitration authority of the Lao PDR or to any other mechanism for dispute resolution of the Lao PDR, a foreign country or an appropriate international organization which the disputants can agree upon.

SECTION FOUR: THE ORGANIZATION OF FOREIGN INVESTMENT MANAGEMENT

Article 22: The Government of the Lao PDR has established a State organization to promote and to manage foreign investment within the Lao PDR titled the Foreign Investment Management Committee (hereinafter called "the FIMC").

The FIMC is responsible for administration of this law and for the protection and promotion of foreign investment within the Lao PDR.

Article 23: All foreign investments established within the Lao PDR shall be assisted, licensed and monitored through the "1-stop-service" of the FIMC, acting as the central focal point for all Government interactions with the investors, with the collaboration of the concerned ministries and the relevant provincial authorities.

Article 24: A foreign investment shall be considered to be legally established within the Lao PDR only upon the investment's receipt of a written foreign investment license granted by the FMC.

Article 25: A foreign investor which seeks a license for a foreign investment shall submit to the FMC an application and such supporting documentation as the FMC may prescribe by regulation.

The FMC may grant preliminary approval-in- principle for investment projects being specially promoted by the Government.

Article 26: Upon receipt of a completed application and supporting documentation, the FIMC shall screen them, take a foreign-investment licensing decision and notify the applicant of the decision within 60 days of the application's submission date.

Within the same overall 60-day period, concerned ministries and provincial authorities consulted by the FIMC for their views shall have a maximum of 20 days in which to reply.

Article 27: Within 90 days of receiving its foreign investment license from the FIMC, a foreign investors shall register that license and commence operation of its investment in conformity with the implementation schedule contained in the investment's feasibility study and with the terms and conditions of the license granted by the FIMC, and in accordance with the laws and regulations of the Lao PDR.

Article 28: The FIMC has responsibility to coordinate with other concerned ministries and provincial authorities in monitoring and enforcing the implementation of a foreign investment in conformity with the investment's feasibility study and with the terms and conditions of the investment license, and in accordance with the laws and regulations of the Lao PDR. he concerned ministries and provincial authorities have the responsibility to perform their respective monitoring and enforcement obligations.

Article 29: If a foreign investor violates the agreement and the terms and conditions of its foreign investment license or the laws and regulations of the Lao PDR, the investor shall be notified of the detected violation and shall be instructed to promptly desist. In the event the investor fails to desist or in case of a serious violation, the investor's foreign investment license may be suspended or revoked and the investor may additionally be subject to other sanctions under the applicable laws and regulations of the Lao PDR.

SECTION FIVE: FINAL PROVISIONS

Article 30: This law shall come into force 60 days after its ratification.

Upon the entry into force of the present law, the foreign investment law of the Lao People's Democratic Republic No. 07/PSA dated 19 April 1988 shall cease to have effect, without prejudice to the rights and privileges granted to, and the obligations imposed upon, foreign investments under the law No. 07/PSA

Notwithstanding this provision, a foreign investor which received its license under the prior law may elect to petition the FIMC in writing, within 120 days of the coming into force of this law, to become subject to the terms of this law. The FIMC may grant such petitions at its discretion. For a foreign investor whose petition is granted, the right and benefits previously granted, and the obligations previously imposed under the law No. 07/PSA shall thereafter prospectively cease to have effect.

Article 31: The Government of the Lao PDR shall, by decree, issue detailed regulations for the implementation of this law.

NOTIFICATION ON PROCEDURE FOR BUSINESS REGISTRATION IN LAO P D R.

- According to additional announcement No.0530/MOC,dated 10/May/2002 & No.0538/MOC,dated 13/May/2002.
 Ministry of Commerce, Domestic Trade Department (Business Registration Division) hereby notify the procedures for Business Registration and documents required for Enterprises.
* Business Registration takes place at 3 Levels

I. MINISTRY (CENTER) LEVEL.

The following are required registered at the Ministry :
1. Foreign investment whose registered capital is more than $ 200.000.
2. Enterprises engaged in import of Vehicles, Gas and export of wood products .
3 . State enterprises and state-owned joint venture enterprises who obtained licenses from the Ministry.

II. PROVINCES, CAPITAL AND SPECIAL ZONE LEVEL.

1. Foreign investors whose registered capital is less than $199,999.
2. Enterprises regulated by or have dealings with other main sectors such as:
-     Agriculture, Industry and Services .
3. Commercial :Enterprises engaged in export--import trade out side administered by the Ministry will be transferred to provinces.
4. All enterprises who have license from provincial governments.

III. DISTRICTS LEVEL.

Small business enterprises who opera out side from the Ministry and Provincial jurisdiction should register with the district office these are:
1. Branches .
2. Small shops.
3. Others

For additional analytical, business and investment opportunities information,
please contact Global Investment & Business Center, USA
at (703) 370-8082. Fax: (703) 370-8083. E-mail: ibpusa3@gmail.com
Global Business and Investment Info Databank - www.ibpus.com

DOCUMENTS TO BE COMPLETED BY FOREIGN INVESTORS

- License from Foreign Investment Management Committee (FIMC)
- Registration form .
- Copy of passport.
- 3 photos of size 3x4 inches .
- Letter of authority from the manager of company .

DOCUMENTS TO BE COMPLETED BY DOMESTIC INVESTORS AND ENTERPRISES OTHER THAN COMMERCE.

- License from the concerned sector.
- Registration form .
- Curriculum Vitae (CV)
- Certificate of Assets
- Criminal noted No 3, copy of ID card,3 photos of size 3x4 inches

DOCUMENTS TO BE COMPLETED BY DOMESTIC INVESTORS AND CONTROLLED BY COMMERCE SECTORS:

- Registration form from commerce
- Curriculum Vitae (CV)
- Certificate of finance
- Criminal noted No 3 , copy ID card, 3 photos of size 3x4 inches .
- Regulation confirmed by commerce sector.
- Economic evaluation.

Fees. See Minister of Finance additional announcement No. 0341/MF,dated 21/02/2002 .
Notes 1: If all documents are complete as required , registration will be completed in 24 hours.
Notes 2: This notification translated from additional announcement No.0530/MOC,dated 10/May/2002 & No.0538/MOC,dated 13/May/2002.

NOTIFICATION ON LIST OF GOODS SUBJECT TO IMPORT-EXPORT CONTROL AND PROHIBITION

- According to the Decree on the import-export management, No 205/PMO of 11 October 2006 .
- According to the Regulation on the Import-Export Licensing of Controlled goods, No 106/MOC.FTD dated 25/1/2002.
- According to Prime Minister Order on import-export facilitation and distribution of goods throughout country No. 24/PMO,dated 24/09/2004..
- According to the list of goods needed approval from related government agencies.

The Minister of Industry and Commerce issues the notification on the list of goods subject to import-export control and prohibition, as follows:

I. GOODS SUBJECT TO IMPORT-EXPORT PROHIBITION

Goods subject to import – export prohibition are dangerous and have a severe effect on national security, peace and public safety in order to protect the social/public order; the standard of living; national cultures and traditions; human, animal and plant life or health; national treasures of artistic, historic or archaeological value; architectural value; and national resource preservation; to comply with the United Nations treaties and national laws and regulations. The list of goods subject to import-export prohibition includes:

A. There are five categories of goods subject to import prohibition
1. Guns, bullets, all kinds of explosives, war weapons and war vehicles
2. Opium seeds, opium flowers, cannabis
3. Dangerous pesticide
4. Game Machines that lead to bad attitudes
5. Pornography and literatures that affect on cultures and national security

B. There are nine categories of goods subject to export prohibition
1. Guns, bullets, explosives, war weapons and war vehicles
2. Opium seeds, opium flowers, cannabis
3. Animals and animal products which are prohibited to export according to the law
4. Log, timber and Akar wood from the forest
5. All kinds of orchids from the forest and Dracaena Loureiri
6. All kinds of rattan
7. Bat manure
8. Antique objects; national treasures of historic or archaeological and cultural value and naturally national historic objects.
9. Old/antique Buddha and angel images; and religiously respectful objects

II. GOODS SUBJECT TO IMPORT-EXPORT APPROVAL OR CERTIFICATE

Goods subject to import-export approval or certificate means that those need to get approval or certification from related government agencies prior to the import – export in order to comply with the national laws and international treaties that Lao PDR is a party member; to ensure the safety of use; to inspect the quality and standards; and to prevent epidemic disease. The List of goods subject to import – export approval is:

A. There are 25 categories of goods subject to import approval or certificate

1. Live animal, fish and aquatic animals
2. Animal meat and other parts for human consumption; and products from animals and processed products from animal meat.
3. Milk products
4. Rice in the husk (paddy); rice
5. Cereals, products from vegetables, other processing for human consumption
6. Beverage, alcohol and orange juice
7. Food for animals
8. Cements, mortars and concretes
9. Fuel
10. Gas

11. Chemicals that are reacted to Ozone and products contained such chemical substances
12. Bio-chemical products
13. Pharmaceutical products, medicine for human and animal as well as medical equipment
14. Chemical fertilizer
15. Some types of cosmetic
16. Pesticide and toxic products for mouse and germs /microbes / bacteria
17. Sawn wood processed by sawmill company
18. Log and seedling
19. Textbooks and books
20. Rough diamonds
21. Silver and gold
22. Steel (long and round piece of steel and other shapes)
23. All kinds of vehicles and parts (except bicycles and tractors)
24. Game machine
25. Explosive substances

B. There are seven categories of goods subject to export approval or certificate

1. Live animal, fish and aquatic animals
2. Rice in the husk (paddy); rice
3. Resin and forestry products
4. Mining
5. Wood and wooden products
6. Rough diamond
7. Gold and silver

Ministry of Industry and Commerce will regularly improve the notification on the list of goods subject to import – export control and prohibition, where it is appropriate, in order to facilitate the business and to comply with the international treaties that Lao PDR is a party member.

This Notification replaces the notification on List of goods subject to import-export prohibition N. 0284/MOC.FTD date 17/6/2004 and the notification on List of goods subject to import-export approval from trade and other related government agencies.

NOTIFICATION LIST OF PROHIBITED GOODS FOR IMPORT AND EXPORT

- According to decree on export and import management no. 205/PMO, dated 11 October 2001;
- According to decree on export and import licensing with trade sectors for control goods, no. 106/MOC.FTD, dated 25 January 2002;
- According to notification on list of goods from related sectors.

Minister of Commerce issues the list of prohibited goods for import-export to notify the trade units, concerned organization and implementing as follow:

A. Prohibited goods for importation:

For additional analytical, business and investment opportunities information,
please contact Global Investment & Business Center, USA
at (703) 370-8082. Fax: (703) 370-8083. E-mail: ibpusa3@gmail.com
Global Business and Investment Info Databank - www.ibpus.com

1. Any kind of explosive, weapons and armament
2. Any kind of drug addict
3. Any kind of products affecting tradition of the nation
4. Industrial disposal and chemical product that dangerous for health and environment
5. Antiques
6. Food, medicine and prohibited doctor equipments from related sectors
7. Wild life, aquatic animals and their parts which are forbidden by domestic law and international subcontract that Lao PDR had signed.
8. All type of right hand side driving vehicles
9. Toys affecting children attitude, growth, safety and peace of the society
10. Literature work, nude publication and other that against Lao PDR
11. Second hand goods that government banned from import
12. Equipment for printing of bank note
13. Dangerous insecticides which prohibited by related sectors
14. All type of log, sawed timber (processed timber), wood and forestry product that banned according to internal regulation

B. List of export prohibition goods
1. Any kind of explosive, weapons and armament
2. Any kind of drug addict
3. Any kind of products affecting tradition of the nation
4. Wild life, aquatic animals and their parts which are forbidden by domestic law and international subcontract that Lao PDR had signed
5. All type of log, sawed timber (processed timber), all type of rattan and unprocessed eaglewood
6. Forestry product such as: Orchids, Ã€Â®Ã‰Â¨-Ã¬Â¾Â¨, Ã•-Â´Ã±-Â¨Â¾Â¤, Â¥Ã±-ÃƒÂ© and etc that prohibited according to internal law
7. Sulfur (bat manure)
8. Equipment for printing of bank note

List of prohibited goods for import and export is goods that badly damaged and dangerous to economic and social situation, politic, peace, safety and traditional of the country. All type of goods mentioned above are prohibited to import and export with an exception to Article 8 of decree numbers 205/PMO, dated 10/11/01 on export and import management. The detail of procedures and regulations are requested to follow the regulation numbers 106/MOC.FTD, dated 25/01/2002 on export and import licensing with trade sectors for control goods.

So this notification is prepared to notify organizations, related business units and be strictly implemented.

REGULATION ON THE IMPORT AND EXPORT LICENSING PROCEDURES OF CONTROLLED GOODS FROM TRADE AUTHORITIES

- Pursuant to the Decree on the establishment and operation of the Ministry of Commerce and Tourism No. 24/PM, dated 24 March 1999

- Based on the Decree on import and export No. 205/PM, dated 11 October 2001

The Minister of Commerce sets out

CHAPTER I GENERAL PRINCIPLES

Article 1. Licensing

An import or export licensing is a measure to administer import and export of goods in the Lao PDR, with an aim:

-   To control the implementation conditions, criteria of the applicants for import or export activities;
-   To monitor the conditions and criteria of import or export applicants, and to collect statistics of controlled-good imports or exports;
-   To avoid a severe adverse impact on domestic production or national balance of payments;
-   To control the import or export of prohibited goods which are occasionally needed for import or export.

Article 2. Applicant

An applicant comprises of importer, exporter as specified in Article 9 and Article 10 of the Decree on Import and Export No. 205/PM, dated 11 October 2001.

Article 3. Goods subject to licensing

The goods subject to an import or export license are controlled goods by which the Minister of Commerce has specified the criteria for import or export. The importer or exporter must strictly follow every procedure and regulation in this Regulation and in the laws and regulations of relevant sectors.

The detail of goods items subject to import or export licensing will be announced later.

CHAPTER II LICENSING PROCEDURES

Article 4. Licensing authority

Importer or exporter who wishes to import or export goods subject to control is required to submit an application with trade authorities as follows:

-   Prohibited goods: approval from the Ministry of Commerce with a permission from the Prime Minister;
-   Some controlled goods: approval from the Ministry of Commerce;
-   Other controlled goods: approval from trade services in provinces, Vientiane municipality, and special zones.

Article 5. Licensing procedures

A license needs to be acquired prior to the import or export where accompanying documents include:

-   Business registration and tax certification;
-   Application form;
-   Buying or selling contract;
-   Technical certification from relevant authorities.

Article 6. Licensing consideration

The consideration of licensing application shall be in time, simple, and transparent for importer or exporter who supplies all required documentation as specified in this regulation.

The delay of licensing process without justification or unjustified reasons is considered in breach of this regulation and penalties shall be applied case by case.

Article 7. Time validity of a license

How long a license is valid depends on types of imports or exports. Related authorities specified in Article 4 of this regulation shall determine the time validity of licensing.

CHAPTER III PENALTIES

Article 8. Breach of licensing regulation

An importer or export who does not adhere to this regulation shall not have the right to import or export.

Article 9. Fraud, claim and other breaches

Any act related to fraud, claim, and other breaches to acquire a licensing shall be penalized according to seriousness or is subject civil penalty.

CHAPTER IV FINAL PROVISIONS

The Foreign Trade Department acts as a focal point to coordinate with related authorities, including trade services in the provinces, Vientiane Municipality and special zones, to implement in detail and for effectiveness of this regulation. The list of additional or reducing imports or exports subject to licensing shall also be provided to the Ministry of Commerce in subsequent notification.

Article 11. Enforcement

This regulation shall be into force from its date of signatory. Any other provisions and regulations inconsistent with this regulation shall be nullified.

DECREE ON IMPORT AND EXPORT MANAGEMENT

- Based on the Law on the Government of the Lao PDR No. 01/95 dated 8 March 1995,
- Based on the Business Law No. 03/94/NA dated 18 July 1994,
- Based on the Decree on the Customs Law No. 04/94 dated 18 July 1994,
- Based on the proposal of the Minister of Trade No. 1165/MCT dated 9 October 2001,
- Based on the Decision of the Government Meeting in November 2001,

The Prime Minister of the Lao PDR has decreed:

SECTION I: GENERAL PROVISIONS

ARTICLE 1:   FUNCTION OF THE DECREE

This decree has the function of stipulating management regulations on exports and imports in accordance with the laws, focused on production and export promotion, reasonable import control, promotion of international trade, improving living standards of people and active contribution to the national socio-economy.

ARTICLE 2: DEFINITION

"Export" means exports of goods from the Lao PDR to other country.
"Import" means imports of goods from other country to the Lao PDR.

ARTICLE 3: BASIC PRINCIPLE OF ORGANIZATION AND OPERATION

Any organization and operation of import and export within the Lao PDR shall be conducted strictly in accordance with this decree and other related laws and regulations.

SECTION II: GOODS CONTROL, CONTROLLED GOODS ON IMPORT AND EXPORT

Article 4: Goods Control

The government of the Lao PDR encourages export and import of all goods except those goods which are under state control specified in this decree or other related laws or regulations.

According to this decree, control on import or export of a certain goods means the implementation of measures on these goods as necessary to maintain the economic and social stability, to preserve the national culture and tradition, and to protect other benefits of the state and society.

Application of import control is to protect the domestic production and consumer, to prevent price speculation in the country, and to maintain equilibrium of imports and exports.

Application of export control is needed to prevent the shortage of goods and to accumulate stocks within the country to ensure the export of some goods according to the international agreements that the Lao PDR is a party.

Article 5: Measures of control

Import and export control may be conducted through the following measures:

- Prohibit import or export;
- Require import or export application;
- Demand documentation such as bill of origin and quality certificate of the imported or exported goods based on the agreement or traditional procedure of the international trade.
- Forbid or restrict import or export of some goods;
- Issue specific conditions for the business license;
- Charge import or export fees;
- Stipulate certain quality including amount, packing, type, kind, size, weight, price, trade name or brand, country of origin and export or import country,

For additional analytical, business and investment opportunities information,
please contact Global Investment & Business Center, USA
at (703) 370-8082. Fax: (703) 370-8083. E-mail: ibpusa3@gmail.com
Global Business and Investment Info Databank - www.ibpus.com

- Apply other necessary measures on import and export such as equilibrium plan, customs and tax policy, organize related group or association.

The measures of control specified in this article, which may be in conflict with the laws and regulations of the international trade systems that the Lao PDR is committed to or is member of, will be cancelled.

Article 6: Controlled Goods

Controlled Goods are those one which the measures are applied on import â€" export control as indicated in the article of this decree.

The list of controlled goods may be changed as necessary.

The Ministry of Commerce shall stipulate, cancel and apply the list and measures on controlled goods periodically, except those goods controlled by other sectors or being covered by other measures.

ARTICLE 7: CONTROLLED GOODS UNDER OTHER SECTORS

Goods under control of other sectors are those under the direct management of the related sectors. Importer and exporter of those goods shall conduct business according to measures issued by the related sectors.

The goods mentioned in paragraph 1 above and controlled measures on them shall be stipulated and issued as necessary by the related sectors. Then the list of these goods shall be reported officially to the Ministry of Commerce to add to the list of goods under the state control.

The Ministry of Commerce shall announce this list to business entity and related sectors.

Article 8: Permission Needed Goods

Goods that need to be permitted before import or export comprise forbidden goods and some controlled goods.

The Ministry of Commerce shall issue approval and lay down regulations on application procedures. The Ministry of Commerce has to coordinate with the related sectors and each approval shall be agreed by the Prime Minister.

SECTION III: IMPORTER AND EXPORTER

ARTICLE 9: IMPORTER

Importer includes individual or juristic entity who has registered as a business according to this decree. Imported goods of these business entities are for sale within the Lao PDR.

Individual or juristic entity who has been registered with a business license may import some goods according to the related laws and regulation to serve their specific purpose as indicated in article 18 of this decree.

ARTICLE 10: EXPORTER

Individual or juristic entity who hold a business license may operate the export business.

Article 11: Importer or Exporter of Goods (for Self Consumption)

Importers or exporters of goods (for self consumption) are individual or organizations who have been authorized temporarily to bring in or out some goods for noncommercial purposes.

SECTION III: ESTABLISHMENT AND OPERATION OF THE EXPORT AND IMPORT BUSINESS

ARTICLE 12: ESTABLISHMENT OF THE IMPORT COMPANY

Individual or juridic entities who want to set up a import company as indicated in the first paragraph of Article 9 above shall apply to the Commercial Section for establishment and business registration and to the Financial Section for tax registration.

ARTICLE 13: ESTABLISHMENT OF THE EXPORT COMPANY

All business entities registered with a business license as indicated in Article 10 above can operate an export business.

Those who do not have a business license as specified in the first paragraph above, but want to operate an export business, shall apply for establishment as indicated in Article 12.

ARTICLE 14: BUSINESS ORGANIZATION

The organization of the import or export company may be set up in accordance with the type and form as indicated in the Business Law.

ARTICLE 15: REGISTERED CAPITAL

Registered Capital to set up an export or import business shall be undertaken as indicated in the Business Law, except for export or import of some commodities, for which the laws and regulations specify for a higher Registered Capital.

ARTICLE 16: APPROVED GOODS ON THE LICENSE

Individual or juridic entity shall submit the goods list along with the application for a import business license. The applied list may consist of one or many goods according to its capacity.

For additional analytical, business and investment opportunities information,
please contact Global Investment & Business Center, USA
at (703) 370-8082. Fax: (703) 370-8083. E-mail: ibpusa3@gmail.com
Global Business and Investment Info Databank - www.ibpus.com

Individual or juridic entity received the import license according to the first paragraph above may trade in export of any kind of goods, except those goods controlled by the state which require the export license, those forbidden by the state and others specified in the laws.

The list of approved goods shall be shown on the import license of importer who is dealing with specific goods, as specified in the second paragraph of Article 9.

The Ministry of Commerce shall indicate goods that require an export license.

ARTICLE 17: CONSEQUENCE FROM NON-OPERATION

A business license of the import or export business entity, which is not operative for one year after approval, will be cancelled , except when a reasonable reason has been reported to the Commercial Section before the end of the one year limit.

SECTION V: IMPORTATION

ARTICLE 18: IMPORT BY THE IMPORT COMPANY

Import by the import company shall be conducted in accordance with the following:

- import according to the goods list specified on the import license;
- holding of a sell-buy contract

ARTICLE 19: SPECIFIC PURPOSE IMPORT

Specific purpose importer has the rights to import equipment, machinery and raw materials which will be used directly in production or business based on plan adopted by the related sectors.

Article 20: Import Procedure

Import company or specific purpose importer who has complied with the conditions specified in this decree can submit the import document directly to the related office at the border station to bring in the goods.

Article 21: Import of goods (for self consumption)

Authorized import (for self consumption) shall be conducted in accordance with the list, limit, type and amount of goods indicated in the customs law.

SECTION VI: EXPORTATION

ARTICLE 22: EXPORT BY THE EXPORT COMPANY

Export by the export company shall be accompanied by the sell-buy contract with the foreign counterpart.

For export of controlled goods, the company shall abide by the specific regulations on each controlled goods.

Article 23: Export Procedure

Exporters as indicated in Article 10 of this decree can submit export documents directly to the related office at the border station to bring out the goods.

Article 24: Export for self consumption

Authorized export for self consumption shall be conducted in accordance with the Customs Law.

SECTION VII: SANCTIONS

Article 25: Individual or juristic entity who breach the regulations on controlled goods, in addition to the withdrawal the license, shall be fined and be subject to legal proceedings.

ARTICLE 26: OTHER VIOLATIONS

Any violation of the importer, exporter and government officer such as falsifying documents or misuse of the position shall be punish according to the law.

SECTION VIII: FINAL PROVISION

ARTICLE 27: IMPLEMENTATION

The Prime Minister Office, the Ministry of Commerce, the Ministry of Finance, Ministries, comparable organizations, provinces, municipality and special zone shall implement this decree throughout the country.

ARTICLE 28: EFFECTIVENESS

This decree takes effect from its signature date. All promulgated decrees and regulations in conflict with this decree are herewith abrogated.

DECREE ON GOODS TRADING BUSINESS

- Based on the law on the Government of the Lao PDR No. 01/95 dated 8 March 1995,
- Based on the Business Law No. 03/94/NA dated 18 July 1994,
- Based on the Tax Law No. 04/95/NA dated 14 October 1995,
- Based on the proposal of the Minister of Trade No. 1165/MTT dated 9 October 2001,
- Based on the decision of the Government Meeting dated 25 December 2000.

The Prime Minister of the Lao PDR has decreed:

SECTION I: GENERAL PROVISIONS

ARTICLE 1: FUNCTION OF THE DECREE

This decree has the function of setting up management regulations on domestic goods trading business in accordance with the law, focused on sufficient goods circulation, promotion of goods production, price and exchange rate stabilization, improving living standard of people and active contribution to the national socio-economic development.

ARTICLE 2: GOODS TRADING BUSINESS

Goods Trading Business means business on goods traffic within the country which covers the first sale of local produced goods or imported goods through the last sale to the consumer of both whole and retail sale.

The first sale is the first ownership transfer of goods from the domestic producer or the importer to a person or entity against money or other benefit.

Article 3: Basic Principle of Organization and Operation

Any organization and operation of Goods Trading Business shall be conducted strictly in accordance with this decree and other related laws.

Section II: Management of Conditional Goods

Article 4: Management on Distribution of Conditional Goods

The Government of the Lao PDR promotes the circulation of any commodity liberally in accordance with the law, except commodities, that the government stipulates conditions on distribution in this decree and other laws and regulations related.

Management on distribution of Conditional Goods is the stipulation for the trading business of a certain commodity according to its nature, specific, important, affect, risk or danger.

Article 5: Control Measures of Conditional Goods

Conditional Goods may be controlled by one of the following measures:
- Forbid or restrict business on trading of some goods as necessary;
- Stipulate Registered Capital higher than indicated in the Business Law;
- Require certain qualification of the director, manager, owner or staff;
- Set up standard, quality of goods, trading mark, accounting and other;
- Indicate part which will be permitted for business;
- Set up the price limits and the margins of stocks accumulation periodically.

The measure indicated for a certain conditional goods should not hinder the mentioned business, which can have a negative effect on supply, price, money and competition at reasonable level.

ARTICLE 6: CONDITIONAL GOODS

Conditional Goods are those controlled by the measures in the above Article 5. The list of Conditional Goods may be change as necessary.

For additional analytical, business and investment opportunities information, please contact Global Investment & Business Center, USA at (703) 370-8082. Fax: (703) 370-8083. E-mail: ibpusa3@gmail.com Global Business and Investment Info Databank - www.ibpus.com

Designate the Ministry of Commerce to set up or cancel the list of Conditional Goods and to issue detail management measures for each type of commodity periodically, except those commodities managed by other sector or being covered by other measures.

Article 7: Conditional Goods under other sectors

Conditional Goods under other sectors are those under the direct management of the related sectors. Traders of those goods shall conduct business according to measures issued by the related sectors.

The related sectors shall set up and issue the type and detailed management measures of Conditional Goods mentioned in paragraph 1 above as necessary, then report its list of Conditional Goods officially to the Ministry of Commerce to compile into the list of Conditional Goods of the state.

Assign the Ministry of Commerce to announce this list of business entity and related sectors.

Article 8: Forbidden Goods Trading

Trading of Forbidden Goods shall be permitted by the Ministry of Commerce based on the agreement of the Prime Minister.

In case the Forbidden Goods are under direct management of the related sectors, the Ministry of Commerce shall coordinate with the related sectors before making proposal to the Prime Minister.

SECTION III: FOUNDATION AND OPERATION OF GOODS TRADING BUSINESS

ARTICLE 9: FOUNDATION

Individual or juristic entities who want to set up a Goods Trading Business shall apply to the Commercial Section for foundation and business registration and to the Financial Section for tax registration.

ARTICLE 10: REGISTERED CAPITAL

Registered Capital to set up a Goods Trading Business shall be undertaken as indicated in the Business Law, except for trading of some commodities which the laws and regulations specify for a higher Register Capital.

Article 11: Approved goods on the license

Individual or juristic entity who want to set up a Goods Trading Business may apply for trading of one or many kinds of commodities.

Article 12: Business Organization

The organization of Goods Trading Business may be set up in accordance with the type and form as indicated in the Business Law.

Article 13: Business Activity

Individual or juristic entities who have been licensed for Goods Trading Business may chose the form of trading according to capacity, but have to conduct business in accordance with the related regulations of the selected form of trading.

Article 14: Consequence from Non-operation

A business License of the Goods Trading Business entity, which is not operative for one year after approval, will be cancelled, except in case a reasonable reason has been reported to the Commercial Section before the end of the one year limit.

SECTION IV: SANCTION

ARTICLE 15: VIOLATION OF THE REGULATIONS ON CONDITIONAL GOODS

Individual or juristic entities who breach the regulations on Conditional Goods, in addition to the withdrawal the license, shall be fined and be subject to legal proceedings.

ARTICLE 16: OTHER VIOLATIONS

Any violation of trader and government officer such as false documentation and misuse of position shall be punished according to the law.

SECTION V: FINAL PROVISION

Article 17: Implementation

The Prime Minister's Office, the Ministry of Commerce, the Ministry of Finance, Ministries comparable organizations, provinces, municipality and special zone shall implement this decree throughout the country.

Article 18: Effectiveness

This decree takes effect from its signature date. All promulgated decrees and regulations in conflict with this decree are herewith abrogated.

DECREE ON TRADE COMPETITION

Based upon the Law regarding the Government No. 02/NA, dated 8 May 2003; Based upon the Business Law No. 03194/NA, dated 18 July 1994;

Based upon the proposal of the Minister of Commerce, No. 0713 /MOC.ERIT, dated 18 July 2003,

**The Prime Minister issues
Decree:**

CHAPTER I GENERAL PROVISIONS

ARTICLE 1   OBJECTIVES

This Decree is issued to define rules, measures and enforcement to regulate monopolization and unfair competition in trade of all forms, aiming to promote fair trade competition, protect the rights and legal interests of consumers and to encourage business activities in the Lao PDR to function efficiently in the market economy mechanism as determined by the Government of the Lao PDR.

ARTICLE 2   DEFINITIONS

In this Decree:

- "acquisition" means the power in business management of one business entity by purchasing the property or buy all or part of the shares of another business entity;
- "business person" means a person who sells goods, buys goods for further processing and sale or buys goods for resale or is a service provider;
- "Commission" refers to the Trade Competition Commission;
- "consumer" means any buyer and/or user of goods and services purchased from a seller;
- "goods" refers to products designed for durable and non-durable consumption, including document certifying the ownership of these goods; "trade" means trade in goods and services;
- "market dominance" means sales volume or market share of any goods or services of one or more business entities is above that prescribed by the Trade Competition Commission;
- "merger" means two or more business entities coming together and forming into one business entity with the result the individual business entity will cease to exist;
- "monopoly" means the dominance of the market individually or in collusion with other businesses;
- "price" means price charged in the sale of goods and services;
- "service" means accepting to perform or performing services, giving for use or interest in goods or any activity for payment in return or other consideration, except wages;

Article 3   *Fundamental principle in competition*

Business activities of all sectors are equal under the law, they cooperate and compete with each other in a fair manner by in compliance with this Decree and concerned Laws and regulations.

ARTICLE 4   SCOPE OF APPLICATION

This Decree applies to the sale of goods and services in business activities.

CHAPTER 2 THE TRADE COMPETITION COMMISSION

ARTICLE 5   THE TRADE COMPETITION COMMISSION

The Trade Competition Commission shall consist of concerned parties of the trade sector and a number of relevantly experienced people.

The Minister of Trade, by virtue of his position, is the Chairman and appoints members of this Commission.

The Trade Competition Commission shall have its office and its permanent secretariat
within the Ministry of Commerce.

ARTICLES 6   RIGHTS AND DUTIES OF THE COMMISSION

The Fair Trading Commission has the rights and duties as follows:
- Determine rules on activities, rights and duties of the secretariat, and supervise the functioning of the secretariat;
- Formulate and stipulate further regulations in enforcing this Decree;
- Establish a sub-commission to implement a specific duty when necessary;

- Consider submissions and give approval for any business person as stipulated in Article 13 of this Decree;
- Determine and publish a list of parties and type of businesses as stipulated in Article 13 of this Decree;
- Call on concerned persons for consultations, advice or clarification on any matter;
- Monitor and control business activities and order any business entity to solve, change, suspend or stop its behavior that is unfair;
- Determine market share, and the total volume amount of a business which is found to be dominating the market;
- Determine market share or assets that are considered to dominate business management of another business entity;
- Consider complaints from business persons and consumers;
- Submit to the concerned organizations to take measures for those who breach;
- Coordinate with the media and concerned business entities to publicise various activities and issues on matter relating to competition;
- Implement any other duties and responsibilities as may assigned by the Government.

CHAPTER 3 COMPETITION IN TRADE

ARTICLE 7   PROMOTING A FAIR TRADE COMPETITION
The Government of the Lao PDR encourages business entities of all economic sectors to undertake businesses under competitive conditions with equality, fairness, and cooperation.

ARTICLE 8   ANTI-MONOPOLY
It is prohibited for a business person to perform any act stipulated in Articles 9, 10, 11 and 12 of this Decree so as to monopolize any market of goods and services.

ARTICLE 9   MERGER AND ACQUISITION
It is prohibited for a business person to monopolize the market in the form of a merger or acquisition that destroys competitors or substantially reduces or limits competition.

ARTICLE 10   ELIMINATION OF OTHER BUSINESS ENTITIES
It is prohibited for a business entity to act or behave so as to cause losses directly or indirectly, by such conduct as dumping, limiting or intervening with intent to eliminate other business entities.

ARTICLE 11   COLLUSION AND ARRANGEMENTS
It is prohibited for a business entity to collude or make arrangements to engage in unfair trade practices in any form, such as:
- Price fixing, and fixing the sale and purchase price of goods and services;
- Stocking goods, limiting, reducing the quantity or limiting the production, purchase, sale, distribution or import of goods and services;
- Colluding in tenders for purchase, sale and supply of goods and services;
- Fixing conditions that, directly or indirectly, force their customers to reduce production, purchase or sale of goods or the supply of services;

- Limiting the customer's choice to purchase, sell goods and receive services;
- Prohibiting their suppliers or retailers from purchasing or selling goods to other   business entities;
- Entering into allocation arrangements of markets, customers or suppliers restricting competition;
- Appoint, or give authority to an individual the for sole right to sell goods or supply services in one market;
- Arrangements to fix conditions or the manner of purchase and sale of goods or services to restrict other business entities;
- Other acts that are contrary to the trade competition regulations prescribed by the Trade Competition Commission.

Article 12   Cartel with foreign business persons

It is prohibited for any business entity to establish and operate a business in the Lao PDR that has business relations with a foreign business entity either by contract, share holding or other form to act to limit the opportunity of local businesses to choose to purchase from or sell goods or provide services directly to, a foreign business entity.

ARTICLE 13   EXEMPTION

Any act stipulated in Article 8, 9,10, 11 and 12 of this Decree may be exempted for some specific sector or business for socio-economic or security reasons.

The Trade Competition Commission is assigned to consider and provide exemptions from time to time.

CHAPTER 4 MEASURES AGAINST OFFENDERS

ARTICLE 14   MEASURES AGAINST BUSINESS ENTITIES WHO COMMIT OFFENCES

A business entity that commits offences under this Decree shall be dealt with as follows;
- Notice to change and rectify its behavior;
- Temporary suspension of activity until the behavior is rectified and changed;
- Close down indefinitely the activity and may be punished according to the law;
- Compensate a business entity that has incurred losses as a result of the offences.

Article 15   Other offences

All civil servants and authorities that commit offences under this Decree will be dealt according to the law.

CHAPTER 5 FINAL PROVISIONS

ARTICLE 16   IMPLEMENTATION

The Ministry of Commerce and the Trade Competition Commission are assigned to implement this Decree.

ARTICLE 17   ENFORCEMENT

This Decree is effective from August 1st, 2004.

All rules and regulations, which are contrary to this Decree, are superseded.

For additional analytical, business and investment opportunities information, please contact Global Investment & Business Center, USA at (703) 370-8082. Fax: (703) 370-8083. E-mail: ibpusa3@gmail.com Global Business and Investment Info Databank - www.ibpus.com

LAW ON LAND IN LAO PDR

NUMBER 05 / 1997

BRIEFING BY MR CHALEUN YIAPAOHEU, CHIEF OF CABINET OF THE NATIONAL ASSEMBLY, ON THE RESULTS OF THE 10TH ORDINARY SESSION OF THE NATIONAL ASSEMBLY (THIRD LEGISLATURE) TO MEMBERS OF DIPLOMATIC CORPS AND OF INTERNATIONAL ORGANIZATIONS IN THE LAO PEOPLE' S DEMOCRATIC REPUBLIC

VIENTIANE, 9 MAY 1997.

Distinguished members of diplomatic corps and international organizations in the Lao PDR,

Ladies and gentlemen,

Today I am extremely pleased and honoured to be entrusted by the President of the National Assembly to brief you, members of diplomatic corps and international organizations accredited to the Lao People's Democratic Republic, on the results of the Tenth Ordinary Session of the National Assembly (Third Legislature). May I take this opportunity to express my sincere thanks and appreciation to all of you for taking your valuable time to attend this briefing.

Distinguished guests,

As you know, the National Assembly held its Tenth Ordinary Session for the beginning of this year, from 28 March to 12 May 1997, and it was concluded with splendid success.

Since this is an Ordinary Session for the beginning of the year, as is normal practice, we did not invite foreign guests, members of diplomatic corps and international organizations accredited to Laos to attend the session. What we did previously was to hold only a press conference to inform our guests of the results of the National Assembly session. I hope you will forgive me for the delay in holding this press conference.

On this occasion, I would like to inform you of the following results:

I. WHAT WAS DISCUSSED AND ADOPTED AT THE TENTH ORDINARY SESSION OF THE NATIONAL ASSEMBLY (THIRD LEGISLATURE)?

This session discussed and adopted new laws and amended an existing law. At the same time, it discussed a number of domestic affairs of the National Assembly:

This session discussed and adopted the following new laws:

- Law on Land;
- Law on Mining;
- Law on Land Transportation; and

For additional analytical, business and investment opportunities information, please contact Global Investment & Business Center, USA at (703) 370-8082. Fax: (703) 370-8083. E-mail: ibpusa3@gmail.com Global Business and Investment Info Databank - www.ibpus.com

- Law on Electricity

Apart from adopting these four laws, the National Assembly discussed and adopted amendments to the Law on the Election of Members of the National Assembly.

The National Assembly assessed its activities over the past six months and set forth its plans for the last six months of 1997. The discussion concentrated on two main issues:

- striving to accomplish   the political tasks of the Third Legislature of the National Assembly, since this is the fifth final year of its term; and
- taking all round preparation for the election of members of the Fourth Legislature of the National Assembly in late 1997.

Generally speaking, this session passed four laws and adopted amendments to the Law on the Election of Members of the National Assembly. We took considerable time to deliberate and adopt the Law on Land because we consider this law a "mini constitution".

II. WHAT ARE THE BASIC CONTENTS OF THESE ADOPTED LAWS? A. LAW ON LAND.

Before the establishment of the Lao People's Democratic Republic, we thought that there would be no major problems in managing and using the land, because Laos has a large land mass and low population density. We therefore did not develop a detailed policy regarding the land.

After the foundation of the Lao People's Democratic Republic, particularly after the ten years of the renovation process, the Lao People's Revolutionary Party and the Government of Laos have ,clearly recognized, he importance of the land. issue, "considering · it a major issue directly involved the basic interest of the Lao people of all strata; it is the nation's precious natural resource, providing necessary conditions and a place to live for the, Lao people; it also serves as a basic means for the, social and economic development of the country".

Based on this consideration, our Party and Government consider the issue of land use and management of paramount importance. We have drawn experiences from various countries concerning the management and use of land and have taken them as our reference .for the management and use of. land in the entire country. :This is why we have set forth a policy and developed legal-documents regarding the management, and use of land. Before the adoption of this Land Law, our Government laid down a number of decrees, namely: Decree No 129/PM of 18 November, 1979 concerning the management of land and houses of people who fled the country and those who were sent for reeducation; .Decree No 22/PM of 21 March 1989 concerning the management and use of :land for agricultural development; and Decree No. 99/PM of 19 December 1992 concerning land.

These government decrees are important legal documents of the State for the management and use, of land which have contributed to national development, ,thus ensuring the fundamental rights and legitimate interests of the Lao people of all ethnic groups have been preserved.

In order to respond to the needs of the renovation process and as a result of implementation of these decrees,: ,in the past few years our government began to study and pr pose a draft Law on Land. for the National Assembly's consideration and adoption.

The National Assembly noted that the draft Law on Land was a new, and important law and considered it a fundamental characteristic of the economy equivalent to a "land . constitution". The National Assembly therefore took considerable time to study the contents of the draft law until it was improved to ensure that it guaranteed the rights and interests of people of all ethnic groups and that it conformed with the market economy mechanism as well as the ' development of regional and international economic cooperation. Taking all these aspects into account, the National Assembly discussed and adopted this law at this Ordinary Session.

The Law on Land contains six parts, fourteen chapters and eighty six articles. I would now like to brief you some of the concepts and basic principles of the Law on Land:

1. OWNERSHIP OF LAND

The law provides that "land is the property of the Lao national community". Why is land defined as "the property of the Lao national community"?

Land belongs to the national community because:

(1) Land within the sovereign right of the Lao People's Democratic Republic which includes the surface, underground, territorial waters and airspace is the result of the arduous and protracted struggle filled with great sacrifices of the Lao people of all ethnic groups from successive generations until the present.

(2) Land within the Lao People's Democratic Republic is the Lao nation's precious natural resource, providing places for living and generating income for the Lao people of all ethnic groups. The land is therefore considered the property of the Lao national community.

(3) Land within the Lao People's Democratic Republic serves as the fundamental means for the social and economic development of the nation.

(4) As land is defined as property of the Lao national community, in real terms it defines the rights to selfmastery of the country of the Lao people of all ethnic groups. The definition is correct and is in conformity with the reality of the situation in the country, with the history and the nation's traditions as well as the aspirations of our people.

2. MANAGEMENT OF LAND

The law provides that the "State represents the centralized and unified management of land in the entire country". The State here refers to the government, various sectors of the central organ and the local administrative authorities.

The State has the following rights of land management:
1. surveying and defining land;
2. land mapping;
3. measurement and valuation of land;
4. zoning of land area;
5. classification of land (including land reserved for the purposes of agriculture, forestry, residential, industrial, communication, cultural, national defense, security, water resources, and unused land);
6. establishing the Master Plan of Land;
7. setting a plan for land use;
8. inspecting and approving the plan for land use;
9. registration of land leases;
10. creating a register of lease documents;
11. transferring leases;
12. issuing land leasing documentation;
13. transferring, renting and leasing of land;
14. inspecting land sites; and
15. the withdrawal and reclamation of land.

The State authorizes the transfer of the right to use land to Lao citizens, families and various organizations for their long term use for living, generating income and conducting productive activities and businesses aimed at turning our natural subsistence economy into a market economy, transforming Laos into a prosperous and strong country as well as creating a life of affluence for the Lao people of all ethnic groups and bringing about justice and civilization to our society.

3. RIGHT TO USE LAND, AND OTHER RIGHTS AND INTERESTS.

The law provides that "the State guarantees the right to use and maintain an interest in land of people who have been authorized a long term use of land including the rights to use, to protect, to achieve gains, to transfer the right of land use and to inherit the land in conformity with the law of the country". However, each right needs to be covered further by detailed regulations and policy so as to implement this law effectively.

The general policy of our Party and Government is to encourage all Lao citizens, families and organizations to use land for their productive activities and businesses in accordance with their own conditions and capabilities, but they are not allowed to buy and sell the land.

The State will allocate the use of land by families and productive business organizations as well as other organizations according to their capabilities based on conditions and disadvantages concerning the land in each locality and region so as to appropriately define the land use rates.

The law provides opportunity for all Lao citizens to be allocated land as follows:
(1) for residential construction: not more than 800 square meters for each member of a

family;

(2) land for rice farming and fish raising: not more than 1 hectare for each labourer in a family;

(3) land for industrial plants: not more than 3 hectare for each labourer in a family;

(4) land for fruit tree plantation and other plants: not more than 3 hectare for each labourer in a family; and

(5) land for animal raising: not more than 15 hectares for each labourer in a family.

The allocation of land in different categories is based appropriately on conditions and the land use capability of each person and the land available in each locality and region.

4. RIGHT OF ALIENS STATELESS PERSONS AND FOREIGNERS WHO COME TO INVEST OR GENERATE INCOME IN THE LAO PDR.

The law provides that "the State will authorize aliens, stateless persons and foreigners to lease the land in the Lao People's Democratic Republic for the purpose of living, generating income, investing and operating businesses aimed at contributing to the social and economic development of the Lao People's Democratic Republic".

The average duration of leases mentioned above is not more than 30 years, but the term of the lease can be extended on a case-by-case basis:

- land leased for building residences: 30 years maximum with a possible extension
- land leased for investment and business activities, based on the scale of each project: 50 years maximum with a possible extension
- land leased as part of a specific economic zone: 75 years maximum
- land leased for diplomatic purposes and international organizations: 99 years maximum or as otherwise provided by agreements reached between the two governments.

5. MARKING LAND FOR OWNERSHIP AND THE PURCHASE AND SALE OF LAND.

The law sets forth certain measures regarding the prohibition of self-claiming land ownership and its purchase and sale: "all acts of illegal marking and buying and selling land done before or after the promulgation of the Constitution have been abolished ".

The inclusion of these preventive measures is aimed at abolishing the haphazard practice of self-claiming land ownership and the subsequent sale of land. It is also aimed at preventing the transfer of the right to land use for undeveloped land.

6. LAND WHICH WAS OFFERED BY REVOLUTIONARY ADMINISTRATIVE AUTHORITIES TO PEOPLE OF ALL ETHNIC GROUPS AND PRIVATE OR ORGANIZATIONS' LAND PRESENTED TO THE STATE FOR MANAGEMENT.

The law provides that land which was presented by revolutionary administrative authorities to the people of all ethnic groups for income generation and the construction of residences, before and after the establishment of the Lao People's Democratic

Republic, is legally binding. Previous owners of the land are prohibited from reclaiming the land.

Former private or organizational owners of land who gave their land to the administrative authorities or the State for management are not allowed to reclaim the land.

7. LAND BELONGING TO PEOPLE WHO LEFT THEIR ORIGINAL PLACES OR WHO FLED THE COUNTRY.

The law provides that people who left their original homeland during the time of the national democratic revolution and those who fled the country have lost their rights to use their former land. Former owners or their agents are prohibited from reclaiming the land.

The above are the major principles of the Law on Land. The law will come into force only after the State order has been promulgated by the President of the Republic and following the release of the Decree of the Prime Minister and other instructions as well as detailed regulations worked out by the various sectors concerned. The most important issue for now is to encourage people of all ethnic groups and organizations to become familiar with the contents of the law to bring the Law on Land into practice.

B. LAWS ON MINING LAND TRANSPORTATION ELECTRICITY.

The Law on Mining comprises eight chapters and sixty four articles. It establishes rules for mining businesses and sets regulations for undertaking both occupational and unoccupational mining activities. The maximum term for leasing land for mining purposes is 30 years.

The Law on Land Transportation comprises eight chapters and forty eight articles. The law aims to regulate the management of goods and their transportation both domestically and internationally; to enhance land transportation business activities; to set rules for specific transportation within domestic business networks or other specified activitiactivities; set regulations for private transports for specific any private works; and to set regulations for both internal and international transportation aimed at increasing international cooperation in land transportation.

The Law on Electricity comprises twelve chapters and fifty six articles. The law sets rules for the management of electricity-related activities and other energy resources for the purpose of national development, improving the living standards of our people and ensuring the preservation of our environment. The law defines which organizations have authority to approve different sized electricity projects:

- large-scale electricity projects are to be approved by the National Assembly
- medium-scale by the government
- small-scale by local administrative authorities and
- micro-scale by village administrative authorities.

The law also provides that the maximum term of a lease for land for hydropower development is 30 years which can be extended by the Government.

C. AMENDED LAW ON THE ELECTION OF MEMBERS OF THE NATIONAL ASSEMBLY.

The amended law has ten chapters and forty articles. The previous had eleven chapters and 37 articles.

The amendments aim to implement the Law on the Election of Members of the National Assembly, ensuring the development of rights and the democracy of Lao citizens in their voting and their rights to stand for election.

The fundamental principles of this law remain the same, such as the general principles, and the principles of equality, direct voting and a secret ballot.

The amendment deleted one of the previous chapters which dealt with the use of a budget in the election, added some new articles and merged repeated articles into a single one so as to make the law clearer.

All the issues I have raised reflect the position, contents and major principles of the new laws and amendment. I hope that my briefing will help you to understand the laws that have been adopted by our National Assembly.

Apart from the consideration and adoption of the laws mentioned above, our National Assembly has also expressed its high appreciation and sincere thanks for the support and assistance given by governments and peoples throughout the world and international organizations to the Lao People's Democratic Republic, thus making important contributions to the development of our country.

If you are interested in raising any questions which are not clear enough to you please feel free to do so.

Finally, on behalf of the National Assembly, I wish you all good health, long life and great success.

MINING LAW

of the LAO People's Democratic Republic

CHAPTER I GENERAL PROVISIONS

Article 1.(Purposes of the Mining Law)

The purpose of the Mining Law is to provide a system of management for the conservation, exploration, mining and processing of minerals, for both local consumption and for export, and for the use of mineral resources in industry and its processes and also to improve the quality of life for the people of Lao PDR.

Article 2. (Minerals)

Minerals are naturally occurring resources which exist in non-renewable chemical and physical forms of solids, liquids or gases, including but not limited to gold, silver, iron, precious stones, sand, gravel, construction materials, coal, oil and gas and other hydrocarbons, and geothermal waters.

Article 3. (Ownership of Mineral Resources)

All mineral resources that exist at the surface or under land or water, within the territory of Lao PDR, are the property of the national community and are subject to the centralized and unified management of the State.

Article 4: (The Promotion, Management and Development of Mineral Resources)

The State will follow a policy of promoting the efficient development and management of mineral resources by persons and entities, both foreign and domestic.

Article 5: (Environmental Protection)

Any person or entity licensed to develop mineral resources shall utilize procedures to limit adverse environmental impacts and to limit the destruction of natural resources.

Article 6: Protection of the Rights and Interest of the Mineral Business Operators and the Local Population

The State protects the interest of the mineral business operators and the local population in compliance with the Laws of the Lao PDR.

Article 7: Scope of the Law's Effectiveness

The Mining Law governs the management of mineral resources and all activities concerning exploitation of mineral resources, including but not limited to, basic geologic surveys of natural resources, prospecting, exploration, development, production and processing of minerals in Lao PDR, with the exception of oil and gas, which will be governed under separate laws.

CHAPTER II GENERAL GEOLOGIC SURVEYS AND MANAGEMENT OF MINERAL RESOURCES

Article 8:General Geological Surveys

General geological surveys are the process by which initial information on mineral outcrops and geologic structures are gathered for the purpose of preparing geologic maps.

The Ministry of Industry-Handicraft shall conduct nationwide general geological surveys in coordination with other concerned agencies and local administrative authorities as the need arises.

Article 9: Categories of Minerals

To promote the development of the minerals industry the Government has classified minerals in the following 4 categories:

1. Metallic Minerals;
2. Non-Metallic Minerals;
3. Hydrocarbons;
4. Geothermal Resources

Metallic Minerals include: Gold, silver, copper, zinc, iron, lead, tin and others

Non-metallic Minerals include: Diamonds, rubies, emeralds, limestone, gravel, sand, gypsum, industrial minerals and construction minerals

Hydrocarbon Minerals include: Coal, natural gas and petroleum

Geothermal Resources include: Geothermal waters

Article 10: Protected or Restricted Minerals

The Government shall issue from time to time, in the interest of maintaining efficient and sustainable use, a list of protected or restricted minerals which may not be exported, exported in raw form or imported.

Article 11: Record keeping and Disclosure of Mineral Resource Information

All persons and entities involved in mineral resource development activities shall keep adequate records and samples according to regulations governing record keeping.

All persons and entities involved in mineral resource development activities shall disclose data, information and samples which reflect mineral resources that have high value, are rare or have scientific significance. Persons and entities are forbidden to conceal, or to report false valuations for or sell or trade such samples. The State shall have the exclusive right to purchase samples which are rare, of scientific value, or high value.

The Government shall establish a list of the minerals and their details which will fall under this provision.

Article 12: Management of Mineral Resources

The Government entrusts the Ministry of Industry-Handicraft with the management and development of the nation's mineral resources, in coordination with concerned agencies, by outlining specific regulations.

CHAPTER III CLASSIFICATION OF MINERAL RESOURCE AREAS

Article 13: Mineral Resource Areas

Mineral resource areas refer to areas where general geological surveys have been conducted and where commercial mineral deposits have been targeted for further detailed investigation.

There are four classifications of mineral resource areas:

1. Mineral business licensed areas;
2. Reserved areas
3. Restricted areas
4. Toxic areas

Article 14: Mineral Concessions

Mineral concessions are areas determined by Government as areas where mineral operations may take place.

Article 15: Reserved Areas

Reserved areas are mineral resource areas reserved for the extraction of a specific mineral.

Article 16: Restricted areas

Restricted areas are mineral resource areas where mineral operations are forbidden, such as areas with cultural significance, protected forest areas, areas important for national defense and maintaining order and others.

Article 17: Toxic Areas

A toxic area is an area within a mineral resource area where there exists toxic substances or toxic minerals. Where a toxic area exists, the Ministry of Industry-Handicraft shall inform and cooperate with concerned agencies and the relevant local authorities to provide protection for the health and security of the people.

CHAPTER IV INVESTMENT IN MINERAL RESOURCES

Article 18: Mining Activities

Mining activities refer to activities including prospecting, exploration, extraction, processing and trading of minerals.

Mining activities may take place in the following forms:

1. Mechanized commercial mining operations;
2. Professional artisanal activities; and
3. Part-time artisanal activities.

Article 19: Mines

Mines are natural mineral reserves holding economic importance and are located at the surface and/or under the ground or water.

Article 20: Forms of Mechanized Commercial Mining Activities

Forms of mechanized commercial mining activities are divided into three levels as follows:

1. Large scale commercial mining operations;
2. Medium scale commercial mining operations; and
3. Small scale commercial mining operations.

The scale of each mining activity shall be determined by the Government based upon the amount of capital investment, the type of mineral(s), the area and the amount of mineral reserves.

Article 21: Investment in Mining Activities

Investment in mining activities in the Lao PDR shall take place under one of the following forms:

1. Sole investment by the State;
2. Joint investment between the State and domestic and/or foreign parties; and
3. Collective or private investment from domestic parties.

Article 22: Mining Operation Procedures

Mining operations shall refer to all stages including prospecting, exploration, extraction, processing and trading of minerals.

Prospecting, exploration and extraction shall be authorized only in areas where no mining activities for the same minerals are being conducted.

Article 23: Requirements for Mineral Development Projects

Persons or entities who seek to undertake mining activities shall apply for a prospecting license. When sufficient information has been gathered to justify further exploration, the person or entity shall apply for an exploration license.

After exploration, if a person or entity seeks to obtain a mining license, the following must be submitted to the Government: a study of the economic feasibility of the mine, an environmental assessment concerning the impacts of the mine on the environment, the ecology and society.

When a mining license is granted, the Government shall jointly invest in the mining operation.

A person or entity who has been granted a mining license shall establish and register their enterprise in compliance with the laws of the Lao PDR.

Article 24: Mineral Prospecting

Mineral prospecting refers to the procedure by which an evaluation of the geologic setting and the quality and distribution of mineral occurrences is determined by field observation.

Mineral prospecting shall require the approval of the Government. The period of mineral prospecting shall not exceed two years but may be extended, with approval of Government, two time with each time for no more than one year.

Article 25: Mineral Exploration

Mineral exploration refers to geological and geophysical studies within a determined area for the acquisition of further detailed data on the geology and geological structures through testing, trenching, exploration drilling, analysis of the physical and chemical features of minerals in order to assess economic potential.

Mineral exploration shall require the approval of the Government.

The period of mineral exploration shall not exceed three years but may be extended, with the approval of Government, two times with each time for no more than two years.

Article 26: Assessment of Mineral Reserves

The assessment of mineral reserves refers to the evaluation of the tonnage and grade of each type of explored mineral.

Article 27: Testing and Analysis of Samples

License holders are entitled to send mineral samples and other mineral-related items for testing and analysis, whether within or outside the country, in accordance with the regulations outlined by the Government.

Article 28: Areas of Relinquishment and Addition

After prospecting and exploration, licensees shall relinquish the undesired portion of the prospecting or exploration concession, in part or in full, and provide to the Government all data acquired from such prospecting and exploration.

If it is discovered that a mineral occurrence extends beyond the licensed area, the licenses are entitled to apply for the addition of such area based on the acquired data.

Article 29: Evaluation of the Feasibility Study for Proposed Mining Projects

An evaluation of the proposed mining project shall include an evaluation of the economics of the proposed mine and the foreseeable negative impacts of the proposed mine on the environment and the surrounding communities.

Article 30: Feasibility Studies

Feasibility studies submitted with an application for a mining license shall include an elaboration on the following:

1. The plans and technical processes to be used in mining, and the tonnage and grade of the expected reserve to be mined;
2. An economic evaluation of the mine and an evaluation of the social impact of the mine.

The timeframe for the development of the feasibility study shall not exceed one year but may be extended for more than one year with the approval of Government.

Article 31: Environmental Impact Assessment

Along with the feasibility study, the investor shall submit an environmental impact assessment which shall contain an elaboration on the following:

1. An estimation of the projected environmental impacts and proposed alternatives and measures to avoid or reduce the adverse impacts on the environment, ecology and communities; and
2. An evaluation of the loss to be incurred and the proposed rehabilitation, including the methods proposed to avoid economic hardship to those people who will be affected by the mineral development project, including plans providing for resettlement and the means of livelihood.

Article 32: Conditions for Obtaining a Mining License

Applicants for a mining license shall meet the following conditions:

1. Demonstrate the financial and technical capacity to undertake the mining project:
2. Demonstrate a suitable history and trackrecord in mining ventures of a similar nature;

3. Demonstrate that the mining project can be operated in an efficient manner and that it will adhere to the national socio-economic plan and be devoid of serious environmental or ecological impacts.

Where applicants can meet the above conditions, the Government will consider the application for a mining license.

Article 33: Mining

Mining, as referred to in this Law, refers to stripping, extraction, removal, processing, grinding, grading and storage of minerals.

The period of the mining license shall not exceed thirty years from the date the concession is granted, but it may be extended twice, each time for no more than ten years as approved by the Government who will consider the request for an extension upon a case by case basis and upon consideration of the scale of the mining operation.

Article 34: Relinquishment of the Mining Enterprise

At the expiration of the mining license, the mining company shall relinquish the mining concession in full, including the mining related assets, such as mining equipment and vehicles, to the Government without any compensation, except where the Government indicates that it will refuse to accept such assets.

Article 35: Artisanal Mining

Artisanal mining refers to the occupation of small-scale mining carried out by manual means with non-mechanized tools. Only Lao citizens using their own sources of funds may be artisanal miners.

Professional artisanal miners shall obtain a license from the relevant Ministry of Industry-Handicraft Provincial, Municipal, or designated Special Zone office, which authority shall report to the Ministry of Industry-Handicraft headquarters.

If an artisanal miner employs workers or uses other means of mining [other] than manual tools, such mining shall be considered a mechanized mining operation.

Part-time artisanal mining refers to an artisanal miner who mines only intermittently and for whom mining is not the sole means of employment.

Part-time artisanal mining shall require a license from the relevant Ministry of Industry-Handicraft District Office, which authority shall report to the relevant Ministry of Industry-Handicraft Provincial, Municipal or Special Zone Offices.

Article 36: Minerals Processing

Minerals processing refers to post-mining value-added treatment such as washing, smelting, refining, cutting and polishing.

Minerals processing to upgrade mineral quality shall require specific approval from relevant Government authorities.

Article 37: Minerals Trading

A mining company shall be entitled to sell its mined minerals provided it obtains a trading license from the Government. Other persons or entities who seek to trade minerals must obtain a trading license or other approvals from relevant Government authorities.

Minerals, as used in this section, refers to minerals that have been washed, ground, graded and processed.

CHAPTER V RIGHTS AND OBLIGATIONS OF MINING LICENSE HOLDERS

Article 38: Rights and Obligations of Mining License Holders

Mining license holders shall have the right to:

1. Be protected by law;
2. Conduct exclusive mining activities along approved procedures within the concession area;
3. Receive priority to conduct further mining activities based upon assessment and approval by the Government;
4. Own assets and obtain returns from mining activities as provided by contract;
5. Receive technical and technological recommendations from the Government on the conduct of mining activities;
6. Apply for the extension of mining licenses; and
7. Build, construct and erect equipment to conduct mining activities in compliance with regulations as promulgated by concerned governmental authorities.

Artisanal miners shall be entitled to transfer their mining operation to members of their families, but may not transfer such operations to other persons.

Article 39: Right of Licensees' to Transfer Mining Activities

Licensees' conducting mining activities shall be entitled to transfer or inherit mining activities as approved by the Government, except where those activities have not progressed past the prospecting stage.

Article 40: Rights of the Licensee in Concession Areas

In undertaking mining operations, the licensee has the right to enter contracts with the Government for the supply of water, electricity and other things necessary to conduct the mining operation, however, the licensee must also obtain relevant permits as prescribed by law. The mining project shall use water and electricity efficiently and wastewater shall be recycled and treated prior to discharge for the protection of the population and the environment. Where the mining activity involves the use of toxic substances, the Government may declare such an area a special or toxic mining area.

For additional analytical, business and investment opportunities information,
please contact Global Investment & Business Center, USA
at (703) 370-8082. Fax: (703) 370-8083. E-mail: ibpusa3@gmail.com
Global Business and Investment Info Databank - www.ibpus.com

A licensee's use of wood in the concession area shall require approval and compensation.

Where a licensee's surface operations interfere with other persons' or entities' land, buildings, or crops, compensation must be provided for their damage and/or removal.

Article 41: Priority of Mining Areas

In the case where a licensee discovers other minerals in its concession other than the minerals it obtained authorization to mine, the licensee shall have priority in applying to the Government to mine the newly discovered minerals, unless those minerals appear on the reserved or restricted mineral lists as published by the Government.

Article 42: Obligations of Mining Licensees

Licensees shall have the following obligations:

1. to conduct mining activities in compliance with any or all prescribed procedures and within authorized timeframes;

1. to guarantee performance by setting up a Fund in accordance with the regulations promulgated by the State Bank of the Lao PDR;
2. to conduct mining activities as described in the feasibility study and mine plans;
3. to preserve and restore the land utilized during mining and to rehabilitate the land after mine closure and to guarantee that the project shall have no serious impacts on the environment, national security or the public and to provide appropriate compensation or damage in the case of casualty of life or property in the community or public.
4. to keep records of mining activities and expenses at each stage and to make timely reports;
5. to provide training and skill development for Lao workers and to guarantee the welfare, health and safety for Lao workers;
6. to keep accounts as provided by the Enterprise Accounting Law;
7. to properly and timely perform custom, tax and other fiscal obligations;
8. to construct roads for mining activities as necessary and to ensure that such roads be open for use by others;
9. to strictly abide by the Laws of the Lao PDR.

Professional artisanal and part-time artisanal mining licensees shall be obligated to pay taxes as prescribed by law, to preserve the environment and to strictly abide by the laws of the Lao PDR.

Article 43: Relationship with Local Administrative Authorities

License holders at each stage of activity shall contact local administrative authorities in the areas in which they are working to obtain goods and services to conduct their mineral related activities.

For additional analytical, business and investment opportunities information,
please contact Global Investment & Business Center, USA
at (703) 370-8082. Fax: (703) 370-8083. E-mail: ibpusa3@gmail.com
Global Business and Investment Info Databank - www.ibpus.com

Article 44: Termination of Mining Activities

Mining activities shall terminate when any of the following conditions are met:

1. The term of a license expires for any or all stages;
2. A licensee voluntarily terminates activities prior to the term of the license; or
3. A license is withdrawn by the Government due to the licensee's severe breach of contract or violation of the laws of the Lao PDR.

Article 45: Standards for mining technique and technology

In the performance of mining activities, the licensee must use techniques and technologies that meet international standards and are approved by the Ministry of Industry-Handicraft and other relevant authorities with the view of ensuring efficiency, security and environmental protection.

Article 46: Relinquishment and Restoration of the Mine Area

Mining licensees shall relinquish area in the mining concession to the Government, including leased land, under the following circumstances:

1. the use of such land is no longer required;
2. the licensee's mining license has been withdrawn due to the licensees' non-performance
3. of contract or serious violations of the laws of the Lao PDR; or the licensee's mining license has expired.

The licensee shall notify the relevant governmental authorities of any such relinquishment in a timely manner.

In the case where the surface of the land has been changed by mining activities, the land shall be restored and rehabilitated before relinquishment, including, where necessary, cleaning, chemical decontamination, and revegetation.

Article 47: Compensation

The licensee shall set up and maintain a fund appropriate under the circumstances of the specific mineral development project for:

1. resettlement of people from the mining area and to ensure their livelihood;
2. compensation for any damage to land, buildings or crops;
3. rental of land;
4. environmental protection; and
5. restoration and rehabilitation of the mining area.

This fund shall be included in the capital investment for the project.

CHAPTER VI ADMINISTRATION AND MINE INSPECTION

Article 48: Authority and Administration

The Governmental authorities responsible for administration of these laws include:

1. Ministry of Industry-Handicraft;
2. Province, Municipality or Special Zone Industry-Handicraft Services;
3. District Industry-Handicraft Offices; and
4. Village administrative authorities.

Article 49: Administration and Mine Inspection

The Ministry of Industry-Handicraft shall have the following duties and authority:

1. Assist the Government in formulating strategic planning for mineral development and in the enactment of rules and regulations to manage and administer mining activities;
2. Conduct scientific and technical research on geology and mining; gather national statistics and establish an information center for geology and mining;
3. Coordinate with other relevant agencies and local administrative authorities;
4. Research and present technical opinions on mining activities;
5. Issue prospecting, exploration, mining and mineral processing licenses;
6. Train and improve geology and mining skills among Lao personnel and workers;
7. Grant approvals for export or import of minerals in compliance with relevant regulations of other concerned ministries;
8. Undertake inspections of geological and mining activities; and
9. Undertake cooperation with external agencies and entities concerning geology and mining.

Article 50: Authority and Duties of the Provincial, Municipal and Special Zone Industry-Handicraft Services

In the management and inspection of mining activities, the Provincial, Municipal and Special Zone Industry-Handicraft Services shall have the following duties and authority:

1. Provide staff support to the Ministry of Industry-Handicrafts and local administration on management and guidance of mining activities within their territories;
2. Coordinate with other relevant agencies and administrative entities;
3. Research and present opinions on mining activities within their area of management;
4. Issue licenses and register professional artisanal mining activities;
5. Undertake inspections of mining activities within their area of management; and
6. Perform other duties pertaining to mining activities as assigned from the Ministry of Industry-Handicraft.

Article 51: Authority and duties of the District Industry-Handicraft Offices

For additional analytical, business and investment opportunities information,
please contact Global Investment & Business Center, USA
at (703) 370-8082. Fax: (703) 370-8083. E-mail: ibpusa3@gmail.com
Global Business and Investment Info Databank - www.ibpus.com

In the management and inspection of mining activities, the District Industry-Handicraft Offices shall have the following duties and authority:

1. Assist the Ministry of Industry-Handicrafts and the Provincial, Municipal and Special Zone Industry-Handicraft Services in the implementation of plans, projects, regulations and instructions of the Provincial, Municipal and Special Zone Industry-Handicraft Services concerning mining activities;
2. Coordinate with other relevant agencies and administrative entities;
3. Authorize and inspect part-time artisanal mining activities within their districts;
4. Provide facilities to lawful mining activities;
5. Perform other duties pertaining to mining activities as assigned by the Ministry of Industry-Handicraft Services.

Article 52: Authority and duties of Village Administration Authorities

In monitoring mining activities, the village administrative authorities shall have the following authority and duties:

1. Duty to monitor and inspect professional artisanal and part-time artisanal activities within village areas;
2. Submit reports concerning mining activities that impact local communities and their rights, traditions and customs;
3. Monitor and report on mineral occurrences within the village area;
4. Provide facilities to mining activities in the village area;
5. Coordinate with other concerned authorities and parties concerning security in the village area; and
6. Inspect part-time artisanal mining activities for compliance with regulations.

Article 53: Monitoring and Inspection of Mining Activities

Monitoring and inspection of mining activities refers to the oversight activities by the Government throughout the stages of prospecting, exploration, mining, processing, trading and after mine closure to ensure proper performance by persons or entities under any relevant contracts, the Mining Law and other laws of the Lao PDR.

The main elements that will be monitored and subject to inspection include the following:

1. Implementation of proper mining procedures;
2. Timely performance of obligations;
3. Preparation of feasibility studies;
4. Compliance with approved plans;
5. Compliance with mine safety and health plans;
6. Compliance with environmental impact mitigation measures;
7. Compliance with record keeping and reporting procedures;
8. Assets of the mining projects; and
9. Compliance with laws and regulations concerning mining activities.

Article 54: Inspection of Mining Activities

Inspection of mining activities may be performed as follows: routine inspections and announced and unannounced inspections, depending on the circumstances.

Routine inspections refer to inspections which are regularly performed at fixed times, and which shall be performed at least once a year.

Announced inspections refer to inspections which are deemed necessary and where the mining project is given advance notification of the inspection.

Unannounced inspections refer to inspections which are deemed necessary and where no advance notice is provided to the mining project.

Inspections may include both inspections of a mining project's documents and data and field inspections.

CHAPTER VII ARBITRATION, AWARDS, DISPUTES AND PENALTIES

Article 55: Arbitration

Where disputes arise between parties to a mining contract, a settlement shall be sought. Otherwise, the parties to the contract may submit the matter in dispute to the Arbitration Committee or the Court of the Lao PDR for further proceedings.

In case of disputes arising between employers and employees, the Labor Law of the Lao PDR shall apply.

In the case disputes arise between foreign investors or between a foreign investor and a Lao investor, Article 21 of the Law on the Promotion and Management of Foreign Investment in the Lao PDR shall apply.

Article 56: Awards

Persons or entities with prominent achievements in the efficient management and preservation of mineral resources according to the Laws of the Lao PDR will receive an award and be granted benefits as outlined by the Government, which can include, *inter alia*, credit policy and extension of mining licenses.

Article 57: Sanctions

Persons or entities breaching this Law shall be subject to sanctions such as education, fines or criminal penalties, including sentences, depending on the nature of the offense.

Article 58: Educational Measures

Persons or entities committing an offense under this Law, whether it is minor or severe, such as failure to submit timely reports, failing to comply with technical standards or failure to obtain mining licenses for professional or part-time artisanal mining, shall receive an official warning and education.

Article 59: Fines

Persons or entities that violate this Mining Law through any of the following:

1. Conducting mining activities without a license or with an expired license;
2. Trading in minerals in violation of regulations;
3. Sale, lease or transfer of a mining license without authorization;
4. False statements in reports;
5. Breach of the principles in the Mining Law and other regulations governing mineral activities;
6. Failure to comply with environmental protection mitigation measures, the discharge of untreated wastewater, or discharge of water containing toxic substances that affects the public's health;
7. Failure to comply with mine safety provisions for workers;
8. Destruction of a mineral resource due to their own fault; and
9. Failure to cooperate with Government authorities and inspectors.

The above shall subject the person or entity to the following fines:

For the first offense: 500,000 kip to 3,000,000 kip.

For the second offense: 3,100,000 kip to 5,000,000 kip.

For the third offense: 5,100,000 kip to 10,000,000 kip.

Offenses under Article 58 which are committed over three times shall be fined from 50,000 kip to 200,000 kip.

Where professional or part-time artisanal miners are in violation of any of the provisions in this section, fines of 10,000 kip to 20,000 kip shall be imposed.

Article 60: Criminal Sanctions

Circumstances which will warrant criminal sanctions under the Criminal Law for violation of the Mining Law include: falsification of mining licenses or failure to comply with technical safety measures which cause death or injury.

Punishment under the Criminal Law will also apply to civil servants who commit criminal offenses including: taking bribes, abuse of power, forgery of documents and the abuse of an official position for personal gain from mining activities.

Article 61: Additional Penalties

Operators who are penalized under Articles 59 and 60 may be subject to additional penalties such as cancellation of the mining license and seizure and liquidation of assets.

CHAPTER VIII FINAL PROVISIONS

Article 62: Implementation

The Government of the Lao People's Democratic Republic shall implement this Law.

Article 63: Effective Date

This Law shall become effective within ninety days after its promulgation by the President of the Lao People's Democratic Republic.

Persons and entities receiving mining licenses prior to this Law's effective date shall be entitled to continue their mining activities.

Where contracts have been signed but which terms conflict with the terms of this Law, the concerned agencies shall be notified within one hundred and twenty days from the effective date of this Law to consider amendment.

Any regulations and decrees inconsistent with this Law are superseded.

TRAVELING TO LAOS

US STATE DEPARTMENT SUGGESTIONS

COUNTRY DESCRIPTION: Laos is a developing country with a socialist government that is pursuing economic reform. Outside of Vientiane, the capital, and Luang Prabang, tourist services and facilities are relatively undeveloped.

ENTRY REQUIREMENTS: A passport and visa are required. Visas are issued upon arrival in Laos to foreign tourists and business persons, subject to certain conditions, at the following points of entry: Wattay Airport, Vientiane; Luang Prabang Airport; Friendship Bridge, Vientiane; Ban Huay Xai, Bokeo Province; and Vantao, Champasak Province. In the United States, U.S citizens may apply for visas and obtain further information about entry requirements directly from the Embassy of the Lao People's Democratic Republic, 2222 S St. N.W., Washington, D.C. 20008, tel. 202-332-6416, fax 202-332-4923, Internet home page: http://www.laoembassy.com. U.S. citizens should not attempt to enter Laos without valid travel documents or outside official ports of entry. Unscrupulous travel agents have sold U.S.-citizen travelers false Lao visas, which have resulted in those travelers being denied entry into Laos.

SAFETY AND SECURITY: The security situation in Laos can change quickly. Please refer to any Department of State Public Announcements for Laos for additional information.

Since the Spring of 2000, a number of bombings have occurred in public places frequented by foreign travelers in Vientiane, and there have been credible reports of other explosive devices found in Savannakhet and Pakse cities. While there is no evidence that this violence is directed against American citizens or institutions, American citizens should be aware that more such incidents could occur in the future. American citizens traveling to or residing anywhere in Laos are advised to exercise caution and to be alert to their surroundings.

Persons traveling overland in some areas, particularly Route 13 north between Kasi and Luang Prabang; Saisombun Special Zone; Xieng Khouang Province, including the Plain of Jars; and Route 7 east from the Route 13 junction, run the risk of ambush by insurgents or bandits. There have been violent incidents in these areas in the past year. Some groups have warned of impending insurgent attacks in these areas. Americans considering travel outside urban centers by road or river are advised to contact relevant Lao government offices and the U.S. Embassy for the most current security information.

American citizens should also avoid traveling on or across the Mekong River at night along the Thai border. In some areas, Lao militia forces have been known to shoot at boats on the river after dark.

INFORMATION ON CRIME: While Laos generally has a low rate of crime, visitors should exercise appropriate security precautions and remain aware of their surroundings. Street crime has been on the increase, particularly motorcycle drive-by theft of handbags and backpacks. The loss or theft abroad of a U.S. passport should be reported immediately to the local police and the U.S. Embassy. Useful information on safeguarding valuables and protecting personal security while traveling abroad is provided in the Department of State pamphlet, *A Safe Trip Abroad*, available from the Superintendent of Documents, U.S. Government Printing Office, Washington, D.C. 20402, via the Internet at http://www.access.gpo.gov/su_docs, on the Bureau of Consular Affairs home page at http://travel.state.gov and autofax service at 202-647-3000, or at the U.S. Embassy in Vientiane.

MEDICAL FACILITIES: Medical facilities and services are severely limited and do not meet Western standards. The blood supply is not screened for HIV or AIDS.

MEDICAL INSURANCE: U.S. medical insurance is not always valid outside the United States. U.S. Medicare and Medicaid programs do not provide payment for medical services outside the United States. Doctors and hospitals often expect immediate cash payment for health services. Uninsured travelers who require medical care overseas may face extreme difficulties.

Please check with your own insurance company to confirm whether your policy applies overseas, including provision for medical evacuation, and for adequacy of coverage. Serious medical problems requiring hospitalization and/or medical evacuation to the United States can cost tens of thousands of dollars. Please ascertain whether payment will be made to the overseas hospital or doctor or whether you will be reimbursed later for expenses that you incur. Some insurance policies also include coverage for psychiatric treatment and for disposition of remains in the event of death.

Useful information on medical emergencies abroad, including overseas insurance programs, is provided in the Department of State, Bureau of Consular Affairs brochure, *Medical Information for Americans Traveling Abroad*, available via the Bureau of Consular Affairs home page at http://travel.state.gov and autofax service at 202-647-3000.

OTHER HEALTH INFORMATION: Vaccination recommendations and prevention information for traveling abroad may be obtained through the Centers for Disease Control and Prevention's international travelers hotline from the United States at 1-877-FYI-TRIP (1-877-394-8747), via its toll-free autofax service at 1-888-CDC-FAXX (1-888-232-3299), or via their Internet site at http://www.cdc.gov.

ROAD SAFETY: While in a foreign country, U.S. citizens may encounter road conditions that differ significantly from those in the United States. The information below concerning Laos is provided for general reference only, and may not be totally accurate in a particular location or circumstance:
Safety of Public Transportation: Poor
Urban Road Conditions/Maintenance: Poor
Rural Road Conditions/Maintenance: Poor
Availability of Roadside Assistance: Poor

Roads are mostly unpaved, pot-holed and poorly maintained in most parts of the country, although there has been a successful effort to improve roads and drainage in the capital in recent years. There are no railroads. Public transportation in Vientiane is generally poor and unreliable, and it is very limited after sunset. Taxis are available. Drivers speak little or no English. Most taxis are old and poorly maintained. Traffic is increasing, and local drivers remain undisciplined. Pedestrians and drivers should exercise great caution at all times. Theoretically, traffic moves on the right, but most cars, like pedestrians and bicycles, use all parts of the street. Cyclists pay little or no heed to cars on the road, and bicycles are rarely equipped with functioning lights or reflectors. This makes driving especially dangerous at dusk and at night. Defensive driving is necessary. The U.S. Embassy in Vientiane advises its personnel to wear helmets, gloves, and sturdy shoes while operating motorcycles.

AVIATION OVERSIGHT: Serious concerns about the operation of Lao Aviation, particularly regarding its safety standards and maintenance regime, have caused the U.S. Embassy to advise its personnel to limit domestic travel on Lao Aviation to essential travel only. Americans who are required to travel by air within Laos may wish to defer their travel or consider alternate means of transportation.

Also, since there is no direct commercial air service at present, nor economic authority to operate such service between the U.S. and Laos, the U.S. Federal Aviation Administration (FAA) has not assessed Laos' Civil Aviation Authority for compliance with international aviation safety standards for oversight of Laos' air carrier operations. For further information, travelers may contact the Department of Transportation within the U.S. at tel. 1-800-322-7873, or visit the FAA Internet home page at http://www.faa.gov/avr/iasa/iasa.pdf. The U.S. Department of Defense (DOD) separately assesses some foreign air carriers for suitability as official providers of air services. For information regarding the DOD policy on specific carriers, travelers may contact the DOD at tel. 1-618-229-4801.

RELIGIOUS WORKERS: Religious proselytizing or distributing religious material is strictly prohibited. Foreigners caught distributing religious material may be arrested or deported. The Government of Laos restricts the import of religious texts and artifacts. While Lao law allows freedom of religion, the government registers and controls all associations, including religious groups. Meetings, even in private homes, must be registered, and those held outside established locations may be broken up and the participants arrested.

MARRIAGE TO A LAO CITIZEN: The Lao Government imposes requirements on foreigners intending to marry Lao citizens. U.S. citizens may obtain information about these requirements at the U.S. Embassy in Vientiane. A marriage certificate is not issued by the Lao Government unless the correct procedures are followed. Any attempt to circumvent Lao law governing the marriage of Lao citizens to foreigners may result in deportation of the foreigner and denial of permission to re-enter Laos. Similar restrictions exist prohibiting the cohabitation of Lao nationals with nationals of other countries.

PHOTOGRAPHY AND OTHER RESTRICTIONS: Police and military may arrest persons taking photographs of military installations or vehicles, bridges, airfields and government buildings, and confiscate their cameras. Confiscated cameras are seldom returned to the owners. The photographers may be arrested. Export of antiques, such as Buddha images and other old cultural artifacts, is restricted by Laotian law.

CRIMINAL PENALTIES: While in a foreign country, a U.S. citizen is subject to that country's laws and regulations, which sometimes differ significantly from those in the United States and do not afford the protections available to the individual under U.S. law. Penalties for breaking the law can be more severe than in the United States for similar offenses. Persons violating the law, even unknowingly, may be expelled, arrested or imprisoned. Penalties for possession, use or trafficking in illegal drugs in Laos are strict, and convicted offenders can expect jail sentences and fines. Local police and immigration authorities sometimes confiscate passports when outstanding business disputes and visa matters remain unsettled.

CONSULAR ACCESS: The United States and Laos are parties to the Vienna Convention on Consular Relations (VCCR). Article 36 of the VCCR provides that if an arrestee requests it, foreign authorities shall, without delay, inform the U.S. Embassy. U.S. consular officers have the right to be notified of a U.S. citizen's detention and to visit the arrestee. Lao authorities do not always notify the U.S. Embassy or grant U.S. consular officers access to incarcerated U.S. citizens in a timely manner. Nevertheless, American citizens who are arrested or detained in Laos should always request contact with the U.S. Embassy.

CUSTOMS REGULATIONS: Lao customs authorities may enforce strict regulations concerning temporary importation into or export from Laos of items such as religious materials and artifacts, and antiquities. It is advisable to contact the Embassy of the Lao People's Democratic Republic in Washington for specific information regarding customs requirements. (Please see sections on "Religious Workers" and "Photography and Other Restrictions" above.)

CHILDREN'S ISSUES: For information on international adoption of children and international parental child abduction, please refer to our Internet site at http://travel.state.gov/children's_issues.html or telephone (202) 736-7000.

REGISTRATION/EMBASSY LOCATION: U.S. citizens living in or visiting Laos are encouraged to register at the U.S. Embassy where they may obtain updated information on travel and security within the country. The U.S. Embassy is located at Rue Bartholonie (near Tat Dam), B.P. 114, in Vientiane; mail can be addressed to American Embassy Vientiane, Box V, APO AP 96546; telephone (856-21) 212-581, 212-582, 212-585; duty officer's emergency cellular telephone (856-020) 511-740; Embassy-wide fax number (856-020) 518-597; Embassy-wide fax number (856-21) 212-584; Internet home page: http://usembassy.state.gov/laos/.

PRACTIVCAL INFORMATION FOR TRAVELERS

The Lao People's Democratic Republic, strategically located at the hub of Indochina-sharing borders with China, Vietnam, Cambodia, Thailand and Myanma ☐ is emerging as the region's newest fledgling economy.

After a lengthy period of political instability, the Lao People's Democratic Republic was established in 1975. As a result of the government's New Economic Mechanism launched in 1986, and with Lao PDR's imminent entry into ASEAN, the past decade has been marked by unprecedented growth. Signs of new prosperity are especially visible in the capital of Vientiane, where advancements in infrastructure and services have been occurring rapidly.

Parallel to this recent economic development is the opening of Lao PDR as a tourist destination. With its rich culture, traditional lifestyle, expanding economy and unspoil natural beauty, the Lao PDR welcomes adventurers and business visitors alike.

Step in and experience the great diversity of cultural sights and attractions, restaurants, leisure activities and shopping areas. The Lao PDR is yours to discover.

CULTURAL FESTIVALS

Colorful religious and cultural festivals involve the whole community ☐ come and celebrate in distinctive Lao style. Some of the major festivals are featured on these two pages. If you are fortunate enough to be here for one of our holidays, we hope you will join in the festivities with us.

Pi Mai ☐ Mid-April

From the washing of religious icons to the drenching of friends and strangers, water is central to *Pi Mai* or Lao New Year celebrations. Wander through temple compounds as worshippers pour perfumed water over Buddha images ☐ and each other. Even if you miss the significance of cleansing and renewal, you won't escape the traditional water throwing. Expect to be ambushed by celebrants with buckets of water. No one stays dry - or really wants to - during *Pi Mai*.

Three days in mid-April are official public holidays. Exact dates are announced by the government.

Boun Bang Fai - May

On the verge of planting season, the Rocket Festival or *Boun Bang Fai* is held to coax rain and fertility back to the earth. Bamboo rockets adorned with brightly colored decorations are carried to the launch in rowdy procession. Some celebrants paint their faces or wear wild masks and outlandish costumes. All come to enjoy Lao music, dance, and drama ☐ especially the bawdy *maw lam* ☐ at its most playful.

Join Boun Bang Fai celebrations on weekends in May at varying locations.

Boun Khao Phansa □ July to October

Boun Khao Phansa is the first day of the Buddhist Lent, which is held from full moon in July to full moon in October. During this time of austerity, monks fast and people make offerings to gain merit. Traditionally, no weddings or celebrations are scheduled during these three months.

Early in the morning on the first day of Lent, people flock to temples carrying silver bowls full of gifts to offer the monks. For a breathtaking sight, go to one of the larger temples, like *That Luang*, where hundreds of worshippers □ mostly women in vividly-colored silks□ kneel row upon row.

Boun Ok Phansa □ October/November

Boun Ok Phansa □ the final and most important day of Lent □ also features an early morning temple ceremony. After dusk, candlelit processions grace temple grounds and buildings glow with candles burning in honor of Buddha.

Also after dusk is *Lai Heua Fai*, a river ceremony during which small hand-made boats is floated down-river by people praying and making vows. The candlelit rafts hob away into darkness, symbolically dismissing bad luck, disease, and sin. This festival is similar to Thailand's *Loy Krathong* festival, which is held in December.

Boun Souang Heua□ October

Held the day after *Ok Phansa*, *Boun Souang Heua* or the Boat race Festival draws crowds of excited spectators to the Mekong River. Fifty-member teams in wooden longboats row to the rhythm of drums as they compete for the coveted trophy. The races are held close to Vientiane. A carnival provides additional entertainment along the riverbank.

Boun That Luang□ November

Held during the time of the full moon in November, the *That Luang* Festival is celebrated in honor of Lao PDR's national shrine. The festival begins with a Morning Prayer and alms giving ceremony on the first day of the three-day festival.

Masses of faithful worshippers come to pay homage to the hundreds of monks gathered at *That Luang*. This ceremony, like *Khao Phansa*, is solemn yet colorful.

A carnival held during these three days offers food and handicraft stalls, bumper cars, a shooting gallery, curiosity booths, pinball, games of chance, and musical entertainment. For sports fans, the highlight of *Boun That Luang* is *tee khee*, or field hockey.

In 1995, two weeks before the actual festival, an international trade fair was held for the first time. Many large local and international companies were present at this important event.

For additional analytical, business and investment opportunities information,
please contact Global Investment & Business Center, USA
at (703) 370-8082. Fax: (703) 370-8083. E-mail: ibpusa3@gmail.com
Global Business and Investment Info Databank - www.ibpus.com

Lao National Day December 2

On this important public holiday, parades and speeches commemorate the 1975 Lao People's Revolutionary Victory over the monarchy.

Vietnamese & Chinese New Year January/February

Firecrackers explode all through this holiday, and mouth-watering sweetmeats and other delicacies are made especially for the occasion. Celebrations are held in January or February, with many business and market stalls closing for three days.

OFFICIAL HOLIDAYS

The following official public holidays for 1996 have been announced by the Prime Minister's Office:

1-3 January International New Year's Day

20 January Military Day (Military only)

8 March Lao Women's Day (Women only)

13-15 April Lao New Year

1 May Labor Day

7 October Teacher's Day (Teachers only)

2 December Lao National Day

VIENTIANE

Vientiane's small size allows easy travel around the city. Most tourist attractions and shopping areas are within walking distance of major hotels. If preferred, most tour operators can organize a one-day tour to these attractions. For day excursions outside Vientiane, it is best to consult a travel agent.

That Luang

The national shrine of the country, *That Luang*, or Great Sacred Stupa, stands 45 meters tall and is believed to contain a relic of the Lord Buddha. The original structure was built by King Setthathirath in 1566, and the present structure was restored in 1953. The gold-colored central structure of this stupa echoes the curving lines of an elongated lotus bud, and the gold is a symbol of the country's wealth. This shrine is the center of the *That Luang* festival held in November.

Revolutionary Monument

Located close to That Luang, this monument stands as a memorial to those who died in the Revolutionary War.

For additional analytical, business and investment opportunities information,
please contact Global Investment & Business Center, USA
at (703) 370-8082. Fax: (703) 370-8083. E-mail: ibpusa3@gmail.com
Global Business and Investment Info Databank - www.ibpus.com

Patuxai

Built in 1962, *Patuxai*, or the Victory Monument, is a memorial to those who died in wars before the Revolution. Known to some as *Anousavali*, or "the monument," the arch and the surrounding park area attract those who wish to relax with friends and watch Vientiane's traffic speed by. For 200 kip, energetic visitors can climb to the top of the monument for a view of the city. The *Patuxai* itself is open from 08:00 to 17:00, but people continue to enjoy the park into the evening.

That Dam

An old legend tells of a seven-headed dragon that protected the people of Vientiane from Siamese invaders during the 1828 war. This dragon is said to be hidden under *That Dam*, or the Black Stupa, and continues to protect the city to this day.

Revolutionary Museum

This impressive example of French colonial architecture houses a collection of artifacts weapons paintings and photographs depicting the history of the Lao People's Revolution. Most captions are written in Lao and English.

Wat Sisaket

Wat Sisaket is the oldest temple in Vientiane-only one to survive the Siamese invasion in 1828. All other temples have since undergone extensive restoration.

The *wat* features a library, which was ransacked during the invasion, as well as unique frescoes and a grand total of 6,840 Buddha images, hundreds of which are framed in small wall niches.

Wat Phra Keo

Once the royal temple of the Lao monarchy, *Wat Phra Keo* was built in 1566. After being destroyed by the Siamese invaders in 1828 it was rebuilt between 1936 and 1942, and has been used as a museum since the 1970s. The main building-which originally housed the *Phra Keo*, or Emerald Buddha-now contains fine examples of Buddhist sculpture and artifacts including antique drums and palm leaf manuscripts. A short description of each exhibit is given in French.

Wat Simuang

Wat Simuang was built when King Setthathirath established Vientiane as the nation's capital in 1563. This temple enshrines the foundation pillar of Vientiane, and is home to the city's guardian spirit.

Local folklore surrounding the temple's construction tells of a pregnant girl who, for the good of the city, sacrificed herself to the spirit by jumping into the hole before the foundation pillar was lowered.

This temple is one of Vientiane's most popular centers of worship, largely because it houses a Buddha image believed to answer the questions of worshippers who lift it three times, repeating the same question each time. The oddly shaped image is always surrounded by fruit and flowers-offerings of thanks from those who have received its answers.

Wat Ong Teu

Wat Ong Teu, or the Temple of the Heavy Buddha, is the residence of the Deputy Patriarch of the Lao monastic order. The Deputy Patriarch directs Vientiane's Buddhist Institute where monks from all over Laos come to study. The temple also houses a 16th century Buddha weighing several tones.

Suan Vathanatham

Located near the Lao-Thai Friendship Bridge, *Suan Vathanatham* (National Ethnic Cultural Park) offers the visitor a taste of Lao PDR's cultural and natural heritage. Shady paths wind past traditional Lao architecture, an small zoo (featuring alligators, bears, monkey, snakes, hawks, civets, and jungle cats), textile and handicraft shops, food and drink stands, towering dinosaurs, and sculptures of Lao literacy characters including *Sinxai* and the Four Eared Elephant.

Wat Xieng Khouan (Buddha Park)

Situated by the Mekong River about 21 kilometers out of Vientiane municipality, *Wat Xieng Khouan*, despite its name, is not a temple but a sculpture park. Created in 1958, the park captivates visitors with unusual and somewhat disturbing Buddhist and Hindu imagery. For a bizarre experience, climb into the three level model of hell. *Wat Xieng Khouan* offers food and drinks stalls, and is a popular spot for picnics and recreation.

SPORT AND LEISURE ACTIVITIES

Golf

Santisouk Lane Xang Golf and Resort

Located on Thadeua Road, out toward the Friendship Bridge, this gold course claims an international standard. Along with a nine-hole course, the Santisouk Lane Xang offers a driving range, gold shoes and club rental, shower room, and restaurant.

Vientiane Golf Course

The first golf course in Lao PDR, the nine-hole Vientiane golf course is located at Km 6 on Route 13 South.

Night Life

Vientiane offers a wide range of nightclubs and bars with an unique blend of Eastern and Western music. The city's dance floors cater to different tastes from the traditional Lao lamvong to rap. Many establishments offer entertaining light and sound shows and feature popular local bands.

Dokmaideng Fun Park

The Dokmaideng Fun Park is Vientiane's choice destination for children of all ages for an afternoon or evening of bumper cars, swing rides, miniature trains, and video games. Plans are underway to expand the park, adding a waterslide and more.

Thoulakhom Zoo

Another place that is worth visiting is Vientiane province's Thoulakhom Zoo. Located fifty kilometers north of Vientiane municipality, this zoo features many exotic and rare animals from Lao PDR's jungles, from magnificent tigers to mouse deer, elephants, monkeys, parrots, and the newly arrived kangaroos.

SHOPPER'S HEAVEN

Lao PDR is treasure trove of exquisite handicrafts and antiques. Silk and cotton textiles, hand-woven baskets, fine silver-work, detailed woodcarvings, traditional musical instruments and pottery are the pride of the Lao artisan tradition. Art galleries in town feature a wide selection of drawings, watercolors, and oil paintings by local artists.

Many small jewelry and handicraft shops dot the city, and the main shopping center, the *Talat Sao*, houses a head-spinning array of woven textiles, antiques, silver items, and gold jewelry.

Talat Sao

The *Talat Sao* (Morning Market) is comprised of three large pavilions, each with its own Lao style green-tiled roof. The *Talat Sao* offers the shopper everything from silk and fine jewelry to toiletries, electronic equipment and hardware.

The second level of this market is crammed with silver and gold smiths, and there is a good selection of handicrafts and antiques both upstairs and downstairs. The Morning Market also has conveniently-located licensed moneychangers.

Credit Cards

Credit cards are becoming more widely used in Laos, with the most common being VisaCard, MasterCard and American Express. Most major hotels, restaurants and some shops will accept credit cards, but many of the smaller shops, even in the Morning Market, only accept cash.

Nongbouathong Village Weavers

Traditional Lao textile weaving is proudly upheld in this village, and the exquisite results are displayed at the local Pheng Mai Gallery. Nongbouathong village is just a ten-minute drive out of town, and lovers of weaving should not miss this opportunity to watch the weavers at their looms.

The Art of Silk

This silk museum is run by the Lao Women's Union and features a variety of traditional silk pieces created by skillful weavers from different provinces. The items on display are also for sale.

Culinary Treats

Visitors are pleasantly surprised by the many excellent eating establishments in Vientiane. From fabulous Lao, French, Italian, Chinese, Indian, Japanese, and Thai restaurants to mouth-watering chicken roasted over open grills in street stalls, even the most choosy eater will find something to satisfy the plate.

Noodle Houses and Street Stalls

Vientiane abounds with noodle houses-just ask a local to point out the most popular places in town. Different restaurants specialize in different types of noodle dishes, so be adventurous and savour the variety.

Street stalls add undeniable character to the city, and most of them start bustling at sunset. For a Lao food extravaganza, visit Khounboulom Road in the heart of town and try sweet sticky rice with cononut, rich Lao cakes, and loti, the egg pastry roll-ups drizzled with sweetened condensed milk... The list goes on and on and you will not be disappointed.

TRAVELLING OUTSIDE VIENTIANE

Major provincial capitals are serviced by regular Lao Aviation domestic flights. Although internal travel permits are no longer required by foreigners travelling to these areas, it is advisable that travel outside Vientiane is organized through one of the major travel agencies listed in the Gold Pages.

Luang Prabang

This lovely town nestled in the mountains was once capital of Laos. A short forty-minute flight from Vientiane, Luang Prabang is a step back to a time when tradition, culture and religion motivated most activities in Lao society.

Visit the Royal Palace Museum for a fascinating glimpse into the past. Personal artifacts of the Royal Family and gifts from foreign governments are especially interesting. Take a boat trip to *Tham Ting* Caves to see the hundreds of Buddha images enshrined there years ago to protect them from invaders.

For additional analytical, business and investment opportunities information, please contact Global Investment & Business Center, USA at (703) 370-8082. Fax: (703) 370-8083. E-mail: ibpusa3@gmail.com
Global Business and Investment Info Databank - www.ibpus.com

Xieng Khouang & Plain of Jars

Xieng Khouang province is home to the Plain of Jars. Scattered across a grassy slope 12 kilometers outside of the provincial capital, are more than 300 ancient stone jars weighing up to six tonnes each. Xieng Khouang was one of Lao PDR's most heavily bombed provinces between 1964 and 1973.

Tham Piu care is a sobering historical sight. *Tham Piu* was used as a bomb shelter by Lao villagers until 1969 when a single rocket fired into the cave killed about 400 people - mostly women and children. Rock debris and human bones from the explosion still litter the cave.

Travelling through the Region

Vientiane is a convenient point from which to travel to other parts of Indochina. The capital is serviced by the national flag carrier, Lao Aviation, and a growing number of foreign airlines, including Air Cambodia, Air Vietnam, Southern China Airlines, Silk Air and Thai International Airways.

Travel from Vientiane to Thailand is convenient with the recent opening of the Australian-built Friendship Bridge, the first bridge across the Mekong River. From the border town of *Nongkhai*, the nearest Thai airport is 60 kilometers away in *Udon Thani.*

BUSINESS INFORMATION

Hotels in Vientiane

There are several excellent hotels and guest-houses in Vientiane offering clean, air-conditioned comfort and genuine Lao hospitality. Most hotels have restaurants, and some of the larger ones have business facilities with facsimile and word processing services. A wide range of prices and features serves the needs of every traveler.

Transport within Vientiane

Vientiane is a small city and easy to move around in. Travelling by jumbo or tuk-tuk is inexpensive and convenient. These vehicles can be hailed from the side of a street or found waiting for customers near markets, restaurants, and hotels. It is wise to know the Lao name of your destination. For most destinations in the city, you should pay no more than 500 kip per passenger. Negotiate the fare before starting on your journey. Taxis are available for hire. Most taxis congregate around the Morning Market and the newer ones have meters. Bicycles and motorcyles can also be hired for a nominal fee.

Clothing and Climate

The climate is tropical, with the monsoons from June until October and the dry season from November to May. The winter months, December to February, can be quite cool and light jackets and sweaters are recommended. If you travel in the provinces during winter months warmer clothing is required as it gets very cold in the mountain areas.

In Vientiane, keep your clothing light, simple and modest. Natural fibers such as silk and cotton are recommended.

Water

Tap water is unsafe for drinking, but purified bottled water is available everywhere. It is not advisable to ear food that has just been rinsed under the tap. Avoid unpeeled fruit and uncooked vegetables.

Electricity

The Lao PDR uses 220 volt power at 50 HZ. Power pints will accept a plug with two flat pins or two round pins. Various adaptors can be purchased at the Morning Market.

SUPPLEMENTS

LAOS GLOSSARY

Asian Development Bank
Established in 1967, the bank assists in economic development and promotes growth and cooperation in developing member countries. The bank is owned by its forty-seven member governments, which include both developed and developing countries in Asia and developed countries in the West.

Association of Southeast Asian Nations (ASEAN)
Founded in 1967 primarily for economic cooperation and consisting of Brunei (since 1984), Indonesia, Malaysia, the Philippines, Singapore, and Thailand. Laos has had observer status since 1992 and applied for membership in July 1994.

ban
Village; grouped administratively into *tasseng* (*q.v.*) and *muang* (*q.v.*).

dharma
Buddhist teaching or moral law; laws of nature, all that exists, real or imaginary.

fiscal year (FY)
October 1 to September 30.

gross domestic product (GDP)
A value measure of the flow of domestic goods and services produced by an economy over a period of time, such as a year. Only output values of goods for final consumption and intermediate production are assumed to be included in the final prices. GDP is sometimes aggregated and shown at market prices, meaning that indirect taxes and subsidies are included; when these indirect taxes and subsidies have been eliminated, the result is GDP at factor cost. The word *gross* indicates that deductions for depreciation of physical assets have not been made. Income arising from investments and possessions owned abroad is not included, only domestic production. Hence, the use of the word *domestic* to distinguish GDP from gross national product (*q.v.*).

gross national product (GNP)
The gross domestic product (GDP--*q.v.*) plus net income or loss stemming from transactions with foreign countries, including income received from abroad by residents and subtracting payments remitted abroad to nonresidents. GNP is the broadest measurement of the output of goods and services by an economy. It can be calculated at market prices, which include indirect taxes and subsidies. Because indirect taxes and subsidies are only transfer payments, GNP is often calculated at factor cost by removing indirect taxes and subsidies.

Hmong

Largest Lao Sung (*q.v.*) ethnic group of northern Laos. This tribal group dwells at higher elevations than other ethnic groups. During the period of the Royal Lao Government (RLG) (*q.v.*), the Hmong were referred to as Meo.

International Monetary Fund (IMF)

Established on July 22, 1944, the IMF began operating along with the World Bank (*q.v.*) on December 27, 1945. The IMF is a specialized agency affiliated with the United Nations that takes responsibility for stabilizing international exchange rates and payments. The IMF's main business is the provision of loans to its members when they experience balance of payments difficulties. These loans often carry conditions that require substantial internal economic adjustments by the recipients. In 1994 the IMF had 179 members.

karma

Buddhist concept of the sum of one's past actions, which affect one's current life and future reincarnations.

khoueng

Province; first order administrative division.

kip(k)

Lao currency. In June 1994, US$1=R721.

Lao Issara

Free Laos. Movement formed in 1945 to resist any attempt to return to French colonial status.

Lao Loum

Literally translated as the valley Laotian. Inclusive term for people of Tai stock living in Laos, including lowland Lao and upland Tai. Group of lowland peoples comprising the majority population of Laos; generally used to refer to ethnic Lao, the country's dominant ethnic group (approximately 66 percent of the population according to the 1985 census), and speaking Tai-Kadai languages, including Lao, Lue, Tai Dam (Black Tai), and Tai Deng (Red Tai).

Lao Patrocitic Front (LPF) (Neo Lao Hak Xat)

Sucessor to Neo Lao Issara (*q.v.*), the political arm of the Pathrt Liberation Army (*q.v.*)--formerly known as the Pathet Lao (q.v.)--is its milituary arm.

Lao People's Army

Formed in 1976 when the Lao People's Liberation Army (LPLA-- *q.v.*) was restructured after the establishment of the Lao People's Democratic Republic in December 1975.

Lao People's Liberation Army (LPLA)

Official title of Pathet Lao armed forces, more commonly known as the communist revolutionaries, or guerrilla forces. The LPLA originated with the Latsavong detachment, formed in January 1949 by Kaysone Phomvihan, and steadily increased in number to an estimated 8,000 guerrillas in 1960 and an estimated 48,000 troops between 1962 and 1970.

Lao People's Revolutionary Party (LPRP) (Phak Pasason Pativat Lao)

Founded secretly in 1955 as the Phak Pasason Lao (Lao People's Party--LPP); name changed in 1972. Seized full power and became the ruling (communist) party of Laos in 1975. The LPRP Central Committee formulates party policy; it is dominated by the Political Bureau (Politburo) and the Secretariat and maintains control by placing its members in key institutions throughout the government and the army.

Lao Sung

Literally translated as the Laotian of the mountain top--those who traditionally live in the high altitudes in northern Laos. In official use, term denotes a category of ethnic groups that speak Tibeto-Burmese, Miao-Yao languages; chiefly the Hmong (*q.v.*) (Meo) group of highland or upland minorities but also the Mien (Yao) and Akha. According to the 1985 census, these groups make up approximately 10 percent of the population.

Lao Theung

Literally, Laotian of the mountain slopes; group--including Kammu, Loven, and Lamet--that traditionally lives in medium altitudes, practices swidden, or slash-and-burn-agriculture, and speaks Mon-Khmer languages and dialects. According to the 1985 census, approximately 24 percent of the population. Regarded as original inhabitants of Laos, formally referred to by ethnic Lao as *kha*, or slave.

mandala

Indian geopolitical term referring to a variable circle of power centered on a ruler, his palace, and the religious center from which he drew his legitimization.

muang (*muong*)

Administrative district; also an independent principality; comprises several *tasseng* (*q.v.*), second order administrative divisions.

Lao Patriotic Front (LPF) (Neo Lao Hak Xat)

Successor to Neo Lao Issara (*q.v.*), the political arm of the Pathet Lao (*q.v.*) during the Indochina Wars (1946- 75). The Lao People's Liberation Army (*q.v.*)--formerly known as the Pathet Lao (*q.v.*)--is its military arm.

Neo Lao Issara

Free Laos Front--organization established by former Lao Issara (Free Laos) (*q.v.*) to continue anti-French resistance movement with the Viet Minh (*q.v.*); succeeded by Neo Lao Hak Xat (Lao Patriotic Front--LPF) (*q.v.*) in 1956.

net material product

Gross material output minus depreciation on capital and excluding "unproductive services." According to the World Bank (*q.v.*), net material product is "a socialist concept of national accounts."

Nonaligned Movement

Established in September 1961 with the aim of promoting political and military cooperation apart from the traditional East and West blocs. As of 1994, there were 107 members (plus the Palestine Liberation Organization), twenty-one observers, and twenty-one "guests."

Pathet Lao (Lao Nation)

Literally, land of the Lao. Until October 1965, the name for the Lao People's Liberation Army (*q.v.*), the military arm of the Lao Patriotic Front (*q.v.*).

Royal Lao Government (RLG)

The ruling authority in Laos from 1947 until the communist seizure of power in December 1975 and the proclamation of the Lao People's Democratic Republic.

Sipsong Panna

Region in southern Yunnan Province, China, from which migrated many groups that now inhabit Laos.

Southeast Asia Treaty Organization (SEATO)

Established in September 1954 as a result of the 1954 Geneva Agreements to stop the spread of communism in Southeast Asia. SEATO never had an active military role and was ultimately disbanded in June 1977 following the success of the communist movements in Cambodia, Laos, and Vietnam in 1975. Original signatories to SEATO were Australia, Britain, France, New Zealand, Pakistan, the Philippines, Thailand, and the United States.

tasseng

Administrative unit; territorial subdivision of *muang* (*q.v.*), subdistrict grouping of ten to twenty villages.

That Luang

Most sacred Buddhist stupa in Vientiane and site of annual festival on the full moon of the twelfth month.

Theravada Buddhism

Predominant branch of Buddhism practiced in Laos, Cambodia, Sri Lanka, and Thailand.

United Nations Children's Fund (UNICEF)

Acronym retained from predecessor organization, United Nations International Children's Emergency Fund, established in December 1946. Provides funds for establishing child health and welfare services.

United Nations Development Programme (UNDP)

Created by the United Nations in 1965, the UNDP is the world's largest channel for multilateral technical and preinvestment assistance to low-income countries. It functions as an overall programming, financing, and monitoring agency. The actual fieldwork is done by other UN agencies.

United Nations High Commissioner for Refugees (UNHCR)

Established by the United Nations in 1949, it did not become effective until 1951. The first world institution to aid refugees, the UNHCR seeks to ensure the humanitarian treatment of refugees and find a permanent solution to refugee problems. The agency deals with the international protection of refugees and problems arising from mass movements of people forced to seek refuge.

Viet Minh

Coalition of Vietnamese national elements formed in May 1941 and dominated by the communists in their movement calling for an uprising against the French colonial government.

World Bank

Informal name used to designate a group of four affiliated international institutions: the International Bank for Reconstruction and Development (IBRD), the International Development Association (IDA), the International Finance Corporation (IFC), and the Multilateral Investment Guarantee Agency (MIGA). The IBRD, established in 1945, has as its primary purpose the provision of loans at market-related rates of interest to developing countries at more advanced stages of development. The IDA, a legally separate loan fund but administered by the staff of the IBRD, was set up in 1960 to furnish credits to the poorest developing countries on much easier terms than those of conventional IBRD loans. The IFC, founded in 1956, supplements the activities of the IBRD through loans and assistance designed specifically to encourage the growth of productive private enterprises in the less developed countries. The MIGA, founded in 1988, insures private foreign investment in developing countries against various noncommercial risk. The president and certain senior officers of the IBRD hold the same positions in the IFC. The four institutions are owned by the governments of the countries that subscribe their capital. To participate in the World Bank group, member states must first belong to the Intentional Monetary Fund (IMF--*q.v.*).

SELECTED TOUR OPERATORS IN LAOS

The following list is issued by the National Tourism Authority of Lao PDR. This is not an exhaustive list of travel companies. You are advised to contact the travel company directly for their up-to-date itineraries and prices.

Dafi Travel Co., Ltd
093/4 Samsenthai St,
P.O. Box 5351,
Vientiane

Lao Tourism Co., Ltd
08/02 Lane Xang Ave,
P.O. Box 2511,
Vientiane

Luang Prabang Tourism Co., Ltd
P.O. Box 356,
Sisavangvong Rd,
Luang Prabang.

Phathanakhet Phoudoi Travel Co., Ltd
Phonxay Rd,
P.O. Box 5796,
Vientiane

**Phathana Saysomboune
Travel & Tour Co., Ltd**
Km 5, 13 South Rd,
12/G Chommanytai Xaysetha DTR,
P.O. Box 7117,
Vientiane

Chackavane Travel & Tour
92 Thongkankham Rd,

P.O. Box 590,
Vientiane

Raja Tour
03 Heng boon St,
P.O. Box 3655,
Vientiane

Sode Tour
114 Quai Fa Ngum,
P.O. Box 70,
Vientiane

LAO PDR EMBASSIES AND CONSULTATE-GENERAL

Country	Address
Brunei Darussalam	Embassy of the Lao PDR Tel : 673-2-345 666 Fax : 456-888
Cambodia	Embassy of the Lao PDR 15-17 Mao Tse Tung Boulvard P.O. Box 19 Phnom Penh Tel : 855-23-982 632 Fax : 720 907
Indonesia	Embassy of the Lao PDR Jl. Patra Kuningan XIV No.1.A Kuningan Jakarta Selatan - 12950 Tel : 62-21-522 9602, 522 7862 Fax : 522 9601
Malaysia	Embassy of the Lao PDR I Lorong Damai Tiga Kuala Lumpur 55000 Tel : 60-3-248 3895, Residence: 245 6023 HP : 60-012 218 0075 Fax : 60-3- 242 0344
Myanmar	Embassy of the Lao PDR NA I Diplomatic Quarters Franser Road Yangon Tel : 95-1-222 482, 227 445 Fax : 227 446

For additional analytical, business and investment opportunities information,
please contact Global Investment & Business Center, USA
at (703) 370-8082. Fax: (703) 370-8083. E-mail: ibpusa3@gmail.com
Global Business and Investment Info Databank - www.ibpus.com

The Philippines	Embassy of the Lao PDR N. 34 Lapu-Lapu Street Magallences Village Makati City, Manila Tel & Fax : 63-2-833 5759
Singapore	Embassy of the Lao PDR 179-B Gold Hill Centre Thomson Road Tel : 65-250 6044 Fax : 65-250 6214
Thailand	Embassy of the Lao PDR 520-502/ 1-3 Soi Ramkhamheng 39 Bangkapi Bangkok 10310 Tel : 539 6667 Fax : 66-2-539 6678 Consulate General of the Lao PDR Khonkaen Tel : 66-43-223 698, 223 473, 221 961 Fax : 223 849
Vietnam	Embassy of the Lao PDR 22 Rue Tran Bing Trong Hanoi Tel : 84-4-8- 25 4576, 29 6746 Fax : 22 8414 Consulate General of the LAO PDR 93 Larteur ST, District 1 Ho Chi Minh City Tel : 84-8-8- 29 7667, 29 9275 Fax : 29 9272 Consulate General of the LAO PDR 12 Tran Quy-Cap Danang Tel : 84-51-8- 21 208, 24 101 Fax : 22 628
Australia	Embassy of the Lao PDR I Dalman Crescent O' Malley Canberra ACT 2606 Tel : 61-2- 6286 4595, 6286 6933 Fax : 6290 1910
China	Embassy of the Lao PDR 11 Salitun Dongsie Jie Beijing 100 600

For additional analytical, business and investment opportunities information,
please contact Global Investment & Business Center, USA
at (703) 370-8082. Fax: (703) 370-8083. E-mail: ibpusa3@gmail.com
Global Business and Investment Info Databank - www.ibpus.com

	IfsTel : 86-1- 6532 1224 Fax : 6532 6748 Consulate General of the Lao PDR Room 3226 Camellia Hotel 154 East Dong Feng Road Kunming 650041 Tel : 86-871- 317 6623, 317 6624 Fax : 317 8556
France	Embassy of the Lao PDR 74 Ave Raymond Poincare 75116 Paris Tel : 33-1- 4553 0298, 4553 7047 Fax : 4727 5789
Germany	Embassy of the Lao PDR Am Lessing 6 53639 Koeningswinter Tel : 49- 2223 21501 Fax : 2223 3065
India	Embassy of the Lao PDR E53 Panchsheel Park New Delhi-17 Tel : 91-11-642 7447 Fax : 642 8588
Japan	Embassy of the Lao PDR 3-3-22 Nishi-Azabu Minato-Ku Tokyo 106 Tel : 81-3-5411 2291, 5411 2292 Fax : 5411 2293
Russia	Embassy of the Lao PDR UI Katchalova 18 Moscow 121 069 Tel : 7-095-203 1454, 291 8966 Fax : 290 4246, 291 7218
Sweden	Embassy of the Lao PDR Badstrandvagen 11 11265 Stockholm Tel : 46-8-618 2010, 695 0160 Fax : 618 2001
United States of America	Embassy of the Lao PDR 2222 S Street NW Washington DC 10022

For additional analytical, business and investment opportunities information,
please contact Global Investment & Business Center, USA
at (703) 370-8082. Fax: (703) 370-8083. E-mail: ibpusa3@gmail.com
Global Business and Investment Info Databank - www.ibpus.com

	Tel : 1-202- 332 6416, 332 6417 Fax : 332 4923 Permanent Mission of the Lao PDR 317 East 51st Street New York, NY 10022 Tel : 1-212- 832 2734 Fax : 750 0039

For additional analytical, business and investment opportunities information,
please contact Global Investment & Business Center, USA
at (703) 370-8082. Fax: (703) 370-8083. E-mail: ibpusa3@gmail.com
Global Business and Investment Info Databank - www.ibpus.com

BASIC TITLE FOR LAOS

IMPORTANT!
All publications are updated annually!
Please contact IBP, Inc. at ibpusa3@gmail.com for the latest ISBNs and additional information
Global Business and Investment Info Databank: www.ibpus.com

TITLE
Lao People's Dem. Rep. Fishing and Aquaculture Industry Handbook - Strategic Information, Regulations, Opportunities
Lao People's Democratic Republic Traders and Investors Handbook
Lao People's Democratic Republic Investment, Trade Strategy and Agreements Handbook - Strategic Information and Basic Agreements
Lao People's Democratic Republic Traders and Investors Handbook
Laos A "Spy" Guide - Strategic Information and Developments
Laos A Spy" Guide"
Laos Business and Investment Opportunities Yearbook
Laos Business and Investment Opportunities Yearbook
Laos Business and Investment Opportunities Yearbook Volume 1 Strategic Information and Opportunities
Laos Business Intelligence Report - Practical Information, Opportunities, Contacts
Laos Business Intelligence Report - Practical Information, Opportunities, Contacts
Laos Business Law Handbook - Strategic Information and Basic Laws
Laos Business Law Handbook - Strategic Information and Basic Laws
Laos Business Law Handbook - Strategic Information and Basic Laws
Laos Business Law Handbook - Strategic Information and Basic Laws
Laos Business Law Handbook Volume 1 Strategic Information and Basic Laws
Laos Business Success Guide - Basic Practical Information and Contacts
Laos Clothing & Textile Industry Handbook
Laos Clothing & Textile Industry Handbook
Laos Company Laws and Regulations Handbook
Laos Country Study Guide - Strategic Information and Developments
Laos Country Study Guide - Strategic Information and Developments
Laos Country Study Guide - Strategic Information and Developments Volume 1 Strategic Information and Developments
Laos Country Study Guide Volume 1 Strategic Information and Developments
Laos Country Study Guide Volume 1 Strategic Information and Developments - Everything you need to know about the country - Geography, history, politics, economy, business, etc.
Laos Criminal Laws, Regulations and Procedures Handbook - Strategic Information, Regulations, Procedures
Laos Customs, Trade Regulations and Procedures Handbook
Laos Customs, Trade Regulations and Procedures Handbook
Laos Diplomatic Handbook - Strategic Information and Developments
Laos Diplomatic Handbook - Strategic Information and Developments
Laos Ecology & Nature Protection Handbook
Laos Ecology & Nature Protection Handbook
Laos Ecology & Nature Protection Laws and Regulation Handbook
Laos Economic & Development Strategy Handbook
Laos Economic & Development Strategy Handbook
Laos Education System and Policy Handbook

TITLE
Laos Electoral, Political Parties Laws and Regulations Handbook - Strategic Information, Regulations, Procedures
Laos Energy Policy, Laws and Regulation Handbook
Laos Export-Import Trade and Business Directory
Laos Export-Import Trade and Business Directory
Laos Foreign Policy and Government Guide
Laos Foreign Policy and Government Guide
Laos Industrial and Business Directory
Laos Industrial and Business Directory
Laos Internet and E-Commerce Investment and Business Guide - Strategic and Practical Information: Regulations and Opportunities
Laos Internet and E-Commerce Investment and Business Guide - Strategic and Practical Information: Regulations and Opportunities
Laos Investment and Business Guide - Strategic and Practical Information
Laos Investment and Business Guide - Strategic and Practical Information
Laos Investment and Business Guide - Strategic and Practical Information
Laos Investment and Business Guide - Strategic and Practical Information
Laos Investment and Business Guide Volume 1 Strategic and Practical Information
Laos Investment and Business Profile - Basic Information and Contacts for Succesful investment and Business Activity
Laos Investment and Trade Laws and Regulations Handbook
Laos Justice System and National Police Handbook
Laos Justice System and National Police Handbook
Laos Medical & Pharmaceutical Industry Handbook
Laos Medical & Pharmaceutical Industry Handbook
Laos Mineral & Mining Sector Investment and Business Guide - Strategic and Practical Information
Laos Mineral, Mining Sector Investment and Business Guide - Strategic and Practical Information
Laos Mining Laws and Regulations Handbook
Laos Recent Economic and Political Developments Yearbook
Laos Recent Economic and Political Developments Yearbook
Laos Recent Economic and Political Developments Yearbook
Laos Research & Development Policy Handbook
Laos Research & Development Policy Handbook
Laos Social Security System, Policies, Laws and Regulations Handbook - Strategic Information and Basic Laws
Laos Starting Business (Incorporating) in....Guide
Laos Tax Guide Volume 1 Strategic Information and Basic Regulations
Laos Taxation Laws and Regulations Handbook
Laos Telecom Laws and Regulations Handbook
Laos Telecommunication Industry Business Opportunities Handbook
Laos Telecommunication Industry Business Opportunities Handbook
Laos Traders Manual: Export-Import, Trade, Investment
Laos Transportation Policy and Regulations Handbook
Laos: Doing Business and Investing in ... Guide Volume 1 Strategic, Practical Information, Regulations, Contacts
Laos: How to Invest, Start and Run Profitable Business in Laos Guide - Practical Information, Opportunities, Contacts

WORLD TAX GUIDE LIBRARY

Ultimate directories for conducting export-import operations in the country. Largest exporters and importers, strategic government and business contacts, selected export-import regulations and more...

Price: $149 each

TITLE

1. Albania Tax Guide
2. Argentina Tax Guide
3. Armenia Tax Guide
4. Australia Tax Guide
5. Austria Tax Guide
6. Azerbaijan Tax Guide
7. Belarus Tax Guide
8. Bermuda Tax Guide
9. Bolivia Tax Guide
10. Bosnia Tax Guide
11. Brazil Tax Guide
12. Bulgaria Tax Guide
13. Cambodia Tax Guide
14. Canada Tax Guide
15. China Tax Guide
16. Colombia Tax Guide
17. Croatia Tax Guide
18. Czech Republic Tax Guide
19. Ecuador Tax Guide
20. Estonia Tax Guide
21. Finland Tax Guide
22. France Tax Guide
23. Georgia Tax Guide
24. Germany Tax Guide
25. Global Offshore Tax Guide (Volume 1)
26. Global Offshore Tax Guide (Volume 2)
27. Global Tax Guide
28. Global Tax Regulation Guidebook
29. Greece Tax Guide
30. Guam Tax Guide
31. Hungary Tax Guide
32. India Tax Guide
33. Ireland Tax Guide
34. Italy Tax Guide
35. Japan Tax Guide
36. Kazakhstan Tax Guide
37. Korea South Tax Guide
38. Kyrgyzstan Tax Guide
39. Latvia Tax Guide
40. Lithuania Tax Guide
41. Luxembourg Tax Guide
42. Macedonia Tax Guide
43. Malaysia Tax Guide
44. Malta Tax Guide
45. Mexico Tax Guide
46. Moldova Tax Guide
47. Netherlands Tax Guide
48. New Zealand Tax Guide
49. Norway Tax Guide
50. Panama Tax Guide
51. Portugal Tax Guide
52. Romania Tax Guide
53. Russia Tax Guide
54. Serbia Tax Guide
55. Singapore Tax Guide
56. Slovakia Tax Guide
57. Slovenia Tax Guide
58. South Africa Tax Guide
59. South Korea Tax Guide
60. Spain Tax Guide
61. Sri Lanka Tax Guide
62. Switzerland Tax Guide
63. Taiwan Tax Guide
64. Thailand Tax Guide
65. Trinidad and Tobago Tax Guide
66. Ukraine Tax Guide
67. United Kingdom Tax Guide
68. Uruguay Tax Guide
69. US Tax Guide
70. Uzbekistan Tax Guide

To order and for additional analytical and marketing information, please contacts
International Business Publications, USA at:
P.O. Box 15343, Washington, DC 20003, USA. Phone: (202) 546-210 Fax: (202) 546-32
E-mail: rusric@erols.com

WORLD
TAX TREATIES AND AGREEMENTS LIBRARY

Ultimate handbooks for conducting export-import operations in the country. Largest exporters and importers, strategic government and business contacts, selected export-import regulations and more...

Please contact Int'l Business Publications, Inc. USA at - ibpusa3@gmail.com

Global Business and Investment Info Databank - www.ibpus.com

Price: $99.95 each

Abkhazia (Republic of Abkhazia) Taxation Treaties and Agreements Handbook
Afghanistan Taxation Treaties and Agreements Handbook
Aland Taxation Treaties and Agreements Handbook
Albania Taxation Treaties and Agreements Handbook
Algeria Taxation Treaties and Agreements Handbook
Andorra Taxation Treaties and Agreements Handbook
Angola Taxation Treaties and Agreements Handbook
Anguilla Taxation Treaties and Agreements Handbook
Antigua and Barbuda Taxation Treaties and Agreements Handbook
Antilles (Netherlands) Taxation Treaties and Agreements Handbook
Argentina Taxation Treaties and Agreements Handbook
Armenia Taxation Treaties and Agreements Handbook
Aruba Taxation Treaties and Agreements Handbook
Australia Taxation Treaties and Agreements Handbook
Austria Taxation Treaties and Agreements Handbook
Azerbaijan Taxation Treaties and Agreements Handbook
Bahamas Taxation Treaties and Agreements Handbook
Bahrain Taxation Treaties and Agreements Handbook
Bangladesh Taxation Treaties and Agreements Handbook
Barbados Taxation Treaties and Agreements Handbook
Belarus Taxation Treaties and Agreements Handbook
Belgium Taxation Treaties and Agreements Handbook
Belize Taxation Treaties and Agreements Handbook
Benin Taxation Treaties and Agreements Handbook
Bermuda Taxation Treaties and Agreements Handbook
Bhutan Taxation Treaties and Agreements Handbook
Bolivia Taxation Treaties and Agreements Handbook
Bosnia and Herzegovina Taxation Treaties and Agreements Handbook
Botswana Taxation Treaties and Agreements Handbook
Brazil Taxation Treaties and Agreements Handbook
Brunei Taxation Treaties and Agreements Handbook
Bulgaria Taxation Treaties and Agreements Handbook

Burkina Faso Taxation Treaties and Agreements Handbook
Burundi Taxation Treaties and Agreements Handbook
Cambodia Taxation Treaties and Agreements Handbook
Cameroon Taxation Treaties and Agreements Handbook
Canada Taxation Treaties and Agreements Handbook
Cape Verde Taxation Treaties and Agreements Handbook
Cayman Islands Taxation Treaties and Agreements Handbook
Central African Republic Taxation Treaties and Agreements Handbook
Chad Taxation Treaties and Agreements Handbook
Chile Taxation Treaties and Agreements Handbook
China Taxation Treaties and Agreements Handbook
Colombia Taxation Treaties and Agreements Handbook
Comoros Taxation Treaties and Agreements Handbook
Congo Taxation Treaties and Agreements Handbook
Congo, Democratic Republic Taxation Treaties and Agreements Handbook
Cook Islands Taxation Treaties and Agreements Handbook
Costa Rica Taxation Treaties and Agreements Handbook
Cote d'Ivoire Taxation Treaties and Agreements Handbook
Croatia Taxation Treaties and Agreements Handbook
Cuba Taxation Treaties and Agreements Handbook
Cyprus Taxation Treaties and Agreements Handbook
Czech Republic Taxation Treaties and Agreements Handbook
Denmark Taxation Treaties and Agreements Handbook
Djibouti Taxation Treaties and Agreements Handbook
Dominica Taxation Treaties and Agreements Handbook
Dominican Republic Taxation Treaties and Agreements Handbook
Ecuador Taxation Treaties and Agreements Handbook
Egypt Taxation Treaties and Agreements Handbook
El Salvador Taxation Treaties and Agreements Handbook
Equatorial Guinea Taxation Treaties and Agreements Handbook
Eritrea Taxation Treaties and Agreements Handbook
Estonia Taxation Treaties and Agreements Handbook
Ethiopia Taxation Treaties and Agreements Handbook
Falkland Islands Taxation Treaties and Agreements Handbook
Faroes Islands Taxation Treaties and Agreements Handbook
Fiji Taxation Treaties and Agreements Handbook
Finland Taxation Treaties and Agreements Handbook
France Taxation Treaties and Agreements Handbook
Gabon Taxation Treaties and Agreements Handbook
Gambia Taxation Treaties and Agreements Handbook
Georgia Taxation Treaties and Agreements Handbook
Germany Taxation Treaties and Agreements Handbook
Ghana Taxation Treaties and Agreements Handbook
Gibraltar Taxation Treaties and Agreements Handbook
Greece Taxation Treaties and Agreements Handbook
Greenland Taxation Treaties and Agreements Handbook
Grenada Taxation Treaties and Agreements Handbook
Guam Taxation Treaties and Agreements Handbook
Guatemala Taxation Treaties and Agreements Handbook
Guernsey Taxation Treaties and Agreements Handbook
Guinea Taxation Treaties and Agreements Handbook

Guinea-Bissau Taxation Treaties and Agreements Handbook
Guyana Taxation Treaties and Agreements Handbook
Haiti Taxation Treaties and Agreements Handbook
Honduras Taxation Treaties and Agreements Handbook
Hungary Taxation Treaties and Agreements Handbook
Iceland Taxation Treaties and Agreements Handbook
India Taxation Treaties and Agreements Handbook
Indonesia Taxation Treaties and Agreements Handbook
Iran Taxation Treaties and Agreements Handbook
Iraq Taxation Treaties and Agreements Handbook
Ireland Taxation Treaties and Agreements Handbook
Israel Taxation Treaties and Agreements Handbook
Italy Taxation Treaties and Agreements Handbook
Jamaica Taxation Treaties and Agreements Handbook
Japan Taxation Treaties and Agreements Handbook
Jersey Taxation Treaties and Agreements Handbook
Jordan Taxation Treaties and Agreements Handbook
Kazakhstan Taxation Treaties and Agreements Handbook
Kenya Taxation Treaties and Agreements Handbook
Kiribati Taxation Treaties and Agreements Handbook
Korea, North Taxation Treaties and Agreements Handbook
Korea, South Taxation Treaties and Agreements Handbook
Kosovo Taxation Treaties and Agreements Handbook
Kurdistan Taxation Treaties and Agreements Handbook
Kuwait Taxation Treaties and Agreements Handbook
Kyrgyzstan Taxation Treaties and Agreements Handbook
Laos Taxation Treaties and Agreements Handbook
Latvia Taxation Treaties and Agreements Handbook
Lebanon Taxation Treaties and Agreements Handbook
Lesotho Taxation Treaties and Agreements Handbook
Liberia Taxation Treaties and Agreements Handbook
Libya Taxation Treaties and Agreements Handbook
Liechtenstein Taxation Treaties and Agreements Handbook
Lithuania Taxation Treaties and Agreements Handbook
Luxembourg Taxation Treaties and Agreements Handbook
Macao Taxation Treaties and Agreements Handbook
Macedonia,Taxation Treaties and Agreements Handbook
Madagascar Taxation Treaties and Agreements Handbook
MadeiraTaxation Treaties and Agreements Handbook
Malawi Taxation Treaties and Agreements Handbook
Malaysia Taxation Treaties and Agreements Handbook
Maldives Taxation Treaties and Agreements Handbook
Mali Taxation Treaties and Agreements Handbook
Malta Taxation Treaties and Agreements Handbook
Man Taxation Treaties and Agreements Handbook
Marshall Islands Taxation Treaties and Agreements Handbook
Mauritania Taxation Treaties and Agreements Handbook
Mauritius Taxation Treaties and Agreements Handbook
Mayotte Taxation Treaties and Agreements Handbook
Mexico Taxation Treaties and Agreements Handbook
Micronesia Taxation Treaties and Agreements Handbook

Moldova Taxation Treaties and Agreements Handbook
Monaco Taxation Treaties and Agreements Handbook
Mongolia Taxation Treaties and Agreements Handbook
Monserrat Taxation Treaties and Agreements Handbook
Montenegro Taxation Treaties and Agreements Handbook
Morocco Taxation Treaties and Agreements Handbook
Mozambique Taxation Treaties and Agreements Handbook
Myanmar Taxation Treaties and Agreements Handbook
Nagorno-Karabakh Republic Taxation Treaties and Agreements Handbook
Namibia Taxation Treaties and Agreements Handbook
Nauru Taxation Treaties and Agreements Handbook
Nepal Taxation Treaties and Agreements Handbook
Netherlands Taxation Treaties and Agreements Handbook
New Caledonia Taxation Treaties and Agreements Handbook
New Zealand Taxation Treaties and Agreements Handbook
Nicaragua Taxation Treaties and Agreements Handbook
Niger Taxation Treaties and Agreements Handbook
Nigeria Taxation Treaties and Agreements Handbook
Niue Taxation Treaties and Agreements Handbook
Northern Cyprus (Turkish Republic of Northern Cyprus)
Northern Mariana Islands Taxation Treaties and Agreements Handbook
Norway Taxation Treaties and Agreements Handbook
Oman Taxation Treaties and Agreements Handbook
Pakistan Taxation Treaties and Agreements Handbook
Palau Taxation Treaties and Agreements Handbook
Palestine (West Bank & Gaza) Taxation Treaties and Agreements Handbook
Panama Taxation Treaties and Agreements Handbook
Papua New Guinea Taxation Treaties and Agreements Handbook
Paraguay Taxation Treaties and Agreements Handbook
Peru Taxation Treaties and Agreements Handbook
Philippines Taxation Treaties and Agreements Handbook
Pitcairn Islands Taxation Treaties and Agreements Handbook
Poland Taxation Treaties and Agreements Handbook
Polynesia French Taxation Treaties and Agreements Handbook
Portugal Taxation Treaties and Agreements Handbook
Qatar Taxation Treaties and Agreements Handbook
Romania Taxation Treaties and Agreements Handbook
Russia Taxation Treaties and Agreements Handbook
Rwanda Taxation Treaties and Agreements Handbook
Sahrawi Arab Democratic Republic - Strategic, Practical Information, Regulations
Saint Kitts and Nevis Taxation Treaties and Agreements Handbook
Saint Lucia Taxation Treaties and Agreements Handbook
Saint Vincent and The Grenadines Taxation Treaties and Agreements Handbook
Samoa (American) A Taxation Treaties and Agreements Handbook
Samoa (Western) Taxation Treaties and Agreements Handbook
San Marino Taxation Treaties and Agreements Handbook
Sao Tome and Principe Taxation Treaties and Agreements Handbook
Saudi Arabia Taxation Treaties and Agreements Handbook
Scotland Taxation Treaties and Agreements Handbook
Senegal Taxation Treaties and Agreements Handbook
Serbia Taxation Treaties and Agreements Handbook

Seychelles Taxation Treaties and Agreements Handbook
Sierra Leone Taxation Treaties and Agreements Handbook
Singapore Taxation Treaties and Agreements Handbook
Slovakia Taxation Treaties and Agreements Handbook
Slovenia Taxation Treaties and Agreements Handbook
Solomon Islands Taxation Treaties and Agreements Handbook
Somalia Taxation Treaties and Agreements Handbook
South Africa Taxation Treaties and Agreements Handbook
Spain Taxation Treaties and Agreements Handbook
Sri Lanka Taxation Treaties and Agreements Handbook
St. Helena Taxation Treaties and Agreements Handbook
St. Pierre & Miquelon Taxation Treaties and Agreements Handbook
Sudan (Republic of the Sudan) Taxation Treaties and Agreements Handbook
Sudan South Taxation Treaties and Agreements Handbook
Suriname Taxation Treaties and Agreements Handbook
Swaziland Taxation Treaties and Agreements Handbook
Sweden Taxation Treaties and Agreements Handbook
Switzerland Taxation Treaties and Agreements Handbook
Syria Taxation Treaties and Agreements Handbook
Taiwan Taxation Treaties and Agreements Handbook
Tajikistan Taxation Treaties and Agreements Handbook
Tanzania Taxation Treaties and Agreements Handbook
Thailand Taxation Treaties and Agreements Handbook
Timor Leste (Democratic Republic of Timor-Leste) Taxation Treaties and Agreements Handbook
Togo Taxation Treaties and Agreements Handbook
Tonga Taxation Treaties and Agreements Handbook
Trinidad and Tobago Taxation Treaties and Agreements Handbook
Tunisia Taxation Treaties and Agreements Handbook
Turkey Taxation Treaties and Agreements Handbook
Turkmenistan Taxation Treaties and Agreements Handbook
Turks & Caicos Taxation Treaties and Agreements Handbook
Tuvalu Taxation Treaties and Agreements Handbook
Uganda Taxation Treaties and Agreements Handbook
Ukraine Taxation Treaties and Agreements Handbook
United Arab Emirates Taxation Treaties and Agreements Handbook
United Kingdom Taxation Treaties and Agreements Handbook
United States Taxation Treaties and Agreements Handbook
Uruguay Taxation Treaties and Agreements Handbook
Uzbekistan Taxation Treaties and Agreements Handbook
Vanuatu Taxation Treaties and Agreements Handbook
Vatican City (Holy See) Taxation Treaties and Agreements Handbook
Venezuela Taxation Treaties and Agreements Handbook
Vietnam Taxation Treaties and Agreements Handbook
Virgin Islands, British Taxation Treaties and Agreements Handbook
Wake Atoll Taxation Treaties and Agreements Handbook
Wallis & Futuna Taxation Treaties and Agreements Handbook
Western Sahara Taxation Treaties and Agreements Handbook
Yemen Taxation Treaties and Agreements Handbook
Zambia Taxation Treaties and Agreements Handbook
Zimbabwe Taxation Treaties and Agreements Handbook